STORMING THE OLD BOYS' CITADEL

STORMING THE OLD BOYS' CITADEL

TWO PIONEER WOMEN ARCHITECTS OF NINETEENTH CENTURY NORTH AMERICA

Carla Blank and Tania Martin

Montréal

ISBN 978-1-77186-013-0 (pbk); 978-1-77186-031-4 (epub); 978-1-77186-032-1 (pdf); 978-1-77186-033-8 (mobi/pocket)

Book design and cover by Folio infographie

Cover photo: iStock

Back cover photos:
Mother Joseph of the Sacred Heart and Providence Academy, ca 1901 (Courtesy of Providence Archives, Vancouver, Washington.)
Louise Blanchard Bethune and Hotel Lafayette, ca. 1930 (Buffalo History Museum, used by permission.)

Legal Deposit, 4th quarter 2014

Bibliothèque et Archives nationales du Québec
Library and Archives Canada

Published by Baraka Books of Montreal.
6977, rue Lacroix
Montréal, Québec H4E 2V4
Telephone: 514 808-8504
info@barakabooks.com
www.barakabooks.com

Printed and bound in Quebec

Baraka Books acknowledges the generous support of its publishing program from the Société de développement des entreprises culturelles du Québec (SODEC), the Government of Quebec, tax credit for book publishing administered by SODEC, and the Canada Council for the Arts.

We acknowledge the financial support of the Government of Canada, through the National Translation Program for Book Publishing for our translation activities and through the Canada Book Fund (CBF) for our publishing activities.

Trade Distribution & Returns
Canada and the United States
Independent Publishers Group
1-800-888-4741 (IPG1);
orders@ipgbook.com

LIST OF ILLUSTRATIONS AND MAPS

CONTENTS

PART II

Saving a Grand Old Lady

FOREWORD

SOME EARLY WOMEN ARCHITECTS achieved a measure of fame, and some are now obscure, and it is certainly possible there are women who have yet to surface in the existing literature. This book focuses on two women who began to practice architecture in North America before the turn of the twentieth century.

Mother Joseph of the Sacred Heart (born Esther Pariseau, 1823-1902) is representative of nameless pioneer women who helped to build nineteenth-century North America.

Louise Bethune (born Jennie Louise Blanchard, 1856-1913) is representative of the "exceptional women" admitted into the architecture profession, following another pattern that continued well into the twentieth century.

Our selection of these two women happened somewhat accidentally.

Carla Blank on Louise Bethune and *Storming the Old Boys' Citadel*

In 2005, as guest speaker at Buffalo's Harlem Book Fair, my partner, Ishmael Reed, was put up at a downtown hotel in the vicinity of Buffalo's Lafayette Square. As he walked into the lobby of another hotel located at the square's intersection of Washington and Clinton Streets, which he noticed had a dilapidated look, he saw a plaque indicating that it had opened in 1904 as a luxury hotel, the Hotel Lafayette (also known as the Lafayette Hotel), designed by the first American woman to be called a professional architect. When Ishmael returned home, he told me about this building and asked if I had heard of its architect, whose work he had never noticed or heard talk of in all his years growing up in Buffalo. Amazed that such a feat had managed to escape even Ishmael's relentless curiosity, I began to investigate this architect's story. As my research continued, I came to understand that Ishmael's experience is typical, as Louise Blanchard Bethune, who without question established many "firsts" for women in architecture, has remained practically non-existent in the nation's historical record. I wondered whether this deteriorating architectural legacy of Mrs. Bethune's, hidden in plain sight for so long, reflected the fact that women have found architecture one of the most difficult fields to enter because, from ancient times, when we think of master builders, we think of men.

Further research turned up evidence of over thirty women who had begun architectural studies, training, or practices before the turn of the twentieth century in the U.S. or Canada, or in territories now within those countries' borders. This fact was the makings of a book.

Shopping the book proposal around to various publishers, all expressed interest in the subject but politely declined because they assessed it as too expensive a project to achieve an acceptable return on their investment. Then, accompanying Ishmael on a book launch and tour of Montreal, Toronto, and New York, I related this experience to Robin Philpot, his publisher, and the head of Baraka Books. He was intrigued with the idea and asked me if any Canadians were among these women. As I reeled off the list of names, including Mother Joseph of the Sacred Heart, Robin immediately said that he bet she was a Quebecer as her order, the Sisters of Providence, was founded by Émile Gamelin in 1840 in Montreal. He took me to visit the Canadian Centre for Architecture, where the young women in charge of their bookstore assured me that there were no books on women practicing architecture in Canada in the nineteenth century. They stated that the earliest Canadian woman architect was Marjorie Hill, who became the first Canadian woman registered as an architect when the Alberta Association of Architects accepted her as a member in 1925. However, a day in the McGill University library proved them wrong, as I found *Constructing Careers: Profiles of Five Early Women Architects in British Columbia*, an exhibition catalogue published in 1966 by the Women in Architecture Exhibits Committee that included Mother Joseph and confirmed her Canadian roots. So Robin said he would publish the book if it was about North American women architects, not just those based in the United States, and if a Canadian co-author could be found who understood French.

How to manage finding the right person to fit this bill? Thinking the best possible co-author would be a Canadian architectural historian bilingual in French and English, as Mother Joseph's correspondence was written in French, I remembered that Kelly Hayes McAloney, one of the Buffalo architects who first introduced me to the Hotel Lafayette, was born in Canada. When I asked her if she could suggest a potential candidate, she put me in touch with Despina Stratigakos, an architectural historian born in Montreal, who sent me to McGill University-based architectural historian Annmarie Adams, who in turn suggested Tania Martin, who not only fit all of my qualifications but goes one better as she has been a long-time specialist in the built environments of Catholic religious communities. We finally managed to meet at Université Laval in Quebec City during Ishmael's second Canadian book tour. Robin, Ishmael, and I climbed the Saint-Joseph staircase, whose wooden steps were worn down into polished curves by students over some two hundred years, to the top floor of the School of Architecture, where we found Tania on a teaching break from her design studio course. After some discussion, we agreed to write this book together.

Neither Tania nor I were prepared for the many discoveries in store for us as we explored the lives of these women. For me, Bethune's career not only told the story of a woman who succeeded despite long odds, but her story is also the story of her times.

Tania Martin on Mother Joseph and *Storming the Old Boys' Citadel*

I first heard rumors that Mother Joseph had been an architect while writing my master's thesis. I hadn't paid much attention to it at the time, figuring that if it were the case, she would show up again; and she did. Deborah Rink, a historic preservation consultant who had been studying the landscapes of the Sisters of St. Ann in Vancouver, British Columbia, contacted me. She was putting together an exhibition on the careers of early women architects in that province and had heard about my Ph.D. work on the Grey Nuns and the Sisters of Providence, both based in Montreal. Although I had not yet collected information on Mother Joseph, my article "Housing the Grey Nuns: Power, Women, and Religion in fin-de-siècle Montréal" featured another sister, Marie-Anne Falardeau, or Sœur Saint-Jean-de-la-Croix in religion. She had produced a series of as-built plans of a number of the Grey Nuns' buildings in Montreal at the turn of the twentieth century using the same architectural conventions employed by contemporary architects on her ink-on-linen drawings.

In June 1998, I embarked on a thirty-day cross-continent trip with my mother, who insisted on accompanying me to visit as many sites as possible where the two French-Canadian Catholic sisterhoods had lived and worked, and that were accessible from the major North American highways. As a graduate student, my meager resources did not allow me to fly into the remote northern locations or to drive five-hundred-mile detours to see first-hand the buildings the sisters had erected, although we did make a number of smaller forays to distant locations. The majority of the Sisters of Providence buildings attributed to Mother Joseph had long disappeared, except Providence Academy, formerly the House of Providence, built in 1873 in Vancouver, Washington, as an orphan asylum, school, and administrative seat of the Sisters in the Northwest. Unfortunately, we were not able to visit the whole of the complex. At that time, the chapel was being readied for a wedding and the auditorium decorated for the reception to follow. So it was a delight in August 2013 when Yvette Payne took Carla and me on a complete tour, from attic to basement, of each of the wings of Providence Academy as well as to the extant secondary structures. From the outside, and the little I had seen of the inside, not much had changed since my last visit fifteen years earlier, although the building was slightly worse for wear.

In the autumn of 1999, I learned that my proposal for a paper on Mother Joseph was accepted for the 2000 meeting of the Society of Architectural Historians' session on Women Architects. Rink kindly sent me documentation that she had assembled on Mother Joseph for her book *Spirited Women: A History of Catholic Sisters in British Columbia*. Jeffrey Karl Ochsner, a professor in the University of Washington Department of Architecture and editor and co-author of *Shaping Seattle Architecture*, having noticed the title of my talk in the Society of Architectural Historians' conference program, wrote to me saying that he and his colleagues in Seattle had some concerns about "a considerable mythology surrounding Mother Joseph." Delighted that someone from outside the Pacific Northwest was interested in Mother Joseph's career, David Rash mailed me copies of the article transcriptions he had compiled in combing

Seattle, Portland, and Walla Walla newspapers for the book project. A good number of these listed local practicing architects with whom Mother Joseph had worked. With this material I could begin to address the question of whether we could consider her as a *bona fide* architect by placing her practice within the history of the profession. My presentation, however, had raised more questions than it had answered. So when Carla invited me to co-author this book, it presented yet another opportunity to untangle the competing claims around Mother Joseph's accomplishments and to discover a bit more about this person.

Who Deserves to be Called North America's "First" Woman Architect?

Although bestowing the honor of who was "first" can have great significance, it is not our intent to center this work around such a discussion because, first of all, it should be clear that any "firsts" we talk about refer to women of European American ancestry who practiced architecture. In terms of simple chronology, it is accurate and fair to say that between Mother Joseph and Louise Bethune, Mother Joseph was one of the first European American women working in architecture. Bethune earned her first building design credits in 1881, the year she opened her architecture office in Buffalo, for two houses, a store, and a stable. By 1881, Mother Joseph was credited with having built at least a total of seventeen schools and hospitals for her order and the communities they served. Mother Joseph died in 1902. By that time she had overseen construction of between twenty-eight and thirty-two structures, not counting renovation work. By Bethune's death in 1913, she and her office had completed at least one hundred and twenty new buildings, renovations, or additions to buildings.

We believe that, besides the fact that women architects are routinely not included in architectural history books, omissions of Mother Joseph and Bethune are likely related to how their achievements are judged. In Mother Joseph's case it may mostly be attributed to believing she does not fit into definitions of what constitutes an architect's job description. A late July 2014 search of the Dynamic National Archive, a Wikipedia-like database created to champion women in architecture that is maintained on the Beverly Willis Architecture Foundation website, had yet to include her name in their now copious database of women architects.

While Bethune was listed in that archive, she has been generally omitted, barely noticed, or dismissed in standard histories of architecture, often according to whether a writer thinks she deserves the distinction of being called the first American woman to practice as a professional architect. However, it is easily verifiable that in 1885, four years after Blanchard opened her own office in Buffalo, New York, (now married and known professionally as Louise Blanchard Bethune), she became the first woman in the United States to be acknowledged by her peers as a professional architect when she was voted into membership in a professional architecture association, the Western Association of Architects (WAA). This distinction was followed in 1888 by the honor of becoming the first woman member of the American Institute of Architects (AIA) and then in 1889, the first woman Fellow of the American Institute of Architects (FAIA). Controversies around the importance of

Mrs. Bethune's FAIA honor are grounded in AIA procedures for granting the honorific of "Fellow" at the time Bethune gained her FAIA status, as compared to different requirements needed to receive that higher distinction later.

Then there are those who question the worthiness of Bethune's work. Those objections appear to be related to a charge of "lack of originality" in her designs, an odd objection, since for close to thirty years she conducted a successful business very similar to many architects of her time, combining time-honored styles with contemporary technological innovations. Design innovators, like contemporaries Louis Sullivan, H. H. Richardson, and Frank Lloyd Wright, were the exceptions then, as they are today.

Beaux-Arts Rules

In considering the question of who can be or has been considered an architect, it might be helpful to discuss the kinds of structures these women were building, because they in fact differed little from those attributed to their male counterparts. In the nineteenth century, almost all architects and builders espoused Beaux-Arts principles in their designs for city halls, schools, banks, post offices, hospitals, and other institutional buildings, and for hotels, country clubs, residential enclave developments, and private estates. Louise Bethune and Mother Joseph were no exceptions. It was the dominant idiom in North America and the hallmark of École nationale supérieure des Beaux-Arts training.

The School of Fine Arts, formed in the late 1700s in Paris, taught its students the appropriate historical styles to employ for particular building types and contexts, drawing heavily upon classical Greek and Roman traditions and their reinterpretations during the Renaissance. It was widely considered the most prestigious and rigorous architectural training Europeans or Americans could find anywhere, although it did not admit women until 1898. Many historians rank Beaux-Arts as the ruling European academy until 1919, when architect Walter Gropius founded the Bauhaus, a school in Weimar, Germany. Its mission to make arts a part of everyday life was dominated by the principles of "form follows function," and that everyone should be able to afford functional, well-designed environments, not just the wealthy. "International Style" is a term that came to be interchangeably applied to works by its teachers and graduates.

Whether they are aware of this or not, most North Americans know the architectural principles of Beaux-Arts intimately, as our ongoing romance with various eclectic, European, period revivals can readily be documented throughout our cities in their twenty-first-century urban and suburban McMansion manifestations. Some of the most famous Beaux-Arts buildings in both the United States and Canada are each nation's landmark government buildings. The 1876 Centennial in Philadelphia and famed White City of the 1893 World's Columbian Exposition in Chicago (realized under the direction of Daniel Burnham as well as McKim, Mead & White) invigorated resurgence of the form, and at the urban scale it took the name City Beautiful Movement. You will find references to many North American buildings that employ Beaux-Arts principles as you read the following chapters.

What's Inside this Book?

The Introduction explains the "citadel" to be stormed—the changing definitions of the term "architect," how the training and business of architecture developed in North America, and how women have made their way into a profession that traditionally functioned more like a gentlemen's club.

Part I, "The Sister with a Hammer," tells Mother Joseph's story; Part II, "Saving a Grand Old Lady," tells Louise Bethune's story. Each of these chapters relate how, working on opposite sides of the North American continent, these women took two very different routes into the field of architecture and how, over the years they were active, their practices demonstrated much about the ways the architectural profession evolved into the standards in place in 2014.

Hotel Lafayette, Louise Blanchard Bethune's signature building, as it was circa 1930.

Both of their signature buildings are currently listed on the U.S. National Register of Historic Places: Mother Joseph's House of Providence in Vancouver, Washington; and Louise Bethune's Hotel Lafayette in Buffalo, New York. Both buildings are still standing although each architect's original structure has been changed by various owners and others involved in their additions, modifications, and renovations. They have become testaments to their ongoing importance to their home communities, in part because of the two women who were a large force behind their existence, but also because the layers of history encapsulated in each building carry essential keys to the identities of each place.

The Fort Vancouver National Trust is working to purchase Mother Joseph's landmark building, now known as The Academy, in Vancouver, Washington. They are proposing a sixteen-million-dollar investment for its preservation and renovation as the centerpiece of a larger mixed-use master plan for the seven-acre campus on which it sits to be developed in partnerships between private and public entities. On an even grander scale, Bethune's Hotel Lafayette in downtown Buffalo, New York, has just benefitted from a forty-three-million-dollar renovation project, which has brought it back from the blighted condition it had deteriorated into during the past few decades. Completed in 2012 and now officially known as The Hotel @ Lafayette, it has been restored to its former glamour as a luxury destination.

In the Conclusion we talk about what we have learned from this project.

Providence Academy, Vancouver, Washington, ca. 1901. (Providence Archives, Seattle, Washington.)

In writing this book, our intention was to go beyond "adding women" to the history of North American architecture. It is our wish to help Mother Joseph's and Louise Bethune's legacies become more secure. Mostly, however, we offer this book in homage to all North American women who pioneered in a profession that to this day is not an easy one to work in, especially if you are a woman.

INTRODUCTION
The Citadel to be Stormed

Carla presumed Tania was an architect, as do most people when they learn she obtained, in 1992, her bachelor's degree in architecture. At that time, the five-year professional program was the entry point into the profession, although the Master of Architecture has since superseded it. Rather than embark on the required internship leading to written exams and registration, Tania earned a post-professional degree from McGill University, specializing in the study of built environments, before earning a Ph.D. in Architectural History from the University of California, Berkeley. These credentials allow her to teach history/theory courses as well as design studio in a school of architecture, although many institutions prefer studio instructors to have an architectural practice, and hence registration with the state or provincial architectural association. The Royal Architectural Institute of Canada, however, offers membership to architecture school faculty. In presenting a history of the architectural profession in North America, we thought Tania's experiences, as a participant in this field, provide a contemporary example of the complexities surrounding the evolution of standards and women's choices within the field of architecture. They punctuate the historical narrative.

Just as you cannot practice as a lawyer until you pass an exam that admits you to the bar, in Canada and the United States you can only be called an architect if you pass a licensing exam and are registered. A provincial or state architecture association only has the legal authority to emit a license to practice within its jurisdiction. It will consider applications once the candidate has succeeded in completing the following requirements: earned a degree from an accredited program in architecture or, more rarely, fulfilled a regimented apprenticeship; passed a battery of exams set by the National Certification Boards of the country where he or she will practice; and served the required number of hours of internship under the supervision of a practicing architect. Upon paying his or her annual dues and liability insurance, the newly approved practitioner retains the privilege of officially stamping his or her drawings as a *bona fide* architect.

This restrictive definition of "architect" is fairly recent. It dates to the late nineteenth century. Professionalization was uneven in its progress, temporally and geographically. The process of professionalization spanned the better part of the nineteenth century. In North America, the rate of formation of associations followed no regional pattern, and licensing laws were not enacted throughout all fifty states and territories until 1968, and in Canada's provinces and territories until 2001, with the passage of the Northwest Territories Architects Act, although all of the provinces had effective legislation by 1933. When Newfoundland and Labrador joined the Canadian Confederation in 1949, it enacted an Architects Act. When it was incorporated in 1980, the Architects Licensing Board of Newfoundland and Labrador took over responsibility for registration matters from that province's architects association.

Moreover, the terms "architect" and "professional" have not always been synonymous. The professions—medical, legal, architectural—initially "a premodern and preindustrial invention of eighteenth-century England," as architectural historian Mary Woods points out in *From Craft to Profession: The Practice of Architecture in Nineteenth-Century America*, had to evolve to respond to new conditions, namely capitalism, urbanization, and industrialization.

The term "architect" has its origins in the Greek word *architekton*, which translates to "master carpenter." Although the term fell out of common usage in the Middle Ages, when those responsible for construction were referred to as master masons and builders and patrons, the term "architect" was re-employed to describe the Brunelleschis, Bramantes, and Michelangelos of the Renaissance. As Woods explains, they "were not building craftsmen and did not belong to the construction guilds." By the eighteenth century, an architect was "a Master Workman in a Building, he who designs the Model, or draws the Plot, Plan or Draught of the whole Fabrick; whose Business it is to consider the whole Manner and Method of the Building; and also to compute the Charge and Expence" according to *The Builder's Dictionary*, first published in 1734 and widely circulated in British America. The definition was perhaps too all-encompassing. As Dankmar Adler pointed out to the architects assembled at the Second Annual Convention of the Western Association of Architects in 1885, "Every man... can constitute himself as an architect by calling himself one... We are architects only because we have called ourselves architects, that is all."

Adler was speaking of the realities of practices in his time, before the passage of distinct laws regulating architecture as a profession. Until architecture became the object of professionalization in North America, anyone who created architectural drawings and supervised construction, be they a designer, draftsman, builder, master artisan, or master mechanic, or a gentleman, planter, or merchant who undertook building contracts, all could call themselves architects as they were ultimately in positions of authority and took responsibility for the building. They directed the tradesmen and artisans actually involved in preparing the materials, assembling the structural members, cladding the exterior walls, covering the roof, installing doors and windows, partitioning rooms, and finishing the interiors. Yet even this elastic description omits those people deemed to have superior skills or knowledge of building within a culture or community, those who had a combination of expertise in assorted crafts, calculation, aesthetics, and rituals and passed them on from one generation to the next, from mother to daughter or through special initiation by elders or through long apprenticeship with an experienced practitioner.

As co-authors anthropologist Peter Nabokov and architect Robert Easton explain in their *Native American Architecture*:

> The three hundred or so tribal groups who lived in North America when Christopher Columbus arrived built their homes and arranged their settlements according to singular patterns and principles passed on from generation to generation...
>
> Men and women's roles in the construction and ownership of dwellings were sharply defined. Over most of central North America, women held sway over home and hearth, either building or supervising construction of their houses. Along the West Coast from Alaska to Southern California and on the eastern seaboard, men were largely responsible for building. In parts of the Southwest, and in pockets of the Great Basin, men and women shared the labor equally. Among the Mandan Hidatsa of the upper Missouri River, women held the right to erect earth lodges, but men cut and erected the frame. Cheyenne women had a 'guild' which convened with fasting and prayer whenever they gathered to cut and sew covers and make porcupine quill ornaments for their tipis.

The much-admired architecture of the Shakers, a religious sect that has its origins in seventeenth-century Protestantism, distinguishable by its simplicity and utility, drew upon and improved existing models, run-of-the-mill domestic, agricultural, civic, and religious structures they would have seen in nearby towns and cities. True to vernacular architecture traditions, one adapted the plans and construction techniques of one's forefathers and neighbors from whom one learned to build.

As architectural historian Dell Upton reminds us, "every building, large or small, [high style or vernacular], is designed. Someone, or some group of people, decided what it should look like," and also the functions to which it was put. Doctors and other specialists expected architects to follow their prescriptions to the last detail for the design of jails, asylums, schools, and hospitals. Today, programming a building's functions and layouts is a specific area of expertise not always held by architects, just as job superintendence is often devolved to site supervisors who coordinate the work of the various construction contractors on-site, solve problems as they arise, and otherwise make sure the architect's plans are being followed.

The definition the Western Association of Architects adopted by 1886, after some members expressed their objections to the number of builders and contractors being admitted, Woods notes, did not include the word 'architect' or discuss the artistic aspects of the job. Coming shortly after Louise Bethune had been accepted as their first female fellow, it furthermore did not use masculine pronouns in its:

> revised membership policy that required all fellows be 'a professional person *whose sole occupation* [emphasis added] is to supply data preliminary to the material, construction and completion of a building and to exercise administrative control over contractors supplying material and labor... and [over] the arbitration of contract stipulating terms of obligation and fulfillment between proprietor and contractor.'

Architecture followed in the footsteps of other professions—medicine, law, and engineering—in delimiting its domain and in determining who could legally enter it. The men who established the profession fought hard battles to circumscribe the range of activities laypersons could perform without recourse to their expertise. Still in 2014, control over many areas of the field of architecture escapes architects. Anyone can design their own house and even certain buildings not exceeding dimensions set by Architects Acts.

If the European tradition of architecture centered on the figure of the gentleman whose "considerations, unlike those of merchants or tradesmen, were never financial" and whose actions were guided by honor rather than by the hope of selling his services, at least in theory, in America money entered into the equation, as Dell Upton emphasizes. Indeed, Louisa Tuthill, author of *A History of Architecture from Earliest Times,* the first architectural history published in the United States, in 1848, counseled young men to consider architecture as a career, because in her analysis it was a "*lucrative* and honorable profession" [emphasis added].

Would-be architects had to identify something that would set them apart from mere builders and artisans in the public's eye. Upton posits that they presented themselves as arbiters of taste, whose command of style and artistic expression lent an image of originality to the designs they sold their clients. While the conception of architect as artist drew its roots from Renaissance ideas, in North America the professional also had to demonstrate sound mastery of technical innovations and apply the managerial theories of modern business in his practice.

Some practitioners working south of the forty-ninth parallel were able to convince Canadian businessmen of their superior abilities in each of these areas, much to the frustration of local architects. Toronto-based Canada Life Company repeatedly hired Buffalo-based architect Richard Waite (1848-1911) "to design its new offices buildings, first in Hamilton (1882), then Toronto (1889), and later in Montreal" (1895-1896, now St. Regis Condos), observed architectural historian Kelly Crossman. Waite had an advantage over Canadian architects in that he was willing to introduce American innovations in commercial building to Canada: new buildings types, such as multi-storey office buildings; new building techniques using fire resistant materials, including the use of iron and steel framing; and new architectural fashions, such as the colored stone favored by Richardson's Romanesque Revival. Other American architects followed suit. Frederick Law Olmsted designed about one hundred projects in Canada; Bruce Price (1845-1903) built railroad stations and grand hotels in revival styles for the Canadian Pacific, most famously Quebec City's Château Frontenac (1893) and Montreal's Place Viger (1897). Beaux-Arts-trained Carrère & Hastings displayed their mastery of historical styles in designs for the Trader's Bank Building (1905) and Bank of Toronto head office (1913, demolished).

The manner in which Waite secured the coveted commission for Toronto's Ontario Legislative and Departmental Buildings (1892) became a controversy among Canadian architects. The only American member of a three-man jury to decide who would win the building's 1880 competition, Waite rejected his Canadian co-members' entries as not competent, and was awarded the commission without undergoing further peer review of his own design. The resulting outrage probably helped motivate Canadian architects to put aside their

The Place Viger building in Montreal, designed by Bruce Price, 1897. (Photo, Robin Philpot.)

professional jealousies that had defeated earlier attempts to form durable professional associations.

Architects sought to establish reliable standards of performance through professionalization, guaranteeing the quality of building to the public and to individual clients, thus giving them some semblance of control over the whole construction process, from initial design through project completion. Professional bodies certified one's credentials and one's character. They also initially presumed that only *men* of good standing having the proper education would join.

The first organization of architects in the United States, the short-lived Association for the Advancement of Architectural Science, was founded in 1836, two years after the Institute of British Architects, predecessor of the Royal Institute of British Architects (RIBA), and was succeeded in 1857 by the American Institute of Architects (AIA). When the forty-nine men signed the constitution, the AIA was little more than a gentlemen's club whose mission, as stated in their 1867 Constitution, was "to promote the scientific and practical perfection of its members and elevate the standing of the

The Canada Life Company building at 275, rue Saint-Jacques in Montreal, designed by Richard Waite, 1895-1896. (Photo, Robin Philpot.)

Profession." Prominent AIA members—such as the Chicago-based architects Dankmar Adler, Daniel Burnham, William LeBaron Jenney, John Root, and Louis Sullivan—dissatisfied with its autocratic practices and unsuccessful in their efforts to have the AIA run democratically by its members rather than a board of trustees, bolted from the AIA and formed the Western Association of Architects (WAA) in Chicago in 1884.The one hundred male architects who joined the new association heralded from the Midwest and the South of the United States.

In Canada, architects began to organize into provincial associations in the last decade of the nineteenth century, well before incorporation by the Dominion Parliament in 1909 of the Royal Architectural Institute of Canada (RAIC). In the province of Ontario, Canada, the proposed Architects Act of 1889, a bill to incorporate the Ontario Association of Architects (OAA), contained licensing provisions restricting practice in that province to those having passed examination or able to present previous evidence of professional training. The Act, which probably drew inspiration from the RIBA's revised Charter of 1887, was officially adopted the following year, minus the principle of compulsory registration. The province of Quebec created a similar organization and enacted a similar law in 1890. British Columbia attempted to do so in 1892-1893, but failed. Architects on the west coast of Canada were unregulated until 1906, Alberta being the first to pass legislation.

Despite the governments' and architect associations' best efforts to make registration obligatory, "unqualified men continued to practice architecture," Kelly Crossman asserts. Moreover, "Whatever the profession felt about the distinctions between registered and non-registered architects, the Canadian public was prepared to ignore the distinction entirely." And this was undoubtedly true south of the border as well.

The OAA would remain, like many architects' associations in the United States and Canada, a voluntary association until 1931, when a new Architects Act was adopted in Ontario making membership obligatory in order to legally practice in that province. Quebec succeeded in securing statutory registration by 1898 requiring architects practicing in that province to pass PQAA exams. The Architectural Institute of British Columbia finally succeeded in establishing itself by provincial statute in 1920. The Atlantic provinces followed suit in the early 1930s.

In the United States, WAA chapters pushed for licensing laws in 1886, but the Illinois, Missouri, Iowa, Texas, and Kansas legislatures defeated those attempts until 1897, when the state of Illinois passed its Architecture Licensing Act, most closely followed by California (1901), and New Jersey (1902). New York was the tenth state to approve a licensing law, in 1915, and Vermont and Wyoming were the last, in 1951, followed by the territories of Guam (1960) and the U.S. Virgin Islands (1968).

Under those laws, architects' associations gained the right to restrict entry into the profession, establish postgraduate and apprenticeship-training criteria, set and maintain standards of architectural education, hold compulsory admission exams, control standards of practice, collect membership dues, and enforce codes of ethics. Once states and provinces did pass licensing laws that established boards to examine applicants, they grandfathered-in those who could prove they had been practicing architecture for a specified number of years prior to the enactment of licensing laws. Registration conferred the exclusive right to the title of architect; the seal with which they stamped all their drawings and specifications signified they were liable for defective construction, injuries, and death. The AIA's first code of ethics was adopted in 1909, after associations had obtained exclusive rights in other areas.

Neither the AIA, which had subsumed the WAA in 1889, nor the RAIC had legal power over its members. Rather, these national organizations, really a federation of local associations, advocated on behalf of the membership, organized platforms for debating issues of importance to the profession, and generally provided a collegial network. As early as 1866, the AIA proposed a fee schedule defining who an architect was and what an architect did (and what he should be paid!). Four years later, it adopted a document ensuring architects would be involved in planning, overseeing, and judging competitions for building design, as reported on the AIA's web site, www.aia.org. In 1888, the AIA helped create standardized construction contracts to be used across the United States, the first being an architect and owner agreement for construction.

Laws passed at the federal level of both countries addressed issues of national concern, such as the highly controversial subject of regulating design competitions. In the United States, the Tarsney Act of 1893 was endorsed by the AIA, who had campaigned for such legislation since the 1870s to discourage abuses of power. It advocated that in competitions to design buildings funded through federal commissions, the selection process should only be presided over by AIA judges, and over the next thirteen years, twenty-some architects received commissions in major U.S. cities under these guidelines. Illustrating how difficult it was to institute regulations, this law's provisions were limited in scope, being advisory rather than compulsory, and it was repealed in 1912.

An Architect's Training and Education

During the nineteenth century, one of the most common and acceptable ways for men to become architects was through apprenticeship. It was a practice that existed earlier in New France (1608-1763) than in the thirteen British colonies. Claude Baillif (c. 1635-1699), a "'stone-cutter, master mason, plasterer, contractor, architect' who emigrated from France to Québec in 1675, had up to twenty apprentices" relates Upton, adding that Baillif's "library included books on mathematics, and civil and military architecture, and his drawings were sophisticated and carefully executed."

In Canada as in the United States, young men started out as draftsmen, ideally under the tutelage of a successful architect. The standard of training and conditions of work varied from one office to the next, so much so, as Crossman recounts, that architect A. C. Hutchison told the Province of Quebec Architect Association in 1890 that he "often advised young men who wished to obtain a knowledge of architecture to go to the United States and obtain education" where collegiate programs of architecture existed. University-centered architectural education was offered by 1910 in Canada.

Efforts to formalize architectural training, especially by instituting college and university programs, preceded efforts to have architecture sanctioned as a *bona fide* profession. An academic degree in architecture, while limiting access to education for many, standardized cultivation of "taste," perhaps the only qualification, Upton argues, distinguishing the credentials of an architect from those of a builder. Formal schooling in the classroom and the design studio was an alternative, and an infinitely more predictable way of inculcating the internal values of the profession than interactions with one's employers and colleagues, even though the design studio replicated to some degree the peer learning that went on in the office. Design studios were also modeled on the École nationale supérieure des Beaux-Arts atelier, where students in varying stages of training were supervised and guided by a practicing architect through a series of design competitions. Junior students helped advanced students represent the project to be submitted. The drawing of plans, sections, elevations, and perspective views was a chance to apply their lessons in architectural history and theory.

Standard histories of architecture in the United States credit the Massachusetts Institute of Technology (MIT) as having implanted the first collegiate program in architecture in 1865, but it was the Polytechnic College of Pennsylvania that paved the way for technically-oriented training in 1861. Before 1900, most architectural programs, like the one Columbia University established in 1881, leaned towards the polytechnic and therefore pragmatic curricula that covered drawing, mathematics, geometry, architectural history and ornament, heating and ventilation, estimating, contracts, specifications, and superintendence—rather than the highly romanticized Beaux-Arts atelier. Its director, William Robert Ware, also a founder of the program at MIT, considered construction and engineering "more germane" to the education of an architect than painting and sculpture. He was more concerned with a student's "thorough knowledge of the building trades, an ignorance of which could not be made up for in an architecture office" than a student's design abilities, architectural historian Michael J. Lewis affirms. Ware did, however, invite practitioners to lead Beaux-Arts-inspired design studios at Columbia, and many other schools would follow the example.

The University of Toronto and McGill University in Montreal were the first to offer university-level architecture programs in Canada, in 1890 and in 1896 respectively, although the Quebec government had introduced architecture courses to the curriculum at the Écoles des Arts et Métiers—schools which had been established throughout the province during the 1870s to improve the quality of Canadian design. The French-language École Polytechnique de Montréal, now affiliated with the Université de Montréal, had also added a course in design to its curriculum. French-Canadian students supplemented this grounding in architectural science by working in an office or studying abroad until an architectural program independent from engineering was established at the École in 1907, explains Crossman.

However, going to Paris to study at l'École nationale supérieure des Beaux-Arts was more prestigious for North American students. Its course of study was based in the traditions and principles laid out in the *Ten Books on Architecture* by the Roman civil engineer and architect Vitruvius (born c. 80-70 BC, died after c. 15 BC), which demonstrated how to render buildings according to the five archetypal Greek and Roman classical orders, namely the Tuscan, Ionic, Doric, Corinthian, and Composite Orders. Architects schooled at the Beaux-Arts, or in programs under that influence in North America, were just as likely to refer to *Regola delle cinque ordini d'architettura* (1563), a book on the five orders by Renaissance architect Giacomo Barozzi da Vignola (1507-1573) and study the buildings by Italian Renaissance master architect Andrea Palladio (1508-1580). Americans Richard Morris Hunt, Henry H. Richardson, Thomas Hastings, and Charles Fuller McKim were École nationale supérieure des Beaux-Arts graduates, as was Canadian J. Omer Marchand (1873-1936); Louis Sullivan and John Merven Carrère attended but left before graduating; Frank Lloyd Wright purposely avoided it; and after being refused admission on her first try, Julia Morgan (1872-1957) was accepted in 1898, and became their first female graduate in 1902.

By 1906, the AIA Committee on Education insisted on the artistic rather than the technical competencies in its definition of an architect as "one ranking in the class of *men* of culture, learning, and refinement, differentiated from the others of his class solely by *his* function as a creator of pure beauty, as an exponent through material forms of the best secular, intellectual, and religious civilization of *his* time, and as an organizer and director of manifold and varied industries and activities [emphasis added]."

Three years of full-time study in a university or college program was prohibitive for most individuals. The United States census identified over 10,500 individuals calling themselves architects in 1900, yet "less than 400 students were attending architecture schools in 1898," estimates Dana Cuff, author of *Architecture: A Story of Practice.*

Apprenticeship or office training remained the usual route for aspiring architects at the turn of the twentieth century and would continue to be an alternative path well into the twentieth century even as formal study in a college or university-level architecture program supplanted it.

Apprentices, who received one-on-one instruction from an experienced practitioner, supplemented their training by enrolling in drawing schools, which were offered as early as 1735 in a number of major North American cities, notes Upton, and their wide-ranging curricula quite possibly inspired collegiate programs. Instructors probably used the same architectural publications that gentlemen architects and practitioners had in their personal libraries. Before William Robert Ware (1832-1915), who Woods calls "the father of American architectural education," authored *The American Vignola* (1902-1906), he required his students to own copies of its inspiration, Vignola's *Rules* (the *Regola* referred to above), which codified the rules of classical architecture for the Italian Renaissance. Abbé Jérôme Demers' *Précis d'Architecture* (1828), the first architectural treatise written in Canada, inspired by Jacques-François Blondel's *Cours d'Architecture* (1771-1777), adapted European teachings to Canadian and American audiences. Illustrated builders' guides and pattern books such as James Gibb's *Book of Architecture* (1728), John Haviland's *The Builder's Assistant* (1821), Asher Benjamin's *The American Builder's Companion* (1806), *The Rudiments of Architecture* (1814) and *The Elements of Architecture* (1843), or Edward Shaw's *The Modern Architect or Every Carpenter His Own Master* (1855), Andrew Jackson Downing's *The Architecture of Country Houses* (1850) circulated widely. They explained the aesthetic rules, ideal proportions, and fashionable styles as well as basic construction techniques and building systems for classical vaults and arches, gabled roofs and domes, doors and windows, walls, wall treatments and ceilings, steps and staircases. Such publications informed the choices of master builders, too.

If one wanted to keep abreast of latest developments, one traveled not only to study canonical masterpieces but also to see newly erected edifices, whether in Europe or leading American cities. Extant buildings inspired many an architect, builder, and client. The man credited as architect of the White House in Washington D.C., James Hoban (1762-1831), modeled his design on Leister House in Dublin, Ireland, an existing building in the Palladian style. The Irish-born builder had studied architectural drawing and apprenticed in the building trades in Dublin before immigrating to America in 1785. Known first in the U.S. for his design of South Carolina's State Capital at Columbia, he may have also consulted Gibbs' pattern book *cum* building manual for his 1792 winning competition entry for the President's House, later renamed the White House.

Professional journals were also a source of continuing education, in addition to being a forum for professional architects and a showcase for their works. Readers could learn how their colleagues had solved design problems and seek inspiration from projects published in their pages. In the United States, *The American Architect and Building News* or *The Inland Architect and News Record* were founded respectively in 1876 and 1883; Canada's first professional journal, *Canadian Architect &*

Builder, was launched in 1888. Early on, these and similar professional journals published articles on drafting, architectural history, sanitation, office management, and building law.

No matter how broad their training and culture, architects nonetheless had to take the expertise of their clients and general contractors into account, as they often possessed greater knowledge of construction, financing, real estate and building law. Architects, at least in the eighteenth century, as Upton points out, "were expected to defer to the wishes of their clients" and "favor ideas that had been proved in practice over those merely theoretical," which differs substantially from late twentieth-century perceptions of 'starchitects' and people's expectations of unique architectural conceptions. But as he, Woods, and Crossman argue, by late nineteenth century, architecture was more than an art or a science; it was above all a totally male-dominated for-profit business enterprise.

Women's Battles and Experiences

The architecture profession remains male-dominated in 2014, despite the great efforts women have exerted to batter down the walls of overt and systemic discrimination. Those walls had been erected during the course of the nineteenth century to exclude persons of the female sex, people of color, and the majority of common builders. Women and all racial and ethnic minorities evidently were not capable of being considered in the same class as "gentlemen," so how could they hope to become architects? In addition, women's ability to properly conduct business was restricted by laws which had their basis in the U.S. Constitution and were of course not limited to the field of architecture. For instance, a person had to be a white male landowner over the age of twenty-one to vote in the country's first presidential election. This meant only five percent of the population was eligible to vote in 1789. Women, men without property, indentured servants, free and enslaved blacks, and Native Americans were excluded. By 1868, when the Fourteenth Amendment granted citizenship to former slaves, it established some precedents through the judicial system for guaranteeing equal protection under the law for all citizens.

In Canada, women were excluded from the vote because only individuals who owned property or significant assets were eligible, with the exception of Québec, where between 1809 and 1849 female property owners were allowed to exercise that right until Québec's franchise act specified only men could vote. At the provincial level, Manitoba, Saskatchewan, and Alberta became the first provinces to legislate in favor of women's suffrage in 1916; Québec would be the last to do so in 1940. Starting in 1918, all Canadian-born women over the age of twenty-one who met the property requirements of their home province, a stipulation that was abolished in 1920, could cast their ballots in federal elections.

Because the U.S. Constitution also followed the British common law tradition of Doctrine of Coverture, in which the husband controlled the body of his wife, women had no right to control their own property, even if inherited, and generally a woman could not sign contracts in her own name. The same was generally true in Canada. Starting in 1872, women in Ontario could keep their wages and their husbands had no control over their earnings, and under the 1884 *The Married*

Women's Property Act, women could make legal agreements and buy property. Manitoba, Prince Edward Island, and other provinces would follow suit in the early 1900s.

By the late 1830s, some states began to pass reforms allowing women the right to inherit property. The exception was in U.S. lands acquired under the Louisiana Purchase of 1803 that had been ruled under Spanish and French law systems, where all property of husbands and wives became "community property." This of course applied to Lower Canada, later the province of Québec. Women living in the community property states of Louisiana, Texas, and New Mexico, and also Arizona, Idaho, Nevada, California, and Washington, had a legal advantage over women in other states, where it could be well into the twentieth century before some removed these restrictive laws.

Architectural historian Mary Woods did nonetheless count 198 women carpenters and joiners and forty-one women brick- and stonemasons in the 1890 census, the first to record women in the building trades in the United States:

> By the 1900 census their numbers had grown to 545 women carpenters or joiners and 167 women masons. Women of color in the building trades were counted separately in the 1900 census. There were 46 carpenters and joiners and 16 brick- and stonemasons who were African-American women. One Chinese woman was either a carpenter or a joiner and one American Indian woman was a mason.

They somehow managed to overcome deep-seated prejudices, as did the exceptionally few women "draftsmen" and designers that appeared in census records from 1870 onwards.

While apprenticeship in an office was the typical route for men, women were usually educated in academic programs, once universities and architecture schools were opened to them. Prior to that, they may have learned from the same textbooks available to male aspirants to the profession. To circumvent exclusionary policies, they may have also taken correspondence school courses—whose curricula covered drawing, mathematics, geometry, architectural history and ornament, heating and ventilation, estimating, contracts, specifications, and superintendence—and attended public lectures, when they were offered. There were limits to self-education, and some young women with sufficient funds hired architectural school faculty as private tutors before they were commonly accepted into university-level programs.

Although as early as 1859, Cooper Union in New York City offered women architectural design and engineering courses, it was not until 1871 that Cornell University became the first university architecture department to admit women. It was followed by the University of Illinois (1873) and MIT (1883), which had opened its school of architecture in 1868. Between 1874 and 1894, only eight women graduated from four-year academic programs in architecture anywhere in the United States. Among these pioneers were Mary L. Page from the University of Illinois at Urbana-Champaign in 1879 and Margaret Hicks from Cornell University in 1880, whose student project for a workingman's cottage was published without comment in the *American Architect and Building News* in 1878, as Upton reports. Cornell and the University of Illinois were federally funded public "land grant" institutions. As stipulated in the 1862

Morrill Act, they had the mandate of providing "the liberal and practical education of the industrial classes in the several pursuits and professions in life," contrasting with most private universities intended for the "male leisure class, government leaders and members of the professions."

Because land-grant schools' funding was dependent in part upon the number of students enrolled (although enrollees were required to pay tuition, board, room, light, and fuel in whole or in part), they were willing to admit women well before some private institutions. The architecture programs at Harvard (founded 1636, first admitted women in 1895), and Columbia (variously said to be founded 1740, 1749 or 1750, first offered architecture courses in 1869, developed into a full department in 1890) maintained restrictions against women into the 1940s, when their male student populations were reduced during World War II. Even at the land-grant institutions, young women had to be as doggedly persistent as Bertha Yerex Whitman; as Upton recounts, the dean of the University of Michigan school of architecture told her in 1914, "'we don't want you, but since the school is coeducational and state owned, we have to take you if you insist.' She did."

In Canada, McGill University would not grant a degree to a woman, so Jean Eleanor Howden, who had tried to enroll in the architecture program in the 1890s, went instead to apprentice in the office of renowned Montreal-based architects Edward and W. S. Maxwell. McGill finally admitted women starting in 1939.

Female employees, apprentices, and architects were generally absent from leading nineteenth-century architectural offices. One of the first women to study architecture at MIT, Henrietta Dozier (1872-1947), attempted entry into office of Charles McKim as a draftsperson, and was rebuffed. Dozier's case might have been more complicated than previously recognized. It's possible she passed for white according to genealogical research by scholars and archivists of African American arts Mary Rose Gentry and Corrine Jennings. They believe she may have had African ancestors who came to the United States in the late 1600s or early 1700s from Barbados and West Nimba, Liberia. Dozier related in a 1939 WPA Federal Writers' Project interview, "My father, Henry Cuttino Dozier, came from Georgetown, South Carolina to Fernandina, Florida with Walter Coachman, Sr., shortly before the War between the States," which usually meant at that time that a slave was brought to a place by a slavemaster. One reason to pass may have been professional, because it was not until 1930 that the historical black land grant school now known as Tuskegee University became the first to accept African American women into their highly respected architecture degree program, thirty-seven years after its opening in 1893. "Passing was a common practice up into the 1960s," Ishmael Reed says, "when blackness became a sort of melanin loyalty test for blacks, regardless of skin color."

The McKim, Mead & White firm, however, could not refuse to accept Theodate Pope's (1867-1946) proposition in 1898 to design a house for her parents. An heiress to the United States Steel fortune, she used this opportunity to advance her own ambitions to become an architect. In effect, she completed an apprenticeship under the guise of a commission, even if architectural historian James F. O'Gorman asserts that she avoided training in an architect's office and did not attempt to enter a school of architecture. As recounted by Woods:

> [Pope] clearly understood business negotiations and dictated the employment terms at the very outset: 'As it is *my plan*, I expect to decide on all matters the details as well as all the more important questions of plan that may arise... In other words, *it will be a Pope house instead of a McKim, Mead and White* [emphasis added]... I am not nearly as difficult to deal with as this would seem, for I am very tolerant of advice and always open to suggestions and good reasoning.' After vetoing the office job captain assigned to her, Pope took [a major] part in supervising construction.

And for this reason, McKim, Mead & White reduced their fees. She was a well-traveled woman, had been active in settlement house work, had hired private tutors to teach her about architecture, and after this initiation in one of the preeminent architectural offices in the United States, she had no need to commission more work from McKim, Mead & White or any other firm for that matter. O'Gorman states Pope established her own office in 1907, was licensed in New York in 1916 and in Connecticut, where much of her work was located, in 1933, and was elected to the AIA in 1918. Her practice lasted thirty years.

Even though half of the schools of architecture in the United States continued to deny admission to female applicants, fifty women had graduated from architecture programs by 1910. This did not necessarily qualify as a success, as Julia Morgan observed five years later in a *California Alumni* paper:

> Few women persevere as architects though many take up the study. Many are impatient to reach the top of the ladder too soon, matrimony takes others, but the greatest lures are the teaching positions in the high schools... as the salaries are good one cannot blame them for accepting unless they are determined to become architects.

Morgan was one of those determined women. As a student in the University of California, Berkeley engineering program, where she was the sole woman, she worked in the office of Bernard Maybeck, a leading architect in the California Arts and Crafts movement. After graduating in 1894 and at Maybeck's prompting, she applied to the École des Beaux-Arts. Finally admitted after multiple attempts in 1898, she was the first woman to achieve entry. Upon her return to California, she registered herself as an architect in 1904, again the first woman to do so in that state, and immediately opened her first office. After it was destroyed in the 1906 earthquake and resulting fires, she opened an office with Ira Wilson Hoover as her junior partner. In 1910 he departed for the East Coast and from then on she maintained an independent practice in the name of "Julia Morgan, Architect." She employed as many as six draftspersons, including many women. Over her forty-seven year career, she designed over seven hundred buildings ranging in size and complexity from the single-family house to schools, churches, and hospitals, in California and elsewhere. As measured against the norms established by her male colleagues, Morgan had distinguished herself.

For Marion Mahony Griffin (1871-1961), the most prominent woman architect active in one of the most influential American architectural styles, the Prairie School, the problem of women's access to the profession lay with familiar stereotypes around the division of labor between men and women and women's supposedly inherent inferior abilities. In a speech reported in Sydney, Australia's *Daily Telegraph* on October 12, 1915, she commented:

> [A]bout women in architecture there was nothing really to say except... [the] notion that "women can't do this and can't do that" was all of a piece that it required special genius on the part of certain men to do this or that. It was a theory that truckled to the vanity of some and the laziness of others...
>
> All our troubles arose from that same fundamental false standard. So long as men considered they were superior to women and so privileged to work, or women considered themselves superior to men and so privileged not to work it would perpetuate the same standard in other fields...
>
> Women could not expect to take up a profession like architecture because it was specially fitted to ladies. As a man did so a woman must—work day times, night times. It must form the basis of her dreams. She must give it her Saturdays and her Sundays and go without holidays... Women could not expect to accomplish it with less than the men had to give. At present men had to give up practically all social life... That did not mean she had no relation with her fellow creatures, but those relations would be in connection with and in relation to her work...

Like Morgan, Pope, and Mahony, many of the women who did persevere came from white, upper-middle-class families and were well educated. Their client base also tended to come from a similar background: women benefactors wanting to erect university pavilions; presidents of clubs, women's colleges, and YWCAs seeking to equip their communities with appropriate facilities; reformers in early public housing; and individuals desirous of a well-planned home. While substantial, this type of work attracted little attention from the architectural press, focused on large-scale, complex buildings. Women architects also probably avoided calling public attention to themselves as it would have been gauche to do so, trained as they were to be genteel. Prevailing conventions of their time considered displays of ego and ambition as "unwomanly." In contrast, their male contemporaries unabashedly exhibited their drive for self-promotion.

Woods compared architectural offices to fraternities. Women were unwelcome in this unfriendly environment where it was presumed "baseball games, gymnasium workouts, costume balls, and dinners were decidedly male affairs." Typically, women struck out on their own in private practice or in partnership with other women or their husbands, often because mainstream offices refused to hire them. Minerva Parker Nichols (1860-1943) started her solo practice in Philadelphia in 1888. Henrietta Dozier hung her shingle in Atlanta, Georgia, in 1901. She practiced there until 1916, before moving to Jacksonville, Florida. A specialist in Colonial Revival work and historic preservation, Woods informs, "she reportedly listed herself as H. Dozier or Harry Dozier to bring in clients." This strategy was not always successful, as Dozier related during her WPA era interview:

> I have always had to compete with men, yes. In submitting designs, plans, bids, I have never asked any consideration at any time because I happened to be

a woman; I put all my cards on the table in fair and honest competition, and ask only consideration on the same basis.

For the most part I have been treated fairly. I remember one instance when designs were asked for the State and County Building in Atlanta, I went to the county officials, in the confidence of youth - it was in 1904 - but I knew what splendid training I had received, and stated brashly I would like to have this job. They said, 'We are sorry, Miss Dozier, but we cannot give it to you because you are not a voter.' Well, that was a new argument and was my first experience with officials' playing of politics with the tax-payers' money.

Marcia Mead (1879-1969) designed numerous YWCAs and planned housing for African-American war workers in Washington, D.C., reports architecture professor Kathryn H. Anthony. She opened an office with Anna Schenck in New York City and the firm mentored other women. As Annmarie Adams discovered, they took in Esther Marjorie Hill (1895-1985), the first woman to graduate from the architecture program at the University of Toronto (in 1920) between August 1923 and November 1924. Waltham, Massachusetts-based Ida Annah Ryan (1885-1960) researched and designed what she proposed to be the model tenement.

Elizabeth Carter Brooks (1867-1951), possibly the earliest African-American woman architect according to Dreck Spurlock Wilson's *African American Architects: A Biographical Dictionary 1865-1945*, received her classical and practical education in "historic styles" of architecture at the Swain Free School (later known as the Swain School of Design), the oldest private school in Massachusetts exclusively devoted to teaching Fine and Commercial Art. Wearing two hats, as social activist and architect, in one of her earliest projects she bought property in 1903, now 396 Middle Street in New Bedford, Massachusetts, for the purpose of erecting a permanent building to house the New Bedford Home of the Aged and in 1908 managed to realize her design for a colonial-styled, clapboard covered, two-and-a-half storey building, still standing in 2014.

From one woman architect in 1870 to twenty-two listed in the 1890 census (none of color), the number of women calling themselves architects climbed to one hundred in 1900. Woods likewise counted 305 women listed as "designers, draftsmen, and inventors" in 1890. Ten years later there were 900 "women involved with design, drafting, or inventing." Louise Blanchard (1856-1913) observed the discrepancy in her March 6, 1891 public address to the Women's Educational and Industrial Union on "Women and Architecture," lamenting:

> The total number of women graduates from the various schools of the country can hardly exceed a dozen, and most of these seem to have renounced ambition with the attainment of a degree, but there are among them a few brilliant and energetic women for whom the future holds great possibilities.
>
> There are also a few women drafting in various offices through the country, and the only respect in which they fall below their brothers is in disinclination to familiarize themselves with the practical questions of actual construction. They shirk the brick-and-mortar-rubber-boot-and-ladder-climbing period of investigative education, and as a consequence remain at the tracing stage of draftsmanship. There are hardly more successful women draftsmen than women graduates, but the next decade will

doubtless give us a few thoroughly efficient architects from their number.

The contributions of the few women who did break into the male stronghold generally remained invisible, sometimes because they were assigned secondary roles, sometimes because men took credit or were given credit for their work. The anonymous contributions Natalie de Blois (1921-2013) made to the famous U.S. firm Skidmore, Owings and Merrill (SOM) over the course of her thirty-year career will never be known, admitted one of the principals of the firm, Nathanial Owings (1903-1984), in his autobiography: "Her mind and hands worked marvels in design—and only she and God would ever know just how many great solutions, with the imprimatur of one of the male heroes of SOM, owed much more to her than was attributed by either SOM or the client."

Similarly, Mary Elizabeth Jane Colter's (1869-1958) name had "disappeared" from architectural records until recently because the man who was chief architect of a company that employed her, the Santa Fe Railroad, signed off on all its jobs. Her signature style, widely imitated during Depression Era Works Progress Administration (WPA) construction projects is generally known by its generic brand name, "National Park Service Rustic." Inspired by architecture of Native Americans as well as Spanish colonial buildings, her best-known works are those along the South Rim of the Grand Canyon, in Grand Canyon National Park, and her contributions to the renovation and expansion of La Fonda, a Santa Fe hotel, from 1926 through 1929. The Fred Harvey Company employed her for almost half a century. Another one of the buildings this contemporary of Frank Lloyd Wright and Julia Morgan designed for that firm, La Posada, a sprawling hotel and railroad station in Spanish Colonial Revival style in Winslow, Arizona, opened in 1930. At least five of her buildings are National Historic Landmarks.

While some of Julia Morgan's designs are quite famous, others, be they private residences or public facilities, may either not display any official acknowledgement or have never been credited as her designs. Renewed interest in her career was in large part spurred by historian Sara Holmes Boutelle's published research. She discovered just how neglected Julia Morgan's work was as late as 1972, when she first visited William Randolph Hearst's famous estate at San Simeon, a project that evolved over twenty-four years. Boutelle had to point out that an official photography book for visitors to San Simeon identified the architect, standing next to her famous client, as Hearst's "secretary."

Many North American women architects found their entry to employment as the wives or relatives of practicing architects. Marion Mahony was first employed as an architect in the Chicago office of her male cousin, Dwight Heald Perkins, after her 1894 graduation from MIT's Department of Architecture, where she was the second woman to earn a Bachelor of Science degree. In 1895, she began her second job, in Frank Lloyd Wright's Oak Park studio in Chicago. In 1898, she was one of the first twelve people to take the Illinois licensing exam, becoming the first woman to gain that distinction in the state and the nation.

Mahony's distinctive drawings and watercolors of Wright's designs are widely acknowledged to have helped Wright gain early critical acclaim, which could have been hers had she adamantly sought recognition for the work she completed first as trusted draftsman (architect) and then as chief designer. The latter appointment was made by Hermann von Holst when he took over the firm in 1909, after Wright abruptly decided to leave his wife Catherine and their six children to go off to Europe with Mamah Borthwick Cheney, a client's wife and Oak Park neighbor. As Mahony once observed, "My specialty is, I suppose, what is called presentation work."

In 1911, Mahony married Walter Burley Griffin, another Wright employee, and spent the rest of her career collaborating on and rendering work under his name. She seemed to have accepted subordination with equanimity, as Mahony wrote in her unpublished, four-volume *The Magic of America*, intended as an homage to Griffin and an autobiography: "I can never aspire to be as great an architect as he, but I can best understand and help him and to a wife there is not greater recompense." However, as Upton reports: "Sources close to the couple contend that some of Walter's major projects in... Australia, were actually his wife's."

Barred from architecture schools, discriminated against in architectural offices, excluded from professional organizations—despite these obstacles, an "exceptional few" women did succeed in attaining the status of registered architects. Not all professions were so slow to allow women into their ranks, although the sciences, engineering, and mathematics were also reluctant to include women. Eight hundred women were practicing as medical doctors in the United States in 1888. Meanwhile, Dr. Jennie Trout became Canada's first licensed woman doctor in 1875.

As of October 15, 1889, shortly before the consolidation of the WAA with the AIA, the AIA had 322 architects recorded in their membership list. In 1890, after the merger, the AIA membership list recorded 465 members, of whom only one was a woman: Louise Bethune. The second woman voted into the AIA was Lois Lilley Howe (1884-1967), who began a solo practice in Boston in 1893 that specialized in the design of low-income housing, which by 1926 had become a thriving practice with two other women architects, known as Howe, Manny & Almy. Research by architectural historian Sarah Allaback revealed that thirteen years after Bethune became an AIA member, Howe "became the second woman voted into the AIA because the electing members assumed 'Lois' was a man."

When Bethune terminated her membership in 1904, Howe was again the only woman member. She gained the status of Fellow of the American Institute of Architects (FAIA) in 1931, the second woman to do so. Because Howe's FAIA status was conferred through a voting process by the membership, some people say she became a Fellow through a more rigorous and prestigious process than the means by which Bethune gained her FAIA rank. She had been elected to the membership of the WAA in 1885 and, like all WAA members, kept her Fellow title when the two organizations merged. But AIA's recognition of women continued to be very slow. Twenty-four years passed before the next woman, Elizabeth Coit, became a FAIA in 1955.

In Canada, it took a letter from Esther Marjorie Hill's father, not an architect but in turn a science teacher, school inspector, and public librarian, to convince the Alberta Association of Architects (AAA) to accept her in 1925. She had initially applied for membership to the AAA in January 1921, but wished to supplement her education and sought additional office experience in Toronto and New York City in the intervening years. In the province of Québec, Pauline Roy-Rouillard became the first woman registered as a professional architect in 1942. Women apparently found it difficult to obtain the office experience required of Canadian registration bodies, though the Canadian census listed women architects as early as 1921.

It appears architecture has been one of the slowest of all professions to welcome women into their ranks. In 1900, for every woman listed as a registered architect in the U.S. census, there were 105 registered male architects. According to architectural historian Matilda McQuaid, "Statistics show that the cumulative total membership of women in the AIA did not top one hundred until 1949 and did not reach one thousand until the early 1980s." In 1950, the AIA listed that only 1.2 percent of its members were women and by 1985, another AIA survey found that 8.5 percent of its members were women. By 2000-2002, women's membership in the AIA had grown to thirteen percent and it continues to grow. The U.S. National Council of Architectural Registration Boards (NCARB) found in its statistical report on architectural licensing, *2014 NCARB By the Numbers*, that the percentage of women applying for NCARB Records increased from ten percent in the early 1990s to forty percent in 2014.

In Canada, women comprised 1.2 percent in 1961 and 10.6 percent in 1991 of the total number of architects registered in the provincial associations. Significantly, although North American schools of architecture reported that thirty-seven percent of their students were women in 2003, only ten percent actually went on to practice the profession in architectural firms. These percentages remain basically unchanged.

Alternative Career Choices

When Tania entered the five-year professional Bachelor of Architecture degree program at the University of Toronto in 1987, Blanche van Ginkel was dean of the School of Architecture, an appointment she had held since 1980. Tania's first encounter with a female instructor was in her second or third year, and that was during a 'charette,' an intensive weekend-long, in-house design competition. Although she did have female professors for optional courses taken in other departments, only one female adjunct professor taught her a half-course on architectural lighting at the School of Architecture. In 1985, approximately ten percent of American architecture faculty were women, and most taught "context" courses, like history of architecture, rather than design studios, so Tania should not have been surprised.

Van Ginkel, the first woman to head a school of architecture in Canada and first female president of the Association of the Collegiate Schools of Architecture, elected in 1986, wrote an article entitled "Slowly and Surely (But Somewhat Painfully), More or Less the History of Women in Architecture in Canada: An Account of the Struggles of Women to Find a Way Into the Architectural Profession in Canada," which appeared in the *Canadian Architect* in November 1993. In the U.S., publications about women in architecture had started to appear almost twenty years earlier, when women began to enter the ivory tower as architecture faculty, in step with gains within the women's movement. Among the earliest works addressing gender issues in architecture were Doris Cole's *From Tipi to Skyscraper: A History of Women in Architecture* (1973); Susana Torre's edited volume, *Women in American Architecture: A Historic and Contemporary Perspective* (1977); Gwendolyn Wright's *Moralism and the Model Home* (1980); Dolores Hayden's *The Grand Domestic Revolution* (1981); and Ellen Perry Berkeley and Matilda McQuaid's anthology, *Architecture: A Place for Women* (1989). These early publications all sought to document women's contributions to the field of architecture. Authors and advocates created archives to preserve women architects' materials, even restoring recognition for work first attributed to or appropriated by men. Furthermore, they sought to discover role models for their female students, nieces, and daughters, and in so doing highlighted women's accomplishments, such as those of Catherine Beecher, Harriet Irwin, and Charlotte Perkins Gilman.

Beecher (1800-1878), the eldest daughter of nationally known Calvinist minister Reverend Lyman Beecher, was arguably the most influential of all nineteenth-century women in American architecture. This was because of the mass market dissemination, popularity, and lasting influence of her suburban home design prototypes that appeared in her hugely successful self-published how-to books and magazines for women, including her bestseller first published in 1869, *The American Woman's Home*. The book was co-authored with her sister Harriet Beecher Stowe, already famous as the author of *Uncle Tom's Cabin*.

Self-taught, Harriet Irwin (1828-1897) was daughter of the founder and first president of Davidson College, sister-in-law of Stonewall Jackson, staunch supporter of the Confederacy, upper-class resident of Charlotte, North Carolina, and mother of nine children. In 1869 she became the first woman to patent an architectural innovation, for her hexagonal house. Motivated by the "lack of progress" shown in Charlotte's building boom after the Civil War, she sought a design providing a clean, well-ventilated, and sun-filled living environment. One of the at least three hexagonal houses built following Irwin's plan remains standing in 2014, at 912 West Fifth Street in Charlotte.

Writer and utopian feminist Charlotte Perkins Gilman (1860-1935) attended Rhode Island School of Design and worked as a commercial artist and teacher before marrying her first husband. Like her cousin Catherine Beecher a generation earlier, she is credited by Annmarie Adams for her contribution through her publication of "radical ideas related to household management that displayed considerable architectural expertise."

None of these women had formal training in architecture. Julia Morgan reflected on women's architectural contributions:

> [T]hey have as clients contributed very largely except, perhaps, in monumental buildings. The few professional women architects have contributed little or nothing to the profession—no great artist, no revolutionary ideas, no outstanding design. They have, however, done sincere good work along with the tide, and as the years go on, undoubtedly some greater than other architects will be developed, and in fair proportion to the number of outstanding men to the number in the rank and file.

Hopeful, she nonetheless acknowledged the entrenched hierarchy between architectural "stars" and run-of-the-mill practitioners. Her remark likely refers to registered architects, and if so, ignores the fact that in 1950, 90,000 unregistered professional employees worked for the 19,000 registered architects in America. The male majority educated in architecture, like their female colleagues, never obtained a license but worked in architectural offices where they had comfortable careers. Only those responsible for signing drawings in an architectural firm or office needed the mandatory "stamp"; those working under their supervision did not. Typical of hundreds of women, 1945 McGill University graduate Sylvia Chaplin, whose student work was published in the *Royal Architectural Institute of Canada Journal* in April 1944, never became a member of a provincial architectural association.

Because of the profession's old boys' club mentality, it is important to note that many women found other ways to make significant contributions to the development of residential, commercial, and civic architecture in North America before the turn of the twentieth century. Like a great many of their unregistered male colleagues, many women took up alternative occupations related to architecture as interior designers, landscape designers, craftspersons, critics, educators, clients, and preservationists, roles that the star-system continues to obscure.

As Morgan admitted, female clients "contributed very largely" to the field of architecture. Even so, "in a toast at a banquet of architects," recounts Woods, prominent Chicago architect John Wellbourne Root "poked fun at 'Madame'... and her 'little plan on scented notepaper she had studied at home.'" But as Urban Studies professor Dana Cuff reminds us, "Clients, be they state, public, church, corporate, or private, provide the function of a building, thereby placing a critical dimension of the architectural product under the client's control." Women holding the purse strings and thus decision-making power were influential. If male clients assumed their jobs were to direct the architect, their female counterparts did so, too.

Indeed, in these roles of givers of work or users of space, as argued by Alice Friedman (*Women and the Making of the Modern House,* 1998), Annmarie Adams (*Architecture in the Family Way: Doctors, Houses and Women, 1870-1900,* 1996), Abigail van Slyck (*Free to All: Carnegie Libraries and American Culture, 1890-1920,* 1995), and others, women collaborated in design, and this despite the paternal attitudes some male architects frequently adopted with their female clients.

In the United States, the field of historic preservation largely owes its beginnings to the women who led active campaigns to champion architectural preservation projects. As early as 1854, the Mount Vernon Ladies' Association, a volunteer organization led by Ann Pamela Cunningham, spearheaded the preservation of Mount Vernon, the Virginia home of George Washington. The Daughters of the American Revolution, organized in 1890, is credited as being the first national organization to protect historic sites throughout the United States. Elizabeth Carter Brooks was responsible for restoring the home of a famous African American Civil War veteran in New Bedford, Massachusetts, around 1930, which became a shrine to commemorate the efforts of black Union soldiers who participated in the Civil War. The first to recognize the potential of Charleston, South

Carolina, as a restored historic district was Susan Pringle Frost, an active member of the Charleston Federation of Women's Clubs, who began purchasing architecturally significant real estate in Charleston, in 1909.

Contrary to the U.S., the history of the historic preservation movement is little documented in Canada. Architectural historian Gordon Fulton says that other than local historical societies that took an interest in heritage conservation and private initiatives, "concerted heritage conservation activities were relatively rare in Canada until the early twentieth century." He says nothing about the role of women in that period.

Mother Joseph of the Sacred Heart and Jennie Louise Blanchard Bethune were but two of the women who essayed entry into the heavily guarded citadel that became the architectural profession. Yet in many ways, both women's careers paralleled those of their male contemporaries. Working in an era and region where the division of tasks among architects, builders, and clients were relatively ambiguous, a person like Mother Joseph could perform more than one or all of those tasks. Attempts to circumscribe the spheres of activity proper to the common builder from those proper to the professional architect demanded continuous negotiation.

So architecture remained highly disorganized, heterogeneous, and unregulated until the eve of the twentieth century in North America when the first states and provinces began to pass licensing laws. It took some time before restrictions as to who could be an architect were put in place and rigorously applied throughout North America. The state of Washington passed its first licensing law seventeen years after the death of Mother Joseph. Bethune, who was among those who lobbied for licensure and regulation of the architectural profession during her entire career, died two years before the first licensing law was passed in New York State.

In the U.S. in 2014, there is no single definition of the term "architect," as each state licensing board creates its own definition of the term. As you read the two following chapters, consider whether these women satisfy the criteria for being architects, as currently defined by their home states (found at www.aia.org):

For Mother Joseph, in Washington State:

> "'Practice of architecture' means the rendering of services in connection with the art and science of building design for construction of any structure or grouping of structures and the use of space within and surrounding the structures or the design for construction of alterations or additions to the structures, including but not specifically limited to predesign services, schematic design, design development, preparation of construction contract documents, and administration of the construction contract."

For Bethune, in New York State:

> "The practice of the profession of architecture is defined as rendering or offering to render services which require the application of the art, science, and aesthetics of design and construction of buildings, groups of buildings, including their components and appurtenances and the spaces around them wherein the safeguarding of life, health, property, and public welfare is concerned. Such services include, but are not limited to consultation, evaluation, planning, the provision of preliminary studies, designs, construction documents, construction management, and the administration of construction contracts."

PART I

The Sister with a Hammer

Tania Martin

MOTHER JOSEPH OF THE SACRED HEART is an enigma. When asked, "Who was the first architect of the region, *in terms of today's standards of architectural design and supervision of building construction?*" [emphasis added], veteran architects of Washington and Oregon attending the 1953 American Institute of Architects (AIA) annual convention readily named Mother Joseph. They pointed out that she had "designed and managed the original buildings of St. Vincent's and Providence Hospitals in Portland, Providence Hospital in Seattle, the Sacred Heart Hospital in Spokane, and many other pioneer projects of large-scale construction." Twenty-three, in fact, before the AIA accepted its first female member in 1888, and seven more before her death in 1902. Despite these achievements, outside of the Pacific Northwest, Mother Joseph is essentially unknown.

West Coast architectural historians contend that Absalom B. Hallock (1827-1892) was first. He had established an architectural practice in Portland, Oregon, as early as 1851, six years before the AIA was founded, five years before Mother Joseph landed at Fort Vancouver, and two years before Washington became a territory. The State of Washington, which joined the Union in 1889, issued its first license to practice in 1921. So, in fact, Hallock is just as vulnerable as Mother Joseph, who was long touted as "First Architect of the Pacific Northwest," as to whether the "architect" moniker can be applied. He, too, practiced architecture, when anyone could hang his shingle.

Obviously impressed by the sheer size, number, and functions of the buildings credited to her (since commissions for large, complex buildings generally distinguish an architect as successful), the architects interviewed by *Seattle Times* journalist James Stevens perhaps inadvertently used nineteenth rather than twentieth-century standards of practice to gauge the career of this "Enterprising Nun of the Last Century." Mother Joseph was never registered with a professional association; at no time did the AIA make any formal declaration about her status. Although she never called herself an architect, Mother Joseph can be favorably compared to John Haviland, one of the earliest architects practicing in the United States. When he died in 1853, *The New York Daily Times* portrayed him as "an artist who served the public in a practical manner which everyone can appreciate... a man who served his time in a useful way... in the erection of buildings which the present state of society requires."

An Architect Named Joseph

Born on April 16, 1823, in Saint-Elzéar, a village north of Montreal in what was then Lower Canada, Esther was the third child of twelve born to Joseph Pariseau, whose grandfather Martin had emigrated from the Lorraine region in France in 1756, and Françoise Rousseau. Also in 1823, construction started on the Erie Canal and the President of the United States announced the Monroe Doctrine, banning European influence in the American continents. Born in the same year was Oblate of Mary Immaculate missionary priest Alexandre-Antonin Taché (1823-1894), who served the Red River Colony centered on today's St. Boniface in Winnipeg, Manitoba and the Île-à-la-Crosse mission in what is now Saskatchewan, and fought for French and Catholic schools in the region. French was the predominant language used in the West up until the last quarter of the nineteenth century, with the defeat of the resistance led by the Métis and Louis Riel, who was hanged in 1885. Moreover, Mother Joseph might have even crossed paths with Louis Riel. The survival of French was threatened by settlement increasingly of English speakers and the policies enacted by the Government of Canada to stymy efforts to conduct business and school children in French.

Construction of Notre-Dame Church on the Place d'Armes in Montreal, an early extant example of a Gothic revival church in Canada, began in 1823. Commissioned by the congregation of St-Sulpice and built to the design of Irish-born architect James O'Donnell, it was completed in 1829. In fact, when Esther Pariseau was born in 1823, the political geography in Western North America was still undefined and would take another eighty years before the provinces and states would all be constituted as they are known today (in 2014).

Young Pariseau's formal schooling was limited to a mere three years. Prior to enrolling at age seventeen in Mlle Elizabeth Bruyère's boarding school at Saint-Martin-de-Laval, near her home village, she had been home-schooled. From her mother Esther had learned the requisite housekeeping skills—gardening, cooking, baking, sewing, mending, ironing, laundering—as well as fancy needlework and reading, relates Catherine McCrosson, Sister Mary of the Blessed Sacrament in religion and author of Mother Joseph's biography. McCrosson portrayed Esther as quite the tomboy in her childhood: she led her siblings in play patriot risings and she aided her father in his carriage shop like her older brother, also named Joseph. Esther finessed her reading, writing, and arithmetic skills under Bruyère's tutelage. This graduate of the Sisters of the Congregation of Notre-Dame College may have also awakened Pariseau's vocation. She quit teaching, one of the few avenues open to unmarried women in mid-nineteenth century North America, in order to enter the congregation of the Grey Nuns of Montreal, a sisterhood devoted to all types of works of charity. In 1845 Bruyère would found the Sisters of Charity (Grey Nuns) of Bytown, the village that would become Canada's capital city, Ottawa.

Esther was the thirteenth young woman to be admitted into the newly created order of the Sisters of Providence in 1843. McCrosson has the Pariseau patriarch saying: "She can read and write and figure accurately. She can cook and sew and spin and do all manner of housework well. She has learned carpentry from me and can handle tools as well as I can. Moreover, she can plan and supervise the work of others, and I assure you, Madame, she will some day make a very good superior" when, on December 26, 1843, he brought his daughter to Émilie Gamelin's "yellow house" near the diocesan see, the Bishop's headquarters in Montreal. Today, an important square in Montreal stands in the place of the Sisters of Providence's original convent and bears Émilie Gamelin's name. Homeless people are often fed there and the square is used as a rallying point for demonstrations for social justice issues such as the student strikes of the *Printemps érable* or "Maple Spring" in 2012. It remains unclear, however, where McCrosson obtained his words. Plausibly she used interviews with sisters who may have personally known Mother Joseph or her beloved younger blood-sister, Julie, who had joined the Sisters of Providence on November 2, 1846, and taken St. Martin as her name in religion. Her older sister took the name Joseph when she pronounced her vows in 1845, thus signaling her new status as a "bride of Christ."

The two sisters were among some 330 women to have entered religious life in the 1840s, according to the *Atlas historique des pratiques religieuses*, a historical geography of religious practices in southwestern Québec. It was a significant jump from the seventy who had joined female orders in the 1820s, the decade of the Pariseau sisters' births. In contrast with the Second Great Awakening, an early nineteenth-century Protestant religious revival in the U.S. that had more or less petered out by 1840, Catholicism had a resurgence in a relatively secular Lower Canada (Quebec) society after the Patriotes republican-inspired revolts of 1837-1838. Monsignor Bourget and other prelates multiplied the foundation of religious orders, either by inviting European religious communities to branch out to Canada or by encouraging Canadian-born men and women to establish religious communities to teach and nurse all segments of society and otherwise care for the most vulnerable people in urban and rural locations. By 1902, at the end of Esther's life, sociologists Nicole Laurin and Danielle Juteau estimate ten thousand of the women in Québec who had opted for the veil in the nineteenth century were still living in 1901, the year with which they began their study of female Catholic religious communities in the province.

Esther chose the name Joseph to honor her father, a rural Québec carriage maker. Given the range of skills attributed to him—designer, wheelwright, body-maker, blacksmith, carver, and painter—he could no doubt manufacture virtually any horse-drawn vehicle, from farm carts to buggies and sleighs as well as carriage parts. To do this, he would have needed knowledge to calculate the flowing curves and intricate joinery that outstripped that of the carpenter or handy farmer, as Thomas A. Kinney's *The Carriage Trade* asserts, in addition to deep understanding of the properties of elm, oak, ash, hickory, and other hardwoods used in making carriage wheels and bodies.

Mother Joseph's biographer imagined young Esther helping her father by putting away tools and cleaning the shop. As she grew older and stronger, she learned by observing her father and then by completing simple tasks under his supervision,

Albumen print of Mother Joseph of the Sacred Heart, 1850s. (Providence Archives, Seattle, Washington.)

much as any apprentice would have done. By age twelve, McCrosson claims in *The Bell and the River*, Esther not only knew the name and purpose of each of her father's tools—the hammer, the knife, the saw, the chisel, the drawknife, the spoke shave, the bit brace, the plane, the square—she also was able to recognize the use of various wood essences. The girl clearly had enough mastery in handling the tools to make a lovely sewing box of red maple, ash, and sugar maple as a gift for her mother.

Incidentally, "Joseph" is also the patron saint of carpenters. It was to him people prayed for a successful construction campaign. Building inaugurations were frequently held on Wednesdays, a day associated with the father of Jesus.

Once admitted to the Sisters of Providence, Esther continued acquiring skills as a postulant and then as a novice, two probationary periods a woman must pass before being allowed to take her vows. The *Dictionary of Canadian Biography* tells us she learned how to care for the sick at the Hôtel-Dieu, the premier Catholic hospital in Montreal run by the Religious Hospitallers of Saint Joseph, and how to do fine embroidery and make liturgical ornaments with the Congregation of Notre-Dame, a teaching order. Sister Joseph put this practical training to good use in the Sisters of Providence sewing room (where she made and mended habits and other items of clothing), the infirmary, and the pharmacy, before being asked to assist the general bursar (or treasurer) "with the daily tasks of marketing, baking and the laundry."

After taking her vows, she served two years as director of the elderly women boarders. She then took charge of the community's financial accounts. In that administrative office, and then as assistant to Mother Caron, the second superior of the order, she was able to exercise her executive acumen towards the growth of the Sisters of Providence. In the thirteen years before Sister Joseph was sent west, the order had implanted eleven Houses of Providence in Montreal and the surrounding region at the behest of Catholic clergy and philanthropists, including an orphanage in Burlington, Vermont. From nine thousand in 1800, the population of Montreal exploded to nearly fifty-eight thousand in 1852 thanks to nascent industrialization and heavy immigration from Britain and Ireland. Rural settlement continued to spread in the Saint-Lawrence Valley.

Sister Stanislaus of the Blessed Sacrament, who arrived in Vancouver, Washington, in 1881 and worked with Mother Joseph before the turn of the century, fondly recalled her "crossing the courtyard, a hammer in the belt of her habit, a saw in her hand—she loved to carry woodworking tools—and praying aloud." It is the very picture of the carpenter Joseph as observed in popular iconography. Furthermore:

> Hers was the gift of organization—the talent of the builder. She designed the big school down to its smallest detail. She hand-carved the intricate altar of the chapel and the big ornate chapel doors. She made wax figures of the Christ child and spent hour upon hour at the fine needlework for the vestments of the priests who said mass there.

Visitors to St. James Cathedral, Vancouver, Washington, can admire her stellar needlework in the reliquary and clothing of St. Lucien. She had made the bust with Sisters Martin and Mary-David when she was at the motherhouse in 1890.

By all accounts, Mother Joseph was a formidable woman. Described by Sister Merilu Vachon in a typescript "Portrait" of 1974, probably in anticipation of a ceremony celebrating the return of the bell to The Academy, the dark-haired, deep-set gray-blue-eyed foundress of the Sisters of Providence in the Pacific Northwest stood five feet, eight inches tall. Her large though well-proportioned frame, her strong broad shoulders, coupled with a straight firm mouth and ruddy complexion, lent her a masculine appearance, further reinforced by her deep, baritone voice. Her "step was measured, her walk was firm and always appeared business-like. Her nerves were of steel that seldom exhibited a shadow of fear... She would undertake the most arduous task without hesitation... [she had an] iron will... [a] woman of determined character, [she] never displayed weakness."

In autumn 1856, Mother Caron named Sister Joseph superior of a new mission to be founded in Vancouver, Washington. Just before departing to lead her contingent of four sisters to the Far West, Monsignor Bourget, then Bishop of Montreal, added *Sacré Cœur*, or "Sacred Heart," to her name. Henceforward she would be known as Mother Joseph of the Sacred Heart.

An "Enterprising Nun"

The *Dictionary of Canadian Biography* gives "builder, architect and artisan" as Mother Joseph's occupation. She may have been counted among the 198 women carpenters and joiners, or perhaps figured among the twenty-two female architects in the 1890 U.S. Census. First as superior and then as community bursar responsible for all financial transactions, the French-Canadian sister was responsible for the construction and maintenance of twenty-nine Sisters of Providence's institutional buildings over her fifty-six year career in the Pacific Northwest. There were to be "no broken fences, no broken doors, nothing out of place," even if it meant scraping and begging to procure sufficient funds to keep up repairs.

It was the hard-won January 28, 1859 Act of Incorporation under the legal title of "Sisters of Charity of the House of Providence in the Territory of Washington" that gave the religious order the latitude it needed to negotiate with the local civic and religious authorities, and the individuals representing them (whether priest, benefactor, doctor, or charitable group sponsoring the institution's creation), to purchase existing buildings or land on which to build, and to sign contracts. In other words, the government recognized the order as a non-profit or voluntary organization, making it the second oldest corporation to be registered in the State of Washington. The only sister named in the Act, Mother Joseph had the authority to take additional sisters of the order into partnership and she could acquire property, so long as it yielded no more than twenty thousand dollars in annual revenue. Prior to incorporation, individual sisters had to conduct business under their own names; afterwards Mother Joseph did so in the name of her order. She decided, with the approval of her superiors, when and where a new institution should be established. It was in that capacity, relate the chronicles, that she traveled in November 1889 with the Mother Provincial to choose a "satisfactory plot of land for the construction of the [future] hospital at Port Townsend," and on her return from Canada that same year "stopped in at Yakima, Washington, to take care of building business." She may have been checking whether St. Joseph Academy needed renovation or scoping out a site for the future St. Elisabeth Hospital in that city.

Many of the Sisters of Providence missions started up in borrowed buildings. Fixing up an existing house or hotel as hospital or school was a common and economical way of proceeding when starting up a new work, particularly a work of charity with few sources of revenue. From 1877 to 1882, Providence Hospital Seattle operated out of a house at Fifth and Madison that Mother Joseph had purchased in 1877. Before it was inaugurated July 30, 1880, Mother Joseph had the hotel she bought in Astoria converted into a hospital. She just had to tell her workmen to tear up that wall there, build this partition here, block up that window, and put a door in this window opening. The builders had the skills necessary to perform these straightforward tasks (even if she sometimes thought their work shoddy).

We can liken Mother Joseph to an in-house architect: she contracted for the supply of materials; she tendered and reviewed bids; she hired tradesmen; she supervised construction; she designed buildings. Rather than hire architects on a job-by-job basis, school boards, municipalities, and even state and federal governments began to employ salaried architects to do similar work. There were no architectural fees to pay when, in using her talents to the benefit of her community, Mother Joseph substituted herself as "architect." The May 8, 1879 *Independent* informed readers that "Sister Joseph... is now in Walla Walla, attending to the building of an academy there" (though she was really attending to St. Mary's Hospital, built adjacent to

St. Vincent Academy, erected in 1864). Although she supervised its construction, the architect of record for the hospital was O. F. Wegener, a local architect and civil engineer. On April 27, 1887, the same paper told readers, "Sister Joseph… has gone to North Yakima [Washington] to look after the building proposed to be erected by the Sisters of Charity in that place."

In some regards she was also like Boston and New York upper-class women directing the architects and builders they engaged to draw the plans and build residences on their Newport, Rhode Island estates that conformed to their vision. Mother Joseph likely instructed Warren H. Williams as to the size of the building, its layout, and the materials of the 1880 north and 1883 south wing additions to St. Vincent's Hospital in Portland, Oregon. He had been responsible in 1874 for the plans of Good Samaritan Hospital founded in 1875 by the Episcopal Diocese of Oregon in the same city. The firm of Allen and Whittemore converted Wegener's St. Mary's Hospital, Walla Walla, into St. Vincent Academy in 1883 and produced new plans for the hospital the same year. Scottish-born Donald McKay (1841-c. 1887) designed and supervised construction of the 1882 north wing of Providence Hospital, Seattle, a three-storey, wood-frame structure sporting a Second Empire roof, although tradition credited Mother Joseph with a part in the design.

As Cheryl Sjoblom, author of the entry on Mother Joseph in *Shaping Seattle Architecture*, admits:

> [N]o architect then in the Northwest could have matched [Mother Joseph's] experience. MacKay [like others] apparently had some experience with buildings of this scale, but the program and design requirements of the Sisters of Providence could have been identified only by Mother Joseph, and although MacKay is credited with production of the drawings and supervision of construction, Mother Joseph clearly was a collaborator and possibly a co-equal participant in the design. She most likely played a similar role in the expansion of the facility in 1887, 1888, and 1893, and possibly the expansion of 1901 as well.

Mother Joseph was similarly given credit for the 1887 St. Peter's Hospital in Olympia in that institution's chronicles, although Father Claissons had assisted "the architect."

A few buildings are solely attributed to Mother Joseph. *The California Architect and Building News* listed her as the architect of record for the 1883 Providence Academy, Olympia, Washington. She is said to have drawn up the plans for St. Vincent Hospital in Portland, where white and black people would be equally treated. Construction started in August 1874, as did a citywide collection encompassing East Portland. The Sisters netted two thousand dollars to help pay for materials and workmen. Oral history has Mother Joseph drawing "the plans [of Sacred Heart Hospital] on [Spokane hotelkeeper Mrs. Gray's] kitchen table" in 1888 and "once she had a work office on site, Mother Joseph had a nail keg for her seat and a rough desk for her drafting board." The prevailing "frontier mentality" may have been a boon to her as it was for the California women architects whose services were, architectural historian Diane Favro posits, readily accepted at the turn of the twentieth century.

Given the sheer number of projects in various stages of advancement, Mother Joseph had

Albumen print of Architect J. B. Blanchet, 1883, removed from the cornerstone of St. Joseph Hospital, Vancouver, Washington in 1972. (Providence Archives, Seattle, Washington.)

to seek outside help. She found a knowledgeable, trustworthy accomplice in Jean-Baptiste Blanchet (1839-1913), who arrived in Vancouver, Washington, on December 8, 1866, in the company of his two uncles, Mgr. Augustin Magloire Alexandre Blanchet, Bishop of Vancouver, and Mgr. François Norbert Blanchet, Archbishop of Oregon, as well as several sisters of Providence with the hope of being of some aid to missionaries and religious communities in the region. Born in Sainte-Flavie de Rimouski, Quebec, Blanchet spent forty-six years working with the Sisters of Providence as a farm employee as well as carpenter, interior decorator, joiner (carving tabernacles and altars for the community's chapels and those of churches in the diocese), architect, and construction supervisor, even after Mother Joseph passed away.

Some say the young Blanchet reputedly had apprenticed under her, developing "the gift which he had the greatest opportunity to perfect... architecture," although no corroborating evidence has been found. As Mother Joseph had very little English—all of her correspondence was written in French—perhaps Blanchet initially acted as her translator and later her representative on construction sites. He took over from Mother Joseph's superintendence on a number of jobs. In January 1887, she was too tired and worn out to continue directing the workmen in the construction of Sacred Heart Hospital in Spokane. Described as "beautiful, commodious... outfitted with all the necessities [yet] nothing superfluous," the sisters' chronicles (the yearly reports sent to the Mother Superior in Montreal) say that Blanchet "had drawn up the plan." But a few weeks later, Blanchet had to take over from MacKay, who had died in a fire during the construction of the hospital in New Westminster. He was charged to see completion of the building and "put in order the business, the contract, etc." In July 1893, Blanchet was sent to replace Mother Joseph in Colfax, where she was supervising the construction of the hospital. He spent seven months there, seeing "about the payments and other measures to take so that everything goes roundly, as much for the furnaces as for the finishing of the interior of the hospital and the outbuildings," perhaps freeing up Mother Joseph to oversee projects elsewhere, as later in the year she was receiving "the work of the contracts for the hospital at St-Ignatius."

The sisters regretted learning "that [Blanchet's] health is diminishing and he carries the germ of a mortal disease: asthma and a complication of an illness of the lungs." In his February 1913 obituary, they remembered how he and Mother Joseph together "formed plans of great merit, to which we are able to bear witness in numerous edifices of ours in the West." In 1889, the chronicles say, they had spent two-thirds of their time supervising construction in Yakima and Olympia, Washington, and Missoula, Montana. While Mother Joseph "busied herself with the plan of an addition to St. Peter's hospital, Blanchet actively worked on that of the hospital in Missoula. Even if the latter was not technically part of Sacred Heart Province, Mother General approved that Mr. Blanchet make the plan of the hospital and go to the site to execute the work." The sisters were grateful for the services he had rendered as a "kind of manager of external affairs of the Sisters of Providence that he administered with wisdom and to the satisfaction of all. He was esteemed and respected for his probity; many others consult him for private or public affairs. With experience and study, he had become an able architect."

Without the benefit of professional associations and meetings, Mother Joseph improved her knowledge through "contact with educated religious and business relations," believed Sister Merilu Vachon. Mother Joseph probably kept abreast of architectural developments and observed new building construction, much as architects and their clients did, during her many journeys to and from Montreal, which often brought her through major East Coast American cities, in addition to her extensive peregrinations from mission to mission in the Pacific Northwest. Indeed in July 1890, she and Sister Marie-Thérèse were sent, with the permission of Monsignor Gross, to expressly visit first-rate modern hospitals in the Eastern United States with the goal of "learn[ing] the best manner in which to build the new [St. Vincent] hospital in Portland, Oregon." Over the several-week-long trip, the sisters toured leading institutions in New York City, Brooklyn, Boston, and Burlington before returning to the Montreal motherhouse. They must also have visited the institutions that Protestants and Catholics had erected in Canada's largest city, which Mark Twain dubbed as the "city of a hundred steeples" in 1881.

Mother Joseph certainly had opinions about what qualified as good architecture and economical construction. In 1884, when the Mother House asked Mother Joseph to give her recollections of the first decades at the mission for posterity and the Sister of Providence's records, she told the sister chronicler about the convent-school that Reverend Brouillet had built in Walla Walla, likening it to a barn erected in the middle of an uncultivated field. St. Vincent Academy had opened on February 18, 1864, in a two-storey, forty-five-by-twenty-four-foot clapboard house, she recalled, adding "the Jewish also sent their children to the sisters' school." Worse, she found the school expensively built, noting the carpenters had earned between five and eight dollars per day and the lumber cost eighty dollars per thousand linear feet. And, she complained, in summer 1868 she had had to return to Walla Walla to "oversee the repairs the Mother General had thought necessary at the mission."

The expenses may have explained why St. Vincent Academy continued to carry a five-thousand-dollar debt.

The "enterprising nun," as she was called by a Yakima, Washington, newspaper in 1953, certainly amassed the wherewithal to direct architects and tradesmen to build according to her vision when she herself was not behind the drafting board literally drawing up plans with ink on linen. She had the knowledge needed to say what type of edifice was needed, give its dimensions, determine the size and layout of the rooms, and identify the materials in which it was to be constructed. Local conventional building methods would have also guided her.

A Heartful Vocation

Mother Joseph was "not an ordinary woman" and allusions to her "male character" recurred frequently in the chronicles kept by the Sisters of Providence. A perfectionist, she was intolerant towards the weaknesses of others. For her, blunt facts spoke for themselves; she put little effort in sweet persuasion, although planting the seed of an idea in the mind of a potential benefactor was not beyond her. Managing large undertakings was by far easier for her than managing people. At the same time, the comfort and well-being of those around her were among her preoccupations.

She may have belonged to a distinct group of women whose tremendous energy and stubbornness catapulted them into successful careers as architects. Architecture was a man's world, and if a woman butted heads with her employer, her client, or any other person in a position of authority, it certainly would not have gone unremarked. The terms "volatile" and "difficult" were frequently employed to describe female architects, usually in order to diminish their contributions to architecture, as Elizabeth Birmingham observed in her analysis of the discourse about American architect Marion Mahony Griffin. When similar language was used to describe male architects, the connotations were positive and referred to their creativity and control over their oeuvre (and employees).

Mother Joseph's "temperament of fire, her half-broken character, her iron will brought her to excess on more than one occasion," remarked Reverend A. Archambeault, canon and Ecclesiastical superior of the Sisters of Providence, in her obituary. In the early years, the sister may have been forgiven for occasionally going ahead with projects without prior authorization from her superiors in Montreal, relying on her own judgment rather than waiting for a written response to travel the three thousand miles to reach Vancouver. It took weeks, if not months, for a letter to arrive before the advent of trains, telegraph, and telephone, which increased the rapidity of correspondence and eased coordination of the sisters' activities across the continent. Under such isolated circumstances, local superiors had to act. They had to be prudent, however, before embarking on building campaigns or accepting new missions that could overly stretch scarce financial and human resources.

Decisions were not always easy to make, especially when ecclesiastical authorities were not of the same mind. Mother Joseph was averse to the idea of accepting a house in East Portland near the train yards, generously offered to them by a Mr. B. Halliday, a controversial tycoon whose reputation was tarnished by questionable relationships and shady politics by some accounts. The grand vicar insisted on the merits of such a plan; the benefactor reputedly offered a fine site, a good house, use of his physician, and funds to cover part of construction. However, even though the arrangements pointed towards success, Mother Joseph hesitated, despite local pressure. While she was in Portland on other matters, she passed in front of the old cathedral. She went inside and threw a medal of St. Vincent into the collection box saying, "I can't do anything for your hospital, fix things as you may." Several months passed. On the feast day of St. Vincent, July 19, 1874, however, Mother Joseph's prayer was answered. Members of the Society of St. Vincent de Paul approached the Sisters of Providence and agreed to their terms, and gave them a well-situated block in Portland for the hospital.

It is very unlikely that a lay architect would have behaved in such a manner, one that betrayed a particular form of Catholic piety, unless he himself were a pious Catholic. Yet Mother Joseph relied on a common rhetorical device in the telling of this story in the chronicles. She could not in so many words say that she questioned a male ecclesiastical figure of authority in his decision-making or that she was in disagreement with him, especially since she was a role model for the sisters. Saying exactly what she thought would humiliate him and show disrespect and a lack of humility on her part. She trusted her own intuition in refusing the first offer as much as she trusted God's will. Asking St. Vincent for his intercession bought time and brought to light an alternative, one that she undoubtedly had a hand in devising as community bursar.

Mother Joseph's talents were widely acknowledged. To mark her golden jubilee—fifty years of vocation—the sisters mounted an exhibition of her skills in washing, cooking, nursing, carpentering, carving, making plans for buildings, making outfits for priests and bishops, molding statues, crucifixes and Infant Jesus, making tapers, candles and hosts, making vestments and embroidering in gold, making garments for the Sisters and the poor, dressing the body-saints of martyrs, etc. A similar formula was used in 1956 to commemorate Providence Academy's centennial. Artifacts associated with the pioneer sister included her spinning wheel, a tabernacle carved in 1857 from orange crates and enameled in ivory and gold leaf, as well as a tabernacle veil of heavy, grosgrain silk, embroidered in gold.

The Mother General and male clergy's letters of condolence highlighted Mother Joseph's "ambitious visions… that stem from genius… [believing] God had bestowed upon her a range of talents rarely encountered in a woman. She excelled not only in the works proper to her sex, from the most vulgar to the finest and most delicate, but also she entered in the domain of the strong and executed work that ordinarily men only can accomplish." Those very extraordinary aptitudes, however, put her in a class by herself. Surprisingly gentle and affectionate with the children, she reputedly had great difficulty communicating "those things that were real and important to her," as many gifted people do.

Mother Joseph must have felt some relief when she was finally able to relinquish her post as superior in 1866 to take up the office of bursar of the Western missions. Technically she should have been called Sister Joseph from then onwards, but the title "Mother" stuck. She had requested replacement five years earlier, fully aware that her bilious temperament, imperious disposition, and tactless heedlessness caused tension between herself and fellow sisters, who may have felt "rancor and resentment against one so clumsy in the art of command." Already in 1859 she had written Mgr. Bourget avowing she used their chaplain as an intermediary between herself and the sisters under her charge since, unlike her, he had gained their confidence. Even if she was quick to excuse herself for her bursts of outrage, harm nonetheless was done, though seldom irreparably.

Mother Joseph burned for urgent activity, so much so that she struggled all her life to learn to temper with stillness and inner quiet those fiery impulses to constantly act. We might imagine such a person having some trouble upholding a degree of humility and daily maintaining a pleasing demeanor, yet her "letters testif[ied] to a deep spirituality and interior life," though she did write with the usual rhetoric, giving thanks to God and saints, underscoring the will of God in moments of tragedy. In a September 27, 1877 letter addressed to the Mother Praxedes, she broached the delicate question of personal relationships among sisters, and more specifically the desire on the part of some not to have Mother Joseph return to the mission. On May 24, 1890, the General Council officially tasked her with overseeing the plans and building affairs of the Sisters of Providence in the Pacific Northwest, but she had been doing this work since 1866, before the administrative reorganization into provinces. It was a job that required her to travel a lot.

Her long absences perhaps relieved any tension her presence might incur among the sisters and employees. They also afforded Mother Joseph a degree of freedom while roaming northern and eastern Washington, Montana, and Idaho. When the local administrative council sent Mother Joseph back to Montreal, ostensibly to take care of the mission's business on September 23, 1863, she would have traveled by sea. To get to the mining and lumber camps, Indian missions, and towns where the sisters opened institutions, she would have initially journeyed by riverboat, horseback, stagecoach, and eventually by train. Mother Joseph had a lifelong pass from the Union Pacific passenger train. It was valid for her and a companion, as she would inevitably be accompanied by one other sister, as well as a male member of the clergy or trusted notable, and at least one guide, often Native American. The prettier her female companion was, the better the chances of succeeding in convincing men in the mines and the camps to donate to towards the construction of hospitals.

Mother Joseph's office kept her extremely active. Between 1881 and 1891, the Sisters of Providence founded eight new missions in the Pacific Rim. In Washington they included St. Mary's Hospital (Walla Walla), Sacred Heart Hospital (Spokane), St. Joseph Academy (Sprague), St. Peter's Hospital (Olympia), St. John-of-the-Cross Hospital (Port Townsend), and St. Elizabeth's Hospital (Yakima). In British Columbia they included St. Mary's Hospital (New Westminster). During the same decade were established in the Intermountain West the Sacred Heart Academy (Missoula) and St. Clare Hospital (Benton) in Washington; St. Eugene Hospital in Cranbrook /Kootenay, British Columbia; and Providence Hospital in Wallace, Idaho. Three were under construction at the same time. The indefatigable sister could be in one town signing a contract to buy the land necessary to build a new mission and a few days later in another town overseeing the enlargement of a school established a number of years earlier, not to mention her fundraising campaigns.

"Nothing could tax [Mother Joseph's] activity or generous initiative," claimed her fellow sisters and the prelates who knew her, though they also admitted that "human fragility must necessarily bring areas of shadow, of darkness." Indeed, Mother Joseph, in periodic moments of despair, complained to her superior, her confessor, and friends in the clergy of her failings and weak discipline, worrying that she was not cut of religious cloth, despite her commitments of firmly implanting the Sisters of Providence in "foreign territory." These episodes of self-doubt, feelings of inadequacy, and plausibly depression punctuated Mother Joseph's life. On February 15, 1898, Mother Mary Godfrey granted Mother Joseph permission to visit Mother House, praying that God would reward the sister with peace and spiritual consolation.

Not unexpectedly, Mother Joseph's incessant activity took a heavy toll on her health, especially as she advanced in age. A chronicle entry on the feast of Corpus Christi in 1894 alerted readers that Mother Joseph had suddenly taken ill, which caused great worry. After two weeks of rest, she quietly and slowly resumed her occupations. A year later she had "all the vigor of a fifty-year-old." Aged seventy-one in August 1895, "everyone is surprised to see her follow the parts of the mass like a youth" on her golden jubilee.

Even in the face of illness, Mother Joseph was determined to look after the affairs of the order.

Cabinet photograph of Mother Joseph of the Sacred Heart (1823-1902), ca. 1900. Photographer, Hofsteater, Portland. (Providence Archives, Seattle, Washington.)

After undergoing surgery for breast cancer in St. Vincent Hospital, Portland, in July 1899, she accompanied Sister Marie-Thérèse to Cranbrook the following spring to discuss the construction of a hospital, and a few months later she went to Spokane after receiving a telegram asking her to take care of urgent matters. Similarly, in early February 1901, she made one last trip to Seattle, returning March 12, "tired and suffering, the tumor in her right eye growing" for which she was operated in late summer. Still, she counseled the sisters, "do not refuse Oakland." Although she was practically blind in her right eye, she persisted in embroidering a tabernacle veil with gold thread, a gift for the centenary celebrations of Mother Gamelin that were to take place in Montreal.

Bedridden the last few months of her life, her agony, which she suffered with dignity and patience, ultimately tested the true nature of her religious vocation. On her deathbed, she did not "stop humiliating herself, as she has done all of her life for the weaknesses that His Divine Mercy left her, undoubtedly, to keep her humble, [to] think little of herself given her rare and great intellectual capabilities. Her boiling nature was her companion unto death, but we have reason to hope that it all served the glory of God and the saving of her soul." When the suffering cancer patient had her last communion on January 16, 1902, the same day J. B. Blanchet, "loyal servant and companion architect of Sister Joseph," came to say farewell after several months' absence, she humbly asked forgiveness of the community one last time for all of her past faults and foibles, recounted the chronicles.

Mother Joseph S. H. Parizeau [*sic*], 1823-1902, R.I.P. Headstone. (Photo, Tania Martin.)

Mother Joseph died on January 19, 1902, on the feast of the Name of Jesus. Aged seventy-eight years, nine months, and two days, she had lived fifty-eight years and twenty-eight days a bride of Christ, forty-six of these years on the West Coast of North America. She is buried in the sisters' parcel of St. James Acre Cemetery of Vancouver, Washington, renamed Mother Joseph Catholic Cemetery in May 2007, just north of Fourth Plain Boulevard at 29th and O Streets. Her plain, white, limestone headstone, indistinguishable from those of 150 other Sisters of Providence, was placed in one of two orderly rows leading to a Calvary. She had brought the crucifix from a trip she made in 1884.

Mother Joseph had an insatiable thirst to immolate herself in doing good works and making immense sacrifices over the course of her life. Membership in a religious community gave her opportunities to exploit her skills. This "sister with a hammer" expressed her faith more through incessant action than divine contemplation. It was her path to God.

Holy Trinity of Settlement

Led by Mother Joseph, five Sisters of Providence arrived in the Oregon Country in 1856 in the midst of Yakima War (1855-1858), waged over Euro-American settlers' encroachment on native lands. Bishop Augustin Magloire Alexandre Blanchet had requested sisters; the Montreal motherhouse acquiesced. They had made the six-thousand-mile journey by sea and by land from Montreal to Fort Vancouver, where the "holy trinity" (namely, the Hudson's Bay Company (HBC) trading post, St. James' mission, and the U.S. Army) was already established.

The sisters had been preceded by French-Canadian and Métis trappers and voyageurs who canoed and portaged through the vast wilderness, camped with their native counterparts, and sojourned at fur-trading posts such as those of the North-West Company, which was later absorbed into HBC, manned by Scottish and English factors. Like the Klickitat, a Shahaptian nation whose ancestral lands lay north of the Columbia River at the headwaters of the Cowlitz, Lewis, White Salmon, and Klickitat Rivers, and who served as intermediaries between coastal and inland tribes, the Walla Walla, Yakima, Cayuse, and other nations in the region had not only encountered the Lewis and Clark Expedition (c. 1805), but also had long-established trade relationships with HBC forts at Vancouver, Walla Walla, and Okanagan. Interestingly, Lewis and Cark's guides included Toussaint Charbonneau—Clark wrote of "Shabono, our interpreter"—from Boucherville, near Montreal, and his wife, Sacagawea. Moreover, many white men stationed in the Pacific Northwest or those who traded within this part of the country had intermarried with native women.

First Chief Factor of Fort Vancouver, Dr. John McLoughlin (1774-1857), named "White-Headed Eagle" by the Chinook, had a Métis wife. Born at Rivière-du-Loup, Québec, of Irish and Scottish parents, he had been baptized Catholic and raised in the Church of England. His dear friend, François Norbert Blanchet, first Catholic missionary in the Pacific Northwest, brought him back to the Catholic faith in 1842, the year McLoughlin took command of HBC headquarters in the Columbia District, which covered the northern half of the Oregon Country. Hudson's Bay Company trade monopoly on the region discouraged massive settlement north of the Columbia River. The waterway marked the boundary between British and American interests until the signing of the Oregon Treaty in 1846, awarding possession of the Oregon Country south of the forty-ninth parallel to the United States.

Before resigning from the HBC in 1846 after twenty-two years of service, he had a tiny residence and a church built just outside the Fort. Prior to its construction, Catholic missionaries were frequently lodged in the "priest's house" within the Fort Vancouver palisade, even though they were not employees of the HBC and relied on the Association for the Propagation of the Faith in Canada and Europe for financial support. Dedicated to St. James on May 31, 1850, the mission would become the episcopal see of Nisqually, the Bishop's headquarters for the Catholic Church in the region.

French-Canadian Catholic priests had ventured as early as 1838 into Oregon Country. Fathers A. M. A. and F. N. Blanchet and Modeste Demers, among others, traveled from post to post, fort to fort, mission to mission, and camp to camp, carrying their religious messages and tending to the spiritual needs of those men and families established there, be they white, native, or Métis. By October 1839, Chief Factor James Douglas had permitted F. N. Blanchet to establish a Catholic mission in the Willamette Valley, dedicated to St. Paul. It was to this mission that McLoughlin sent James Sinclair's party in 1841. Twenty-three families (120 settlers, mostly Métis) had set out with Sinclair westward from the Red River Colony (today Saint-Boniface, Manitoba) to the Oregon Country with the aim of reinforcing British claims in the area. Rather than settle the newcomers on the Puget Sound Agricultural Company farms centered at Nisqually (today Seattle), established in 1840 for this purpose as well as to provide HBC employees with produce, dairy, and livestock, McLoughlin instead encouraged them to claim lands in the Willamette Valley alongside Euro-American settlers. Marcus Whitman arrived with the first successful large-wagon train to Oregon in 1843 to take advantage of the provisional government's offer of 640-acre allotments for settlement.

Only when the United States controlled the area south of the forty-ninth parallel did the area known today as Washington State open to Euro-American migration. In 1849, when the HBC transferred its headquarters to Victoria, British Columbia, leaving several employees to operate the post before finally abandoning it in 1860, the region was still "Indian country." Two companies of the First Artillery arrived in May 1849 under the command of Major Hathaway. The contingent built barracks on a rise of twenty feet above the trading post and the army quartermaster negotiated to rent a number of HBC structures. From this United States Army base, the military attempted to keep order as settlers streamed into the area, upsetting long-standing native ways of life and relationships to their lands.

The discovery of gold in the newly created Washington Territory (1853) exacerbated problems between First Nations people and new settlers. Prospectors attracted by the promise of immediate riches tramped across the native peoples' recently reserved territory in south-central Washington. After having practically coerced Yakima chief Kamiakin, along with thirteen other tribal chiefs, to sign the 1855 Yakima Treaty that effectively removed the natives to reserved lands, the first governor of Washington Territory, Isaac Stevens, blatantly ignored the conditions guaranteed by the Treaty. He had agreed to give the chiefs two years to relocate their peoples; instead, he opened settlement immediately. The Yakima, the Cayuse, the Walla Walla, and other nations joined forces under the exhortations of Kamiakin. Earlier that year, the army had fought with the Klickitat, a nation numbering between three hundred and five hundred. By mid-November, Major Gabriel Rains had destroyed Kamiakin's camp at Ahtanum Creek and the Catholic Oblate Sainte-Croix mission, the first among many that would be destroyed in the Yakima region. Although armed conflict cooled following the order of Colonel Edward Steptoe preventing settlers from returning to Walla Walla Valley, by 1858 war erupted again. The Yakima fought side by side with the Cœur d'Alene and

Spokane. Within fifteen months of their arrival, the Sisters of Providence adopted three-year-old Emily Lake, a fatherless waif of mixed blood whose mother could not continue to care for her. Thirty years later, reminisced Mother Joseph, she was living with the Sisters in Astoria, Washington, and played music in that town's Catholic church.

During this same period, the army supervised the surveying and construction of freighting roads, such as the one that linked the head of navigation on the Columbia to that of the Missouri, which probably followed old native and voyageur trade routes. The Sisters of Providence would use these same roads, over which goods could be transported, to institute schools and hospitals among the native and settler communities of the Pacific Northwest. Captain John Mullan notes in *The Bell and the River* the nefarious impact of white civilization on the Indians:

> [T]he only good... that I have ever seen effected among these people has been due to the exertion of these Catholic missionaries. Many of these missions might have benefited by the government allowing them the charge of the schools and hospitals, for they actually take care of the Indians when sick and educate them when well, and all this with the mere pittance at their disposal, not a moiety of what they need; while hundreds and thousands are squandered on paper for the benefit of the Indians which they never receive.

The arrival of the Sisters of Providence in 1856, then, was as critical to Bishop A. M. A. Blanchet's effort to provide the burgeoning Nisqually diocese with fundamental religious and temporal services as it was to the army in "pacifying" the natives.

Providence Faubourg

When Mother Joseph and her four female companions landed, the HBC trading post was located on the northern bank of the Columbia River opposite the mouth of the Willamette River and outside the floodplain. The Fort not only controlled an important navigation route, since it was at the mouth of the Willamette on the Columbia Rivers, but it was also the major trading hub on the Pacific slope west of the Cascades mountain range. Ships and supplies arrived from London and elsewhere. Goods were transported inland through a network of rivers and portages and overland on the primitive, army-built roads extending into the hinterland.

The Fort's twenty-foot-high palisade enclosed up to forty buildings, including houses, warehouses, a school, a chapel, a library, a pharmacy, a blacksmith, and a manufacturing facility, according to the *Fort Vancouver Historic Structures Report* (vol. 1, 1972, vol. 2, 1976). Houses, a distillery, a tannery, a sawmill, and a dairy had been built outside of the palisade amidst gardens, orchards, fields, and a shipyard near the river. A "village" known then as Kanaka, home to French-Canadians, Métis, English, Scots, Irish, Hawaiians, and Native Americans including Iroquois and Cree in the employ of the HBC, skirted St. James Mission nearby. "*La jolie prairie*" around Fort Vancouver proved fertile farmland, thus decreasing the men's reliance on expensive, shipped foodstuffs.

The sisters called the Bishop's residence home for the first eight days. Because the cook left, they moved into the kitchen ell, a ten-by-sixteen-foot room attached to the house, and furnished the space with five plank beds, a table, and three or four chairs. They divided the dormitory from the refectory and community room with a thin, fabric partition. Although cramped, they preferred this relatively private space to hearing the men snore through the floor of the attic. It would be a temporary arrangement.

On Ash Wednesday 1857, the sisters moved into a freestanding sixteen-by-twenty-four-foot house, said to have been an old barracks that had housed Klickitat Indians who had been removed from their dwellings on the Lewis River the previous winter. The three-bay, gable-roofed wood structure sat on a river-stone foundation; it would become the priests' house, labeled D on an 1866 plan of the mission. Like the rebuilt buildings outside of the reconstructed Fort Vancouver, its one-inch-thick plank boards were covered in clapboard, perhaps "double lapped cedar siding." A stair gave access to the attic under a shingled roof. Before leaving this house to the priests, the sisters covered the rough planks with cotton and a thin tapestry. They did the same in the two rooms behind the sacristy where the Bishop had taken up lodgings during the summer, and, with the help of the soldiers, did the interior walls of the church, lending them an appearance of propriety.

A twenty-by-forty-foot structure, built against the back half of the east wall of the church under construction when the sisters arrived, was destined to serve as the boys' classroom. The women took up residence here when they moved out of "the old barracks," necessitating the construction of an addition to that building, located between the Bishop's residence and Holy Angels College. Also annexed over the years to the priests' house were a library, a carpenter's shop, a tool room, and a room where male employees lived, each with their own entrance. A front gallery helped to unify the disparate additions. Once this game of musical chairs was played out, the sisters were finally able to accept student boarders in addition to operating the girls' school and orphanage for boys and girls out of their convent. It had a kitchen wing onto which the schoolchildren's refectory was attached. The convent would be expanded in 1860.

Mother Joseph had a bakery and laundry built in 1858. This twenty-by-eighteen-foot wooden structure was almost immediately partitioned to accommodate a hospital under the auspices of the Ladies of Charity, an auxiliary whose members were mainly Catholic, although Methodist, Episcopalian, and Jewish women joined too. They were tasked with furnishing the hospital room, which at the time took up half of the floor area. Once the ceiling of rough boards was put in, the women covered it with a thin muslin and tapestry; they brought in four beds and four small tables and chairs. The Ladies paid a twelve-and-a-half-cent subscription per week, collected funds to support the poor, and every two weeks gathered at the convent to sew. They also agreed to pay one dollar a day for every patient recommended to the sisters by the President of the Auxiliary, Mrs. Rodgers, a Protestant. While this system worked for a period of time, the sisters, unhappy that expenses exceeded revenues, decided to "buy out" the Ladies' Auxiliary for fear of future conflict over the ownership of the hospital. It was dedicated to St. Joseph.

That same year, the Bishop had built a tiny house for the husband-and-wife team employed to help with chores at the mission. A year later, in 1859, he had a residence erected for his use. The twenty-four-by-thirty-two-foot, one-and-a-half

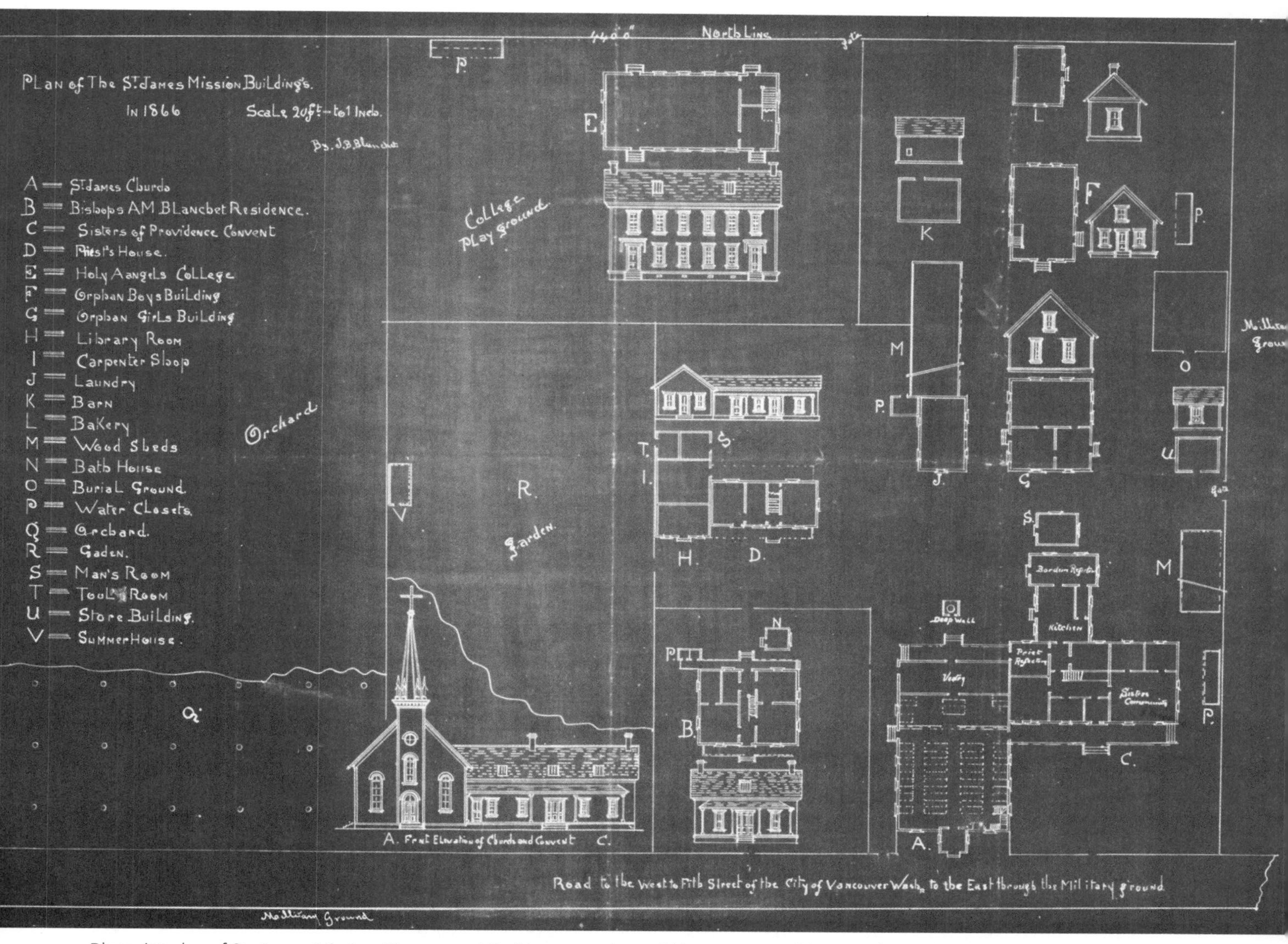

Blueprint plan of St. James Mission, Vancouver, Washington, as it would have appeared in 1866, drawn by J. B. Blanchet. (Providence Archives, Seattle, Washington.)

storey central passage house had four rooms of roughly equal size that opened directly into the hall. One of these was subdivided, probably into a bedroom and office. A staircase led to the attic lit by two dormer windows. Like the convent, it had two chimneys and four-over-four or six-over-six guillotine windows. Successive bishops lived here until 1885, when a new residence built next to the 1884 Cathedral was ready.

The two rooms the bishop vacated were put at the disposal of the sisters who used one as a novitiate, reserved for young women wanting to enter religious life, and the other as a music room where they gave private lessons for a fee.

Captain Rufus Ingalls attributed much of the consolidation and expansion of St. James Mission to Mr. Brouillet rather than Mother Joseph, with whom the Vicar General of the Diocese and head of Holy Angels College for boys certainly collaborated. Yet judging from Ingalls's January 1859 commentary he was pleased with the improvements carried out with the army's consent, as was Mother Joseph. Her 1859 letter to Mgr. Bourget in Montreal reports that the small, religious community cared for aged men and women; seven day-school students; five orphan girls and three orphan boys; seven male college students, and one seminarian. This contrasted with the 1860 Clark County census that reported "eleven nuns, twenty-two female orphans, and six domestic servants" living in a building associated with the St. James Mission. It also mentioned a structure housing "two 'preceptors' and fifteen male orphans."

Holy Angels College was a private school for boys. It was the only two-and-a-half-storey building within the compound. It was a symmetrical, six-bay, two-pile edifice entered by four doors at each end of the north and south façades. A classroom took up most of the ground floor; stairs in the last bay led up to the second and third floors. As was typical, the dormitory was probably located in the attic.

Mother Joseph informed her superior in Montreal that by summer 1861, the sisters were overseeing the running of daily affairs such as cooking, cleaning, and washing at the Bishop's residence and acted as sacristans for the church, and were now able to provide separate accommodations for the pensioners, the students, the sick, and the orphan boys and girls. Nonetheless, the sisters took their meals and gathered in a room attached to the kitchen and slept in the attic of the church. If they were to take in postulants to expand their work, they would require additional space. So the Bishop offered to provide the workmen if the sisters obtained the materials to build an addition. Other sources, however, say construction was for a separate house for orphan girls (they were housed in part with the women pensioners and in part with the sisters) and the Bishop covered both wood and labor costs. Seeing that the Bishop had already given up his former rooms behind the sacristy for a novitiate, this would make sense. Also, a letter dated October 21, 1860, mentioned readying the orphanages, boys' and girls', for a visit by Orphan's Welfare Association.

The important thing was to have enough space to house everyone as the Sisters of Providence welcomed more and more people into their "*faubourg*." Procuring timber was expensive. Mother Joseph had complained as early as 1856 of the prohibitive cost per linear foot of good quality lumber. A workingman's salary was high at eight dollars a day compared to rates in Montreal, she wrote not long after she arrived. No wonder, then, that she immediately thought of salvaging the structures abandoned by the Hudson's Bay Company standing on the military reserve. She wrote to Colonel George Wright, commander of the post, asking if they could "pull off the planks of the old, dilapidated houses." He acquiesced, ordering Major Babbit to "give as much of the lumber as the superior required." The workmen completed the building during course of the summer, for which the Bishop paid 232 dollars in salaries; the sisters painted the ell, which contained the community room in the front half, the novitiate, and Mother Superior's room in the back half. They dedicated their newly enlarged convent Providence Holy Angels.

The workmen probably used Canadian Red River framing common to HBC structures, mortising the ceiling beams or joists "into, or through, the heavy fixed headers that ran around the building directly over the door and window openings. These headers were usually pegged to the upright posts so that there would be no movement when the timbers shrank," explains the *Fort Vancouver Historical Structures Report*. Additional headroom could be gained by continuing the walls two or more feet above the ceiling joist level, or higher if a whole second storey was to be built, as at Holy Angels College. The posts rested on deep, squared log sills and the spaces between the posts were filled with horizontal pieces of three or six-inch-thick sawn planks with tongues sliding into the grooves made in the sides of each post. The plank walls were sometimes sheathed with clapboarding. The solid wood plank sheathing nailed to the timber roof structure was usually covered with shingles. Hip boards and ridge boards would have been applied over the shingles. Floors were made of three-inch-thick planks. Also known as *pièce-sur-pièce* or grooved post construction, the technique survived through the first third of the twentieth century in Montreal and Quebec, where wood was plentiful.

The *Fort Vancouver Cultural Landscape Report* (1992) argues that the U.S. Army inventory of HBC structures in 1860 "makes no mention of any stockade building's use as a convent, nor does there appear to be any reference to it in any communications from Company employees," invalidating a legend that the sisters had established by spring 1857 a convent in "an old [abandoned HBC] fur storage building, later converted into a barn." Yet the sisters did salvage Fort buildings for the materials needed for their growing institutional compound, as mentioned contradictorily later in the same report. Mother Joseph had recognized the value of the timber, even if the HBC buildings were in a poor state of repair. The skeleton crew at Fort Vancouver could not upkeep the buildings, complained Chief Trader James Allan Grahame on September 19, 1859, adding that even the more recently built warehouses were "beginning to show the effects of wind and weather, and are so ponderously put together that when any part gives way it is very expensive and laborious to patch it up." If Ingalls, assistant quartermaster of the army's Fort Vancouver, had had his way, all of the structures would have been torn down in the summer of 1860. Lucky for Mother Joseph, he was prevented from so doing, as the British government protested their demolition.

The "New Store," one of two warehouses that survived the military's destruction of the HBC

Reconstructed Hudson's Bay Trading Post building at Fort Vancouver National Historic Site illustrating the Red River framing construction method. (Photo: Tania Martin.)

establishment in the summer of 1860, was perhaps one of the structures that Mother Joseph eyed as suitable for her own purposes, even if the author of the Report supposes that the building had fallen "prey to firewood scavengers, to decay, and perhaps to fire during the next several years." The gabled-roof, one-and-a-half or two-storey fur store built in 1841 had served as a military warehouse until about the end of 1857, when it reverted to the HBC's control. Authors of the *Historical Structures Report* say that "vandalism and the ravages of time reduced nearly all of the fort building [*sic*] to heaps of rubble" by the end of 1865. While the sisters had obtained authorization, perhaps other settlers served themselves when the army was busy elsewhere.

Once the orphans had been moved into separate buildings, the sisters' convent could better accommodate pensioners and boarders, as Mother Joseph noted in her letter of 1861. In January of that year, one hundred people occupied the five buildings on the two-acre St. James Mission plot as well as a sixth building, Mr. Petrain's house, located in town. As early as 1859 or 1860 (the dates vary in the sources and one even says March 6, 1858), the Sisters of Charity of the House of Providence had acquired one half of block 33 at Eighth and Reserve Streets for 1500 dollars. They used what was left of the five-thousand-dollar gift that Bishop Blanchet had awarded Mother Joseph for taking over the economic administration of St. James Mission in 1857, once she had paid the necessary repairs to the mission buildings.

The two-storey, white-painted, wooden Petrain house was a stone's throw from the public square, located in the block delimited by Fifth and Seventh streets and H and J streets. The square was baptized in the twentieth century as Esther Short Park in honor of the widow of Amos M. Short, whose allotment overlapped land claimed by Clark County for its county seat and the town of Vancouver in 1859, two years after its incorporation. The eastern portions of their claims encroached on the 640 acres that Bishop A. M. A. Blanchet had claimed in May 1853, as allowed by the Oregon Territory Organic Act of 1848 guaranteeing claims made by religious missions prior to passage of the law. Both the HBC and the Army contested the bishop. The Army attempted to evict the Catholic mission from the military reserve in 1870, but the order was suspended. The dispute was finally resolved, after much litigation, on December 26, 1895. Bishop O'Dea received thirty thousand dollars in compensation for the land occupied by the St. James church building, less than 0.44 acres. The Sisters of Providence's Seattle Archives have not only conserved a series of maps and land titles partially documenting this saga, but also their own real estate transactions.

The Petrain property on the outskirts of the growing town of Vancouver was initially destined to become St. Vincent's orphanage, but in 1861 the Sisters won a three-year government contract to care for the alienated and they had two loges, or apartments, outfitted for that purpose. It was dedicated on June 5 to Saint-Jean-de-Dieu, recalling a similar mission or work in Longue-Pointe, just outside of Montreal.

That left the problem of where to lodge the orphan boys. They returned to Providence Faubourg. Mother Joseph had had officers and volunteers lift and roll a recently built, empty, forty-five-foot storehouse and a shed, which would become the boys' refectory, and move them to the site. They were set in line with the girls' Ste. Genevieve Orphanage. With the Civil War raging, the owner, a merchant of the Fort, was only too happy on February 3, 1863 to sell the two structures for two hundred fifty dollars. Similar in size, the orphan boys' and orphan girls' houses stood one-and-a-half storeys tall. The ground floors contained classrooms and the attics housed the sleeping areas. A reporter visiting the Sisters' facilities commented favorably in a *Vancouver Register* article dated January 30, 1869:

> The neatness of everything about the premises was very striking in this age of carelessness and inattention... The healthiness of the children speaks volumes in favor of the good Sisters. Everything moves on like clockwork... The Sisters showed us the kitchen and the dining rooms, pictures of neatness and order. The dormitories are well ventilated and each little separate cot was well supplied with blankets, sheets, pillowcases, etc. of spotless linen.

He was also impressed by the politeness of the children.

By 1866, gable-roofed St. James church was fronted by a tall tower that was topped by a spire terminating in a cross. Its plan followed a type common in ancient-régime Quebec, although St. James' simple, five-bay-long rectangular nave simply ended at the back wall of the sacristy instead of terminating in an apse, as was usual in the Maillou plan. The rounded-arched, double-paneled door echoed the rounded-arched windows in façade and elevation. A host of secondary buildings completed the Providence Faubourg. They included the bakery north of St. Vincent's orphanage for boys and the barn to the west; a laundry west of Ste. Genevieve's Orphanage for girls and the hired men's house, which they shared with the aged men, to the south; as well as a bath house, privies, and

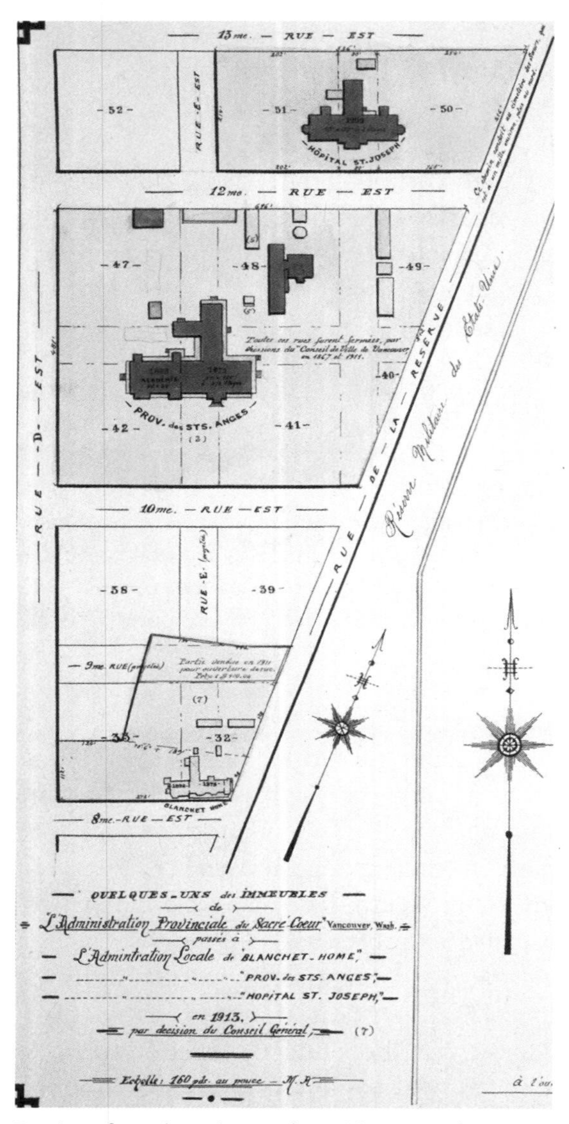

Portion of a cadastral map of Providence Academy, Vancouver, Washington, July 1919, drawn by Sister Anatolie (Mary Elizabeth Eugenie Desroches, 1861-1940) of Montreal, showing Blanchet Home on blocks 33 and 32, where the Petrain House once stood, in relationship to the House of Providence and St. Joseph Hospital. (Providence Archives, Seattle, Washington.)

wood sheds. Although not indicated on the plan of the mission compound, the yard was divided into separate areas for the boys and girls. Mother Joseph had built a shelter early on out of four posts and two blankets for "*la vieille Marie*," a woman who served Mother Gamelin in Montreal before devoting nineteen years to the Pacific Northwest mission. There she could manufacture soap outdoors yet remain dry in the wet climate.

The sisters succored the many needy who came to their door, even if they sometimes lacked space in the seventeen wooden structures near the Fort and those on their property on block 33. The sisters had added a wing to the Petrain House in 1862, remodeled it in 1866 when they moved the sick and the aged there, and extended the two-storey, white, wooden house again in 1872, doubling the capacity of St. Joseph's hospital. Burned to the ground in 1878, a two-and-a-half-storey, thirty-by-fifty-foot hospital with an eighteen-by-forty-six-foot wing was rebuilt on the same site. Two more additions were built, twenty-one by thirty-nine feet in 1879 and thirty-two by thirty-nine feet in 1898. In 1911, when construction of a new, brick, five-storey St. Joseph's Hospital on blocks 50 and 51, north of 12th Street and east of C Street, was complete, it would become Blanchet Home, a hospice for elderly men and women. St. Joseph's Hospital was integral to Providence Holy Angels up until 1893, when it was awarded independent administration and expected to hold its own bookkeeping and chronicles and manage its own revenues and expenses.

Move to Higher Ground

Given the crowded conditions at Providence Faubourg, Mother Joseph had convinced her superiors the time was right to erect a purpose-built structure. She had finally, over the course of a decade, assembled the land needed to build an ornament to the city. Early in 1861, Mother Joseph had asked French-Canadian John Predmore, a gentleman she trusted, to purchase two two-hundred-square-foot adjoining blocks, fell the largest trees, fence the holdings, and build a small cabin on each lot, thus fulfilling the requirements of the Homesteading Act. Then he would cede his rights for 325 dollars through a Quit Claim contract, which he did several months later on June 11, 1861. This gave her ownership of blocks 41 and 48, and fractions of blocks 40 and 49. She proceeded in the same manner with a Mr. D. J. Thornton for adjacent blocks 42 and 47. He signed a Quit Claim deed on January 19, 1867, although another document says it was October 21, 1862. Because the Farnsworth Survey had plotted streets between the blocks, each subdivided into eight fifty-by-one-hundred-foot lots, the sisters submitted an application to City Council as early as 1869 to acquire the eighty-foot wide rights of way. The majority of the councilors objected. The sisters argued the area of an individual two-hundred-foot block was insufficient for an institution of the size they were planning. They also insisted the projected House of Providence would embellish the city, which seemed to have convinced the councilors who passed Ordinance 76 on July 7, 1873, granting the sisters permission to purchase the land set aside for streets. They now had ten clear acres between 10th and 12th Streets, and C and Reserve Streets, on which to build their convent and orphan asylum.

Mother Joseph favorably compared 10th Street, today Evergreen Boulevard, situated on the highest point in Vancouver, with the fashionable Sherbrooke Street in Montreal. She hoped that the celestial president St. Joseph would keep their land always under his protection.

Although the process clearing title to all the portions lasted through 1911 with the inauguration of St. Joseph's Hospital, the sisters had enough of a guarantee to proceed with construction in 1873, seventeen years after arriving at the mission. When Mother Joseph had first made known her plans for the substantial edifice, the pioneer settlers of the area were amazed and urged her to modify her plans. She, however, refused.

Providence House Vancouver

On June 9, 1873, Mother Joseph accompanied the Mother General, who had come from Montreal on her periodic visit of the western missions, Bishop A. M. A. Blanchet, Reverend Aegidius Junger, and Jean-Baptiste Blanchet to measure out the dimensions of the building. The following day, she awarded the contract for the brick, and the following Wednesday, June 12, a day associated with St. Joseph, Mother General was given the honor of digging the first shovelful of earth for the foundations. All of the orphans had their turn afterwards. The hired workmen accelerated their pace from June 16 onwards so that by August 3 the first brick was laid on the completed stone foundation. As was the tradition, the sisters organized a special ceremony for the blessing of the cornerstone held on September 21 in the presence of "soldiers and assorted-sized orphans… clergy in garments of ritual and a motley array of Vancouver area residents."

Stories circulating about Mother Joseph suggest that she was the one making sure everything was

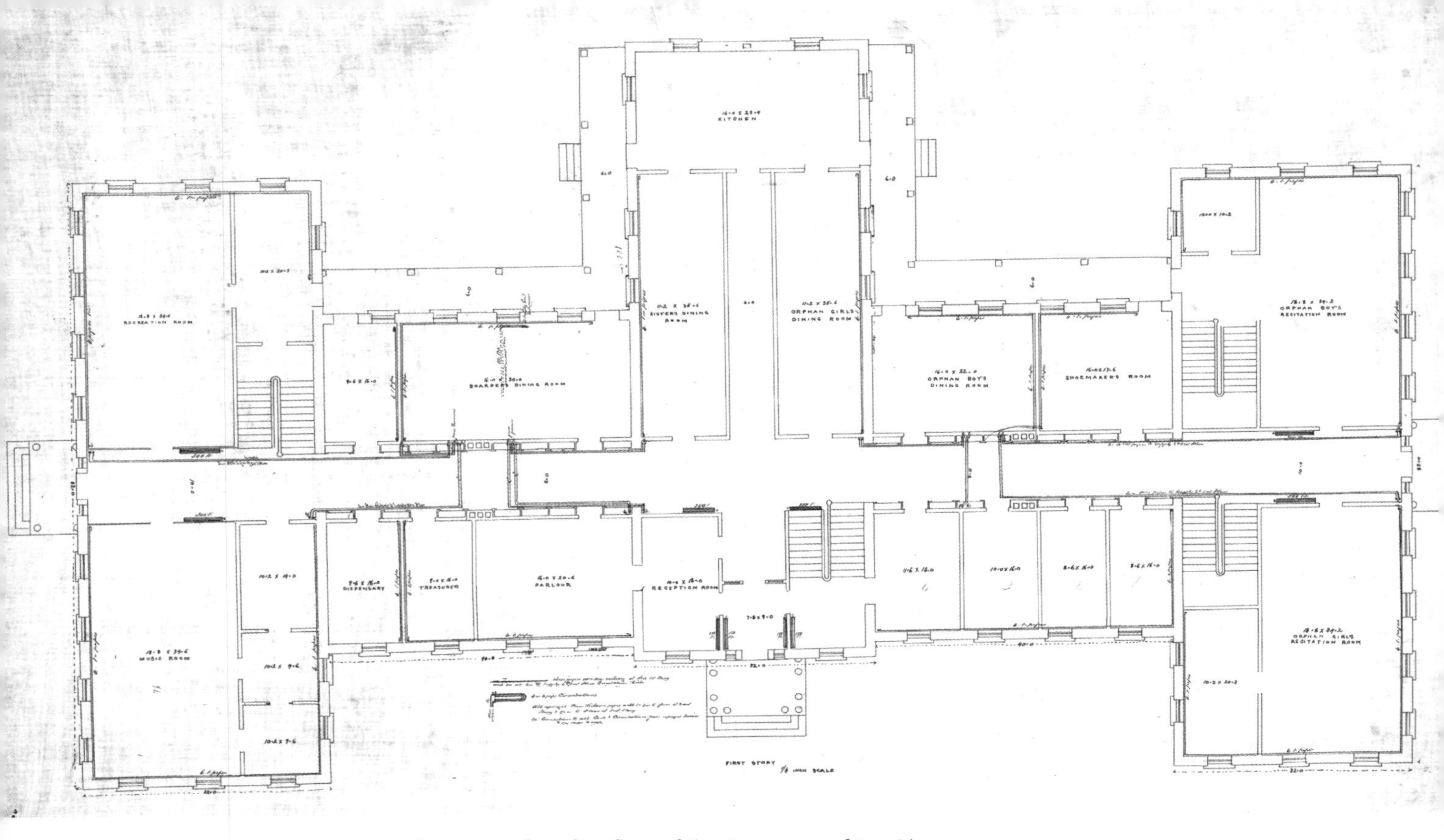

Undated and unsigned ink-on-linen plan of the first floor of the 1873 House of Providence. (Providence Archives, Seattle, Washington.)

square. Curiously, the chronicles make little mention of her activities on the Vancouver construction site; rather, it appears "Mr. JB Blanchet supervised the workmen [and] paid the workers" while Mother Joseph was presumably attending other affairs. Two new institutions were founded the same year, not to mention repairs and renovations at other sites. As the House of Providence was nearing completion, "Blanchet, looking at an unfinished assemblage at the… House [of Providence], was nearly hit by a falling piece of lumber from 40 feet above; the shocked workers almost fell down." Mother Joseph may have been too preoccupied with financial worries to be present daily on the job site. Of the fifty thousand dollars estimated, the sisters had amassed only 11,500 dollars when construction began. The first winter was particularly difficult and Mother Joseph was discouraged. The cold threatened to kill the animals, water froze in the pipes, and a twenty-thousand-dollar debt hung over her head. Although the interior walls were left unfinished for a number of years and the parlor served as the chapel during the first few months, her order, the Sisters of Providence, had succeeded in erecting a structure that rivaled institutional buildings in the region.

The new, fire-resistant, T-shape structure was impressive. As befits a building as imposing as the House of Providence, the façade is particularly striking. Symmetrically organized around the *avant-corps* marking the front entrance, itself accentuated by a brick portico reached by a short flight of stone steps, the redbrick walls, laid in running bond, are articulated vertically with pilasters and horizontally with corbelled belt courses. While the segmental-arched window openings regularly punctuate the façade, those of the central pedimented entrance bay stand out. They are topped with corbelled brick hoods and ornamented with keystones and acanthus scrolls that are recalled in the stone brackets above the Doric columns supporting the curved roof of the porch. Each of the wooden window sashes framing four-over-four lights rest on stone sills. A statuary niche is inset in the middle of a broken pediment defined, like the roofline, by painted wood entablatures and pilaster caps. On either side of the entrance bay, three storeys of galleries enclosed with balustrade railings run the length of the façade, their slender wooden columns supported at ground level on brick piers.

Contemporary newspapers praised the Catholic convent and orphan asylum as the largest, most beautiful building north of San Francisco, as related in a 1979 article in *The Columbian*. Its longest arm, the façade, measured 135 by 50 feet, surpassing the Portland Courthouse (1864-1875), which measured 118 by 66 feet, and the Medical College (1864-1867) at the Oregon Institute (later Willamette University), which measured 84 by 44 feet in size. This educational institution traces its beginnings from the first Protestant (specifically Methodist) mission for Native Americans in the

Avant-corps of the House of Providence, August 2013. (Photo, Tania Martin.)

Pacific Northwest. Like the Sisters of Providence, the Methodists initially "offered health care, food and shelter to several Indian children who had been orphaned when their parents, grandparents, aunts and uncles succumbed to… deadly diseases." Indeed, smallpox wiped out over sixty-five percent of the Pacific Northwest Native population between 1770 and 1840. The missionaries then "began to shift their focus… to serving the rapidly increasing number of white settlers" (although the Sisters of Providence would also open Indian missions when asked to).

The courthouse, a rectangular nine-bay by three-bay, stone-clad, brick masonry, load-bearing structure, sat in the center of its two-hundred-foot block; the convent, in contrast, stood in the middle of an almost 480-foot frontage. The designer of the courthouse was Alfred Bult Mullett, then Supervising Architect of the United State Treasury (1866-1874), who was working on the design of the United States Mint in San Francisco. With the input of local supervising architects E. B. St. John and John J. Holman, he marked the formal entrance with an *avant-corps*, a projecting group of three bays crowned with a gabled pediment and an octagonal wood-framed and clad-domed cupola with arched windows in the center of the roof, recalling the architecture of civic and government buildings in San Francisco and Portland. Like the convent, the five-storey, redbrick Medical College impressed the residents of the "sparsely settled Oregon country." It cost forty thousand dollars to build plus seventeen thousand dollars to finish and furnish the classrooms, library, parlors, recitation rooms, chapel, and dormitories. The top of the cupola at the center of Greek-cross plan soared one hundred feet from the ground, as did the cupola and bell tower of the House of Providence. Both the courthouse and college drew upon the Renaissance Revival, a style that borrowed from Greek and Roman architectural vocabulary and emphasized symmetry. So did the House of Providence.

Mother General or a visiting Bishop could have possibly brought plans from Montreal, but archival records make no mention of this. More likely Mother Joseph was inspired by known models of institutional and civic buildings of similar stature and conventional construction technologies familiar to the majority of tradesmen on construction sites she saw in the many towns and cities through which she traveled, such as San Francisco and Portland, Oregon. Had she business in nearby St. Paul (today a city included in the Salem Metropolitan area), where Bishop F. N. Blanchet had established a Catholic parish, she very likely saw or heard that the five hundred thousand bricks needed for construction of the Salem, Oregon Medical College "were fired on University grounds and were made from clay excavated for the foundation." That fact may have sparked an idea, one Mother Joseph seems to have shared with Lowell Mason Hidden.

A Brickworks is Born in Vancouver

The story of the Hidden Family is nearly inextricable from that of the construction of the House of Providence and of the city. Lowell Mason Hidden (1839-1923) arrived in Vancouver from New England via California in 1864. As with most migrants, he had worked in a series of jobs before purchasing nine acres of woodland and building a log cabin at present-day 14th Street and Main. He was among those who had surveyed the city and helped to plot the community's first, early streets.

Purportedly, in anticipation of the construction of the three-storey convent, it was to this pragmatic entrepreneur that Mother Joseph turned. As Sister Mary Mildred, who entered the order in 1897, recalled:

> Mr. Hidden did not work for a brick company. There were not bricks in town. Mother Joseph wanted to use bricks for the new Academy. Mr. Hidden told her, "You won't find bricks in Portland or anywhere." Mother Joseph said we have the clay here and we'll use it to make our own bricks. Mr. Hidden, a friend of the sisters, assisted her.

The determined Catholic Mother Superior convinced the staunch Methodist that the clay in Clark County was suitable for brickmaking. She needed the high-quality building material in ample quantities as she intended the new House of Charity to be fire resistant and a civic monument. As recounted in the Sisters of Providence's Sacred Heart Vicariate chronicles, started in 1884 and relying on "the pen and memories of Sister Joseph of the Sacred Heart," the signing of the June 10, 1873 contract was "a stroke of providence" as "no brick had ever been made in Vancouver until that moment. An individual opened an oven especially for us." At Mother Joseph's urging, Hidden started firing bricks in 1871. According to a 1989 article in *The Columbian*, the contract for three hundred thousand bricks for Providence House considerably boosted his business. More commissions followed. As *The Vancouver Independent* informed its readers in June 1877, he had "reconstructed his brick yard preparatory to active work this summer making brick" and would "begin work as soon as the weather will permit."

The first Hidden brickyard was located at 15th and Main Streets, just two blocks east and three blocks north from the northeast corner of the Providence House property. Bought at Hidden's standard price of eight dollars per thousand, the bricks were hauled to the construction site in wagons. In fact, "when construction started, all public works stopped so the sisters could purchase materials at a reasonable price," recalled Mother Joseph for the chronicler, who also noted that Reverend J. B. Boulet and Mr. J. B. Blanchet had paid for the brick for the orphans' department. The contractors had also contributed a gift, probably in service. Since "St. James [Catholic] Church was closer… [Lowell Hidden] sold those bricks for $7 per thousand," his grandson Robert told *The Columbian* in 1979. The house of worship was situated one block south of the brickyard. Hidden operated there for sixty years.

Hidden Brick Company supplied red bricks for a number of institutional buildings in Vancouver. An 1898 black-and-white photograph shows his sons, William Foster and Oliver Hidden, among other workers, in front of an enormous pile of bricks protected from the elements, and behind these, cords upon cords of stacked wood. "A kiln containing 400,000 bricks… [would have] consumed a small pile of 150 cords of fir wood in the burning," stated *The Vancouver Independent* in 1879. The same newspaper announced Hidden furnished brick for Hazard & Co.'s brick building, later in the same "brief mention," it was indicated by the newspaper that "W. C. Hazard's new house is rapidly assuming shape and will be one of the fine

Hidden Brick. (Photo, Tania Martin.)

dwellings of Vancouver when completed." Hidden also supplied the bricks for St. James Catholic Church (formerly the Cathedral, 1884-1885); the Masonic Temple (1886); the Washington School For Defective Youth (later State School for the Deaf), a four to five-storey, cruciform building apparently designed by Lowell's son, Oliver Moody Hidden; St. Joseph's Hospital (1911); the United Methodist Church and the Carnegie Library (1909); in addition to Portland-area hospitals and facilities at Oregon State University. In the 1920s, Hidden produced over a million bricks annually, to supply customers including Portland and Vancouver merchants who built large warehouses with eight-inch walls.

After Lowell Mason Hidden retired in 1905, his two sons continued operations as the Hidden Brothers Brick Company, until Oliver retired in 1929. Foster moved the manufactory to 2610 Kauffman Avenue at 27th Street, near rich clay deposits, in 1929, when his son Robert (1910-1992) joined the company. A 1961 Metsker Map identifies the brickyard as a long, narrow band running from 26th to 36th Streets along Kauffman. In 1965, *The Columbian* reported that the Hidden Company was the only brickyard north of San Jose, California, that made molded brick, a special process in which clay was pressed by use of a machine into wooden molds. The raw material for the brick, undersoil clay, was taken from a vast supply of iron-rich material beneath the surface at the Kauffman plant, reported the journalist. It was then dumped into a conveyor system, which carried it to a trough where water was added and the clay mixed before going into the machine where it was pressed into molds. Manual operators knocked the clay bricks from the molds onto an outdoor cable conveyor where the brick was channeled into drying frames. Air-drying of a batch of brick took one week, after which the bricks were then stacked in an updraft kiln were they were burned. Iron in the clay, the reporter continued, gave the brick a distinct salmon-red color when bricks were underburned, but when they were fully burned, they turned into a cherry-red hue. Over-burning, in contrast, brought a dark red or black color to the brick.

In 1981, the Hidden Brick Company was the only brick maker turning out manually made bricks west of the Mississippi. It closed in 1992, when the grandson of Lowell Hidden, Robert, passed away. He had succeeded his father, William Foster, and his uncle, Oliver Hidden, in 1963 as head of the business.

From House of Providence to Providence Academy

Walking through downtown Vancouver, people understand immediately why the city was referred to as a city of bricks—Hidden Bricks. When Mother Joseph acquired the first parcel of cleared land for the future House of Providence in 1861, the town of Vancouver boasted a steam sawmill, a hotel, and two wharves along its riverfront. Hotels, seven stores—including a tobacco store, a drug store, a bakery, and a grocery—two saloons, and two residences had their addresses along the first two-hundred block of Main Street. A law office, a tailor, a market, a fruit store, a hotel, two saloons, and a Chinaman's residence (as labeled on the plat map), lined the block between Second and Third Streets. Going northwards towards Fifth Street, one could stop in at the bakery, the confectionery and fruit store, the book store and post office, the general store, another saloon, the cabinet shop, the blacksmith and wagon shop, or call at one of the six residences. Settlement pretty much stopped at Fifth Street, which turned into Upper Mill Road once inside the military reservation, although one could do business at the jewelry store, be entertained in one of the two halls, stay overnight at the hotel, or drink in the saloon. Twelve residences had been built between Eighth and 26th Streets by 1860.

Mother Joseph had also bought farmland that year, three miles from town. Prone to flooding, she sold it in 1866 to buy a 240-acre plot of land on the outskirts of Vancouver. Having their own source of produce and livestock helped lower the sisters' expenses, justified Mother Joseph. Occasional trips to the farm added "a little variety to the daily life," recalled one orphan for *The Columbian* journalist Ted Van Arsdol in 1966. "We marched west [in twos] on 12th Street and then turned down to the bank of the Columbia River. There was a wagon road and we would follow this road west along the riverbank until we came to the Sisters' farm. There we could break ranks and play until it was time to go back to the House of Providence. The round trip was quite a treat to the boys."

The only orphan asylum north of San Francisco in the early 1880s, its main mission was the "free and gratuitous raising and educating of destitute orphans" to whom they gave "not only shelter, food and clothing, but also a Christian education, without any pecuniary assistance from the government." The sisters deplored the divorce rate and the fact that Catholics were emulating Protestants in this practice. Single mothers left their children; fathers brought their offspring of a first marriage before finding a second wife. Parents who placed their children under the sisters' care paid ten dollars a month for board, tuition, washing, and other essentials. Clothing and stationery cost extra.

Twinned with the orphanage was a private Catholic boarding school. All were welcome as an August 1865 advertisement explained: "no undue influence will be exercised over the religious opinions of the pupils; however, for the maintenance of good order, all are required to conform to the external discipline of the house, $40 for 11 weeks of board and tuition, $10 for washing, $17 for music and use of instrument, $3 for French, $25 for board during vacation, $8 for washing during vacation." In contrast, Holy Angels College, a Boarding and Day School for young men and boys, asked fifteen dollars a month for board and an extra two dollars for tuition for boarders with no extra charge for Latin,

French, English, bookkeeping, etc., according to an 1879 advertisement in *The Vancouver Independent*. Orphans had classes separate from student boarders.

Girls enrolled at Providence School for Young Ladies wore a white muslin and sky blue *de laine* dress as a uniform and in 1878 they came "from every side of the Territory to Vancouver to receive an education." The sisters recruited far and wide; Holy Angels' College and Providence Academy competed with Protestant and public schools to attract the best students. "Studies were resumed at the convent on Monday and at the college yesterday," announced *The Vancouver Independent* on September 2, 1880:

> Both of these institutions have always proved themselves worthy the patronage of the community, and the best advertisement of their merit is the large number of respectable young men and women which both institutions have sent forth and who are at present discharging the duties of good citizens in a creditable and honorable manner. Both institutions are conducted on much the same principles. Both are boarding and day schools, and the tuition in both is almost nominal, while the education is second to none. It is scarcely necessary to remind our readers of the many advantages, moral and intellectual, enjoyed by young ladies confided to the Sisters of Charity, whose fame is deservedly world renowned, as the moral and social virtues of the young ladies of Vancouver speak volumes in that regard... *Mother Joseph, under whose direction many improvements have been made this year, cannot be too highly complimented on her architectural skill and taste* [emphasis added]. Everything is done to secure the health and comfort of the scholars; and taking both institutions all in all, we pronounce them worthy the patronage of the aristocracy of any land.

One of the improvements could be found in the basement, where a new furnace heated water before it circulated through the pipes that snaked through the corridors and the radiators installed in every room of the House of Providence.

Portland, a city that straddled the Willamette River, dwarfed Vancouver in 1887. It was three times as big. Vancouver had been granted an exclusive franchise in 1888 for transporting people back and forth across the Columbia River on steam ferryboats. A year later, passengers were carried from the ferry landing to Main Street and northwards by streetcar, which had replaced the horse car line. An early twentieth-century rooftop view shows rails in the middle of busy Main Street lined with one to three-storey commercial buildings and telephone poles. Visible in the distance to the east and west of the thoroughfare that linked the port to the hinterland were the House of Providence and St. James Cathedral. In an 1890 photograph, the steeple towered above the evergreens not yet cut down to make way for Vancouver's urban expansion. The religious buildings acted as prominent landmarks, as a notice published on July 5, 1877, suggests: "The undersigned wishes to sell her cottage home in Vancouver. It is situated in the block south of the Sisters' Convent and has a good house, 4 lots, barn and all other necessary outbuildings." Vancouver grew in the 1880s and 1890s as families settled and built east of the Military Reservation on newly-platted subdivisions. With Vancouver being situated at the head of deep-water navigation on the Columbia River and host to harbor shipping and river steamers, all trains from Puget Sound to Portland and San Francisco had to pass through "the city before the bridge to Portland," as the city in Washington was then known. It had been eclipsed by its sister-city as a major shipping port in 1890, after the Willamette River was dredged and deepened.

By 1891, The House of Providence could no longer contain all of its population, a situation that had already lasted several years. Every corner of the building was used, and even the laundry accommodated orphans. All of the sisters' apartments, as well as those of the novitiate, were overflowing. It was a pity to see those children in the attic in the heat of the summer, remarked the sister chronicler. One young boy who called the north wing "home" for a couple of months in fall 1889 described his daily movements to journalist Ted Van Arsdol for his June 1, 1966 article in *The Colombian*, "Closing Sparks Memories, Student of an Earlier Era Recalls Days at Providence Academy." Their father had brought the former student and his brother to the sisters when he was age six, after their mother died in October. He recalled the orphan boys' dormitory located in an upper floor where they slept each in their own small, single bed. The supervising sister had a tiny room partitioned off from the larger, full-building-width room. An assembly room, where the boys kneeled in long rows across the full length of the room for daily prayer service, play, or lessons, opened off of the ground-floor dining room. They would be marched up a flight of stairs and around to the chapel door for mass, which was chanted in Latin. An enclosed playground extended north from the building to 12th street. This young boy had been lucky. As early as 1885, Providence House had been judged too small. The sisters occasionally had no choice but to refuse orphans due to lack of space where they could sleep.

The sisters had nonetheless completed a number of improvements despite having to put off construction of an addition until 1891 when the Mother General, having seen the dire situation for herself, finally agreed to give the contract for the foundations and prepare the materials and the site even if they lacked monies needed for construction. In 1873, none of the door and window frames had been installed and only a layer of rough plaster and one coat of paint had been applied to the walls, which made cleaning difficult. In 1887, thirteen years after moving into the new convent, the sisters finally had the unfinished interiors of the ample, well-lit, and ventilated rooms properly plastered and painted. The following summer, they had hardwood flooring laid, the laundry building extended to include additional space for the steam-powered machines for washing and ironing, lodgings for male employees, and furnaces in the adjoining powerhouse. "Underground sewer pipes were also laid, the old ones renewed; the work was hard and difficult, the expenses considerable, but the good it does, especially on the health of our sisters should prevail, outweigh the costs," recounted the chronicles. They contracted Mr. Gardner to install a new six-thousand-dollar hot-water heating system in 1889, the same year Mr. Corbett of Vancouver was contracted to dig a well, as they had judged the water from the city insufficient and incommodious.

Before construction of the new one-hundred-by-fifty-seven-foot wing could start at the end of June 1891, workmen had to chop down the mainly fruit-bearing trees in the pensioners' yard and move several little buildings to clear the area for the new wing and building materials. As described in the chronicles, the addition was to be similar in

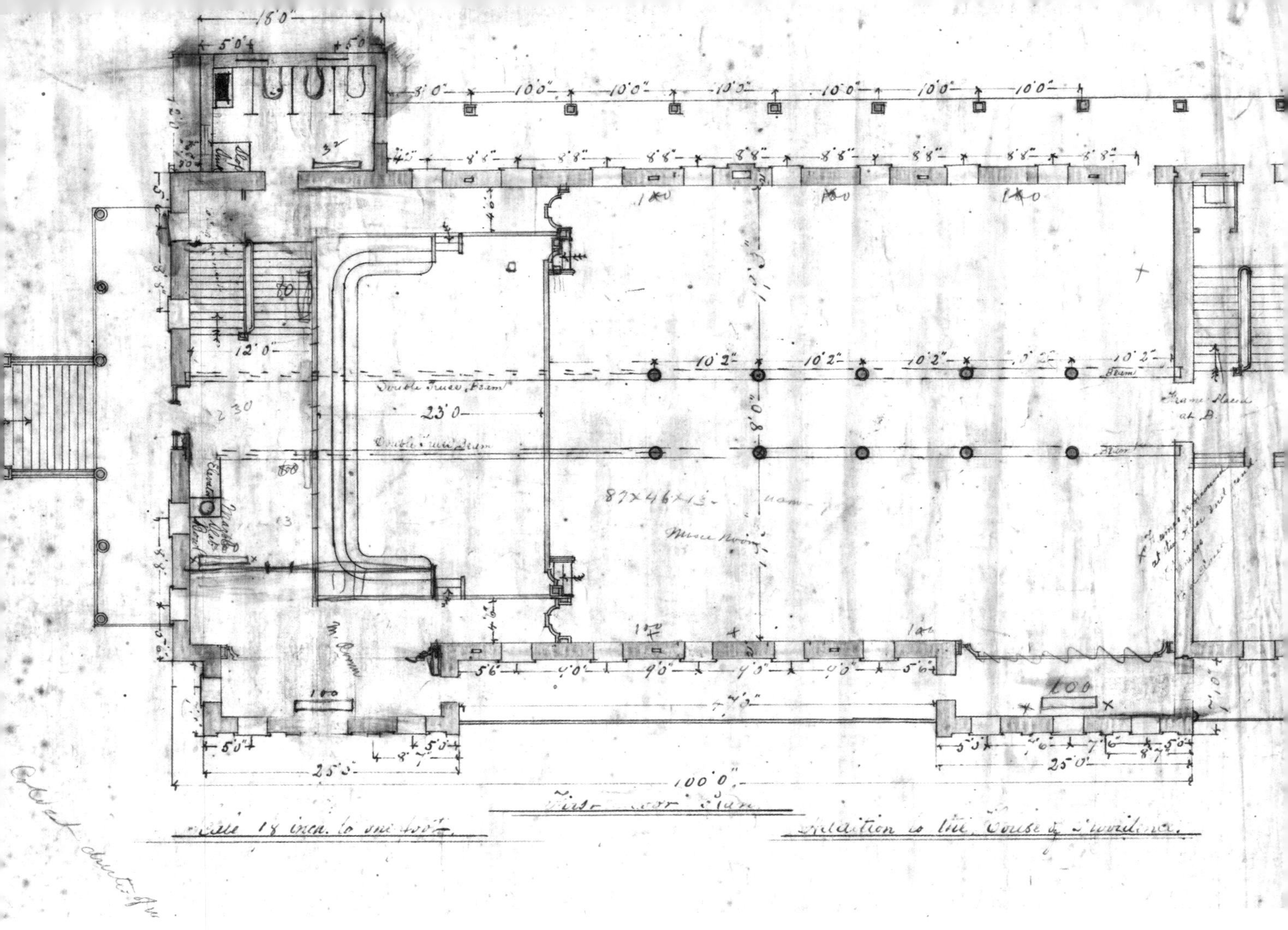

Undated and unsigned ink-on-linen plan of the first floor of the 1891 addition. (Providence Archives, Seattle, Washington.)

all manners—the same height and same proportions—to the original redbrick building, except for the internal divisions and the galleries. Lavatory towers were built as part of the 1891 addition in the northwest and southwest corners. Plans of the 1891 building also indicate a dumbbell elevator near the west end wall; it was probably used to send dirty laundry down to the basement and clean linens up to the dormitories. The second floor of the 1891 wing, when originally built, contained schoolrooms on both sides of the central hallway. One room spanned the full length of the wing on the north but could be subdivided by a series of folding doors. There were two classrooms on the south, one of which could be subdivided in the same manner.

Local legend says Mother Joseph "didn't claim [the design of the 1891 wing] as her own" and was quite upset to find, upon returning from Canada, that the building was no longer symmetrical. The archival materials suggests that not only did she lobby for its construction, she "[did] not rest until she [was] sure everything [was] perfect; she examine[d] every detail and [was] helped by Mr. Blanchet for the immediate supervision of the building site." Furthermore, extending the 1873 building in this manner was logical and conformed to standard practice of the day. Had a second addition been built on the east side, it probably would have mirrored the 1891 wing, thus establishing anew the desired symmetry.

Interior of a classroom circa 1901. (Providence Archives, Seattle, Washington.)

Work interrupted during the winter resumed in the second week of April 1892. Teachers and students finished their school semester in the comfortably finished attic of the new wing. The inconveniences caused by workmen renovating the 1873 building had repercussions on student morale. Orphan girls, pensioners, and music pupils rotated through the same room; they had to share use of the grounds.

Five English and one French classroom in the boarding section and two in the orphan girls' section officially opened in the new wing on September 9, 1892, as did a kindergarten. It was a new mission for the sisters. The orphanage would be discontinued in 1917, as were the distinctions between orphans and boarding students, probably leading to the name change to Providence Academy.

As historic photographs reveal, a student in 1896 would have typically walked down a central allée of two rows of machine-turned wooden bedsteads to get to her bed in the dormitory. Her desk would have been one among those aligned to a five-by-six grid in a classroom ringed with glass-enclosed bookshelves and adorned with religious pictures hung above the high wainscoting. The rugs on the wooden floor and gas lighting of the music room interior echoed a certain formality of the parlors.

Over a period of ninety-six years, the sisters continuously repaired or remodeled House of Providence, not because of any construction faults, but because they needed their environment to adapt to new needs and technologies. In the summer of 1894, they purchased a forge and asked one of their orphans, who became an engineer, to administer the factory. A cost-saving measure, the hands-on industrial training at the forge likely complemented the boys' schooling, partially resurrecting initial plans to operate a boot and shoe factory and a small woolen factory in connection with the boys' orphanage. June and part of July 1895 were spent on necessary, even urgent, repairs in the sisters' areas. The partition between the community room and the Superior's room, moved into of the washrooms was changed into a library for the use of the director of classes.

Electric lighting was installed in the auditorium in 1899, the same summer as a printing press and bookbinding shop were outfitted in the St. James Mission priests' house, a structure the sisters had called home for a few months and which would eventually be used as a museum. It was inaugurated with a favorite prayer of Mother Joseph, a petition to the Sacred Heart, and a hymn to St. François Xavier.

September 7, 1874, marked the first time since 1856 that everyone shared the same roof, rather than being scattered among different buildings as at the Providence Faubourg. As Mother Joseph remarked ten years later, some of the sisters and orphans had been a bit sad to be leaving the familiar old shacks, whose roofs, at the time of her writing in 1884, were overshadowed by large acacias and covered in moss. They had stood as reminders of the sacrifices and privations of their first years along the banks of the Columbia River. Like the priests' house, however, a good many of them had been moved.

In 1902, the Sisters paid thirty dollars a month for municipal water, an amount they believed excessive. So they contracted J. Healy to dig them a new well approximately 110 feet in depth, and Mr. Goss of Vancouver to erect a ten-thousand-gallon tower reservoir, perhaps heeding Mother Joseph's advice in undertaking these necessary improvements.

In 1905, Vancouver boasted a population of five thousand, which five years later had doubled to ten thousand, perhaps an effect of the construction of a substantial double-track railroad bridge built by the Spokane, Portland and Seattle Railway in 1908 to cross the Columbia River. The same year, an electric railway spurred the extension of Vancouver

Photograph of the priests' house circa 1920, when it stood next to the laundry building. It had been moved to the House of Providence property from St. James Mission. Note the water tower in the background. (Providence Archives, Seattle, Washington.)

the converted priests' refectory, was demolished, enlarging that room by six feet. The music room was divided into a community room for tertiary sisters (as there were two classes of sisters at the time) and the priests' refectory. A bath and sink were installed for the use of the sisters on the first floor. A sewing room, used as a linen and dress closet, was partitioned off from the pensioners' dormitory, reducing that space to forty beds. One city limits towards the northeast to the Orchards-Sifton district.

Providence Academy was the provincial seat for the Sisters of Providence in the Pacific Northwest until 1924, when the Montreal motherhouse introduced changes in the administrative structure of the order and removed provincial administration, the infirmary, and novitiate to Seattle. The high school took over the empty rooms.

Enrolment peaked at 350 boys and girls by 1930, which helps explain a new spurt of renovations. That year, the dilapidated St. Vincent's boys' school was demolished, which occupied one of the old wooden buildings that had been moved from St. James Mission, to make way for a lawn and children's playground. The four classrooms had been transferred the year before to the renovated and painted three-storey bakery, then being used as a dormitory during retreats. In 1931, the sisters had a three-storey service tower containing lavatories, lockers, and drying and shower facilities built on the northwest corner of the "boys' department," located in the back half of the chapel wing, as well as an electrical refrigeration system and a new gas range installed in their kitchen. In spite of the Great Depression, the sisters borrowed ten thousand dollars for the construction campaign. The weather-beaten belfry and roof of Providence Academy were repaired, after sixty years, and painted red, as were the roofs of the laundry and pump house. Following the advice of Mr. Hilburn, an architect, the porch railings were strengthened in 1934 by clamping iron bars to the posts, although some porches had been removed entirely. All of the exterior woodwork was painted silver-gray. On the interior, the worn floors were replaced and the walls repainted.

Kaiser Shipyards attracted armies of workers during World War II; the sisters, unable to accept all of the students who wanted to attend their school, had no choice but to turn away non-Catholics. After the Second World War, many workers and their families who had migrated to the city settled in the growing Vancouver suburbs where new parishes were established. St. Joseph School, constructed in the parish of the same name in late 1953-1954, and St. James School built in 1956, took in a considerable number of children born in the period we now call the baby-boom, who might have otherwise attended Providence Academy. For that reason the grade school was closed in the 1950s; Providence Academy would from then on receive only high school students.

Nonetheless, the sisters continued modernizing the boarding school to keep up with latest technologies. They had an intercommunicating telephone system installed in the name of increased efficiency; the apparatus was still visible to *The Columbian* reporter Ted Van Arsdol when he visited Providence Academy in November 1963. In 1956, they expanded the resident students' quarters into two high school classrooms; they converted two spacious rooms into the high school's Home Economics Department, a project financed by the parents' club; they enlarged the library (the space that was once the novitiate); they removed the partition between the 1873 and 1891 building from the third-floor hall; and they made four rooms out of the former cells of the sisters' "second floor north" sleeping quarters.

Thirty-three sisters, whose ages varied from twenty-one to eighty-four, lived at the Academy in 1956, the centennial year of the arrival of Mother

Joseph and her companions to the region. Sister Stanislaus, who had attended Providence as a student and entered the sisterhood as a postulant in 1891, was the most senior among them. They woke to the 5 a.m. bell and before the 6:30 Mass, then spent an hour in meditation and listening to a sister read from a theology book. From the chapel, it was off to the dining room for a breakfast of eggs, hot or cold cereal, fruit, toast, and coffee. Each sister then went to her own office, that is, to the place where she was to carry out her assigned work. Teachers entered their classrooms; those given household tasks such as dusting and sweeping took up the implements they needed. Classes started at 9 a.m. Lunch was served in two shifts, at noon and at 12:30 p.m., so that the children were not left unsupervised. At 4:30 p.m. the sisters went to the chapel for meditation and recitation of Holy Rosary before a 5:30 p.m. supper. From 7 p.m. to 8 p.m. sisters were expected to study in their own rooms or in the school library, depending on the nature of their work. Afterwards, they gathered in the community room, located at the east end of the Academy, for recreation and night prayers before finally retiring to their beds at 9 p.m., after a sixteen-hour day.

The sisters followed a number of rules. If a sister needed to leave the Academy, she had to sign out. If she required money, she had to ask the Superior. Seldom did sisters travel alone. Sometimes they broke the rules. Alumnae reunion attendees recalled "sneaking up to the roof to smoke a forbidden cigarette, or to just enjoy the thrill of trespassing… or catching [the teachers, mostly sisters] bending the rules themselves." Some sisters sewed, others read newspapers or magazines (*Newsweek*, *Life*, *Time*, or purely Catholic publications), listened to records, or played Scrabble or card games during their thirty-minute evening recreation period. Other leisure activities included playing tennis on the Providence courts; singing and folk dancing; and when there were special events going on, listening to the radio, watching television, or viewing motion pictures.

Changes in room use continued despite a dwindling student body. The chronicles reported in January 1958 the senior class renovated and converted the television room, formerly the little boys' dining room, into a visual aids room. The cost of painting the walls and woodwork, installing draw drapes, and purchasing a crucifix totaled 130 dollars. The room housed "the moving picture projector, the filmstrip machine and the television set; a large new wall screen is on a roller and may be lowered easily for the showing of any type of film"—albeit a film previously approved by Church censors. In the following summer, the sisters undertook repair work on the auditorium stage. They replaced the "time-honored buff sateen curtains" with a "rose-beige cyclorama"; painted the stage and proscenium arch a matching rose-beige. These efforts were made to "modernize and beautify the school." When Van Arsdol toured the Academy in 1963, a basement room had been remodeled for a science laboratory, the typing room occupied a former junior girls' dormitory, and a high school lounge had been outfitted in a previous senior boarders' dormitory.

Perhaps as much in anticipation of the sale of the property as out of the danger that the deteriorated structure presented to the public, the sisters hired workmen in March 1959 to dismantle the build-

In the top right corner of this 1956 photograph of visitors filing into Providence Academy for the centennial celebration of the arrival of the sisters in the northwest, we see the Post Hospital in its original T-plan configuration. Before the construction of Interstate 5, there was a strong visual connection between the Sisters' property and the military reserve. (Providence Archives, Seattle, Washington.)

ing that had originally been built as the bakery, used as a dormitory for retreats, and since 1929 as St. Vincent's school for boys. The demolition crew salvaged the materials in lieu of wages.

Providence Academy for Sale

Construction of the Portland-Vancouver bridge and the widening of "old 99," also known as the Pacific Highway, into Interstate 5 in the late 1950s and the 1960s chopped older Vancouver neighborhoods.

The new highways encouraged the growth of suburbs, radically changing the ways people lived and worked. The proximity of Portland, Oregon, now a few minutes' drive away, condemned Vancouver to become a bedroom community. Urban renewal also contributed to changing the face of downtown, as it had in most American cities. Families moved to outlying districts. Two new Catholic parishes were hived off from the historic St. James parish. Schools were built in both St. Joseph of the East, opened in 1953, and Our-Lady-of-Lourdes in the northwest quarter of the city. A new school was also built for St. James at 47th Street and Franklin. Providence Academy became redundant in providing instruction to Vancouver's Catholic children.

By the mid-fifties, the boarding school was operating at a loss; the kindergarten no longer had a teacher and hiring a lay teacher was too expensive. Approval to close both became effective on June 3, 1960. A couple months before, on April 18, Vancouver realtors Whitfield Brothers had announced the sale of Providence Academy and the adjacent St. Joseph's Hospital in the local newspaper *The Columbian*. The sisters asked 1.5 million dollars for the properties, a fraction of estimated costs for the major rehabilitation work needed to keep the buildings up to contemporary fire, health, and safety codes. Many a convent has been closed, even demolished in the twentieth century because of this recurrent issue. Religious communities, justifiably, cannot single-handedly financially support the burden of bringing their buildings up to code, knowing they themselves would have little future use for them. A new sprinkler system alone would have cost some sixty thousand dollars in 1966. The sisters estimated they needed 87,225 dollars yearly to pay the salaries of four lay teachers and four maintenance people, to light and heat the building, and otherwise run the place. Providence Academy was already two hundred thousand dollars in debt.

Despite the general decline in Vancouver's downtown and increasing impoverishment of its population, an effect of urban renewal policies, day students continued to attend the school and, until Providence Academy shut definitively, the sisters yearly readied the building for the start of classes every September: refurbishing floors, cleaning, and painting where needed. They installed a large canopy over the west entrance and, in August 1962, purchased a new pump for the well. But these were minor expenses compared with the more than thirty-five thousand dollars in repairs they had to pay after ninety-mile-an-hour hurricane winds tore off the roof, destroyed the galleries of the east wing, and uprooted trees the following October. "Water from a leaking roof and a broken sprinkling system… saturat[ed] the third and fourth floors," reported the chronicles. As luck would have it, three months later, two frozen pipes burst on the third floor, requiring "replastering and repainting work amounting to $3641.23." All these costs only increased the institution's debt.

Because the sisters were unable to rent facilities in October 1963 as they usually did, volunteers helped transform the old, unused kindergarten building in the east yard into a gymnasium for the high school physical education classes; "Pratka Construction Co. donated time, equipment and services;" parties interested in the lumber removed the hardwood flooring; "another person installed the electric fixtures;" and several Providence Academy employees painted and stippled walls and ceilings. The Parent-Faculty association had the school gymnasium's concrete floor covered with asphalt tile.

As a contribution towards civic enterprise and public relations, the Superior offered the Washington Artists' Association, "an organization of men and women and three high school boys interested in art," free use of Marion Hall, the former girls' dormitory over the laundry. In April 1964, probably in anticipation of the eventual closure and move, "Sister Superior presented to the Fort Vancouver Historical Society for their museum, some artifacts given to the Academy by the Dr. David Wall family. These articles had been given to the Academy with the intention that they remain in Vancouver."

The provincial administration had annually absorbed the school's deficit and Providence Academy simply could no longer generate the twenty-five-million-dollar subsidy needed to keep the school going. One hundred fifty-six girls attended the Academy. Each paid fifteen dollars monthly. Vancouver parents could not afford increased tuition for private schooling.

The provincial superior traveled to Vancouver to personally make the announcement of the school's definitive closure on January 25, 1966, first to the sisters, then over dinner to the priests of the area as well as two gentlemen of the Seattle Development office, Mr. Joseph Greeley and Mr. William Tobin, and finally to the parents at an evening meeting. The students were informed the following day that the 1966 class would be the last to graduate.

The sister-administrators had coolly considered the matter, admitting, "it is a sad prospect to demolish this building, the cradle of our western missions, but we must not yield to our emotional feelings." As any savvy businessman, the women questioned their obligation to maintain operations in Vancouver knowing the school was running at a loss, the building had sustained substantial storm damage in 1962, and many of the personnel had lately fallen sick. In addition, the order wanted to build a new hospital with the income from the sale of the Academy and St. Joseph's Hospital. Remodeling the latter was financially unfeasible due to the "outmoded physical plant," new regulations stipulating land-to-bed ratios, and the limited chances of receiving funding, as they were in competition with Vancouver Memorial Hospital. Finally, the 14th Avenue interchange proposed by the Washington State Highway Department in 1967 would no doubt affect the hospital site.

Besides, other Sisters of Providence institutions also had to be renovated and enlarged. Sister Susanne Hartung, who was chief mission integration officer of Providence Health and Service Strategic Services of eight thousand employees of Providence Health and Services System, numbering seventy-three thousand employees and the only Sister of Providence presently working in the administration of the non-profit corporation, believes that another deciding factor or consideration concerned the application of an ethical standard: "Is someone else going to take care of those poor people?" The two new parishes created in the 1950s could cater to the same population.

The Highway Department's plans notwithstanding, Providence Academy was situated in a prime location, contiguous to the downtown core area of Vancouver to the west and south, the interstate freeway on the east, and residential uses on the north. Zoning classification of the property had been changed from residential to commercial uses, paving the way for high-density development on the sisters' site and the area generally between D Street and the freeway, extending north to McLoughlin Boulevard, as tabled in Clark, Coleman & Rupeiks, Inc.'s 1963 Central Business District plan. Other possibilities were floated, including luxury apartments, a shopping center, a historical monument, and a new City Hall, a suggestion that would resurface in 1997 when the City Manager had an architect begin to study this option.

Most of the sisters, like Hartung, who at the time of closure was teaching fifth grade in Olympia, had little attachment to Providence Academy. It was a building just like any other in which they accomplished their mission. Hartung remembered how the floors creaked, thus alerting one to people's movements within the silent building, but otherwise had little recollection of the physical environment, having lived there three months in summer 1957. Probably few within the religious community were affected by the announcement of the sale. After all, this was not the first of the twenty-nine institutions attributed to Mother Joseph to have been sold. Six institutions opened during her lifetime still operate today, but in modern physical plants.

The reaction of the parents, however, "was one of concern and sorrow." Some "wanted to do something to save Providence Academy." Managing editor of *The Columbian*, Mr. Erwin O. Rieger, summarized for readers in February 1966 the importance of the school in the community: "For among other things that will die with Providence is graciousness, a touch of some of the finer things of the human spirit, that is difficult to find in many of the modernistic and brightly functional abodes of education that are in vogue today."

Salvation of the Building

Soon after the official declaration to close the Academy in 1966, local media started publishing articles about the building's history. It took a couple of years for interested citizens to muster themselves into a preservation committee, even though *The Columbian* had carried a series of six articles November 5 through 14, 1963, detailing the history and works of the Sisters of Providence in Vancouver, Washington. Two days earlier, the Fort Vancouver Historical Society had sponsored a memorial program in memory of the first superior of the Pacific Northwest mission, on November 3, the day Mother Joseph and her companions had left Montreal. After having researched the history of the building, Ann King, a descendant of the family of Sister Stanislaus of the Blessed Sacrament, had elaborated the day's program. The thousand attendees started at Mother Joseph's gravesite in St. James Acres Catholic Cemetery and thence to Providence Academy to see firsthand her works and the display of artifacts she would have used in her daily life. King, who was 1963 Woman of the Year of the Westward Ho Chapter of the American Business Women's Association of Vancouver, wanted to generate interest in the pioneering sister and raise funds towards the preservation of the former convent and orphan asylum. She confided to a journalist in 1963 that she hoped to persuade Walt Disney to film a movie on Mother Joseph. In May 1964, Providence Academy again opened its doors, from 2 to 4 p.m., this time "in honor of Mother Gamelin [foundress of the Montreal-based order] as mother of orphans. The academy bell was rung at 3 p.m. for the occasion." On their November 3, 1965 tour, students pointedly stopped at "the room where Mother Joseph died." Novices and postulants from Providence Heights, Issaquah, Washington, toured Providence Academy in May 1966 because of the building's historical importance to the community, and probably to say farewell. In parallel, the Sisters of Providence were made an institutional member of the Fort Vancouver Historical Society. The Fort Vancouver chapter of the Daughters of the American Revolution reviewed McCrosson's *The Bell and the River* at their January 1964 meeting and then visited the Academy, where they saw some of the historic items described in the biography. Vancouver Fourth Degree Council of the Knights of Columbus renamed their chapter Mother Joseph of the Sacred Heart Council.

A registered general carpenter, possibly a man by the name of Howard Smith, was one of the first to manifest interest in purchasing Providence Academy, according to a 1968 account by Sister Barbara Scheller. He proposed to demolish the building, brick by brick, in anticipation of selling the salvaged materials, sparing only the chapel. Other parties had indicated a desire in its preservation. The sisters would keep the bell and the statue of St. Joseph, however, as mementos of their cradle in the Pacific Northwest. This proposition must have been well received: not only was the general contractor fully insured, selling an empty lot would certainly be easier than one with a standing structure. Demolition was scheduled for February 1, 1968. However, county office worker Si Sheeley alerted Robert Hidden, grandson of brick manufacturer Lowell Mason Hidden, about the demolition contract, who then contacted his buddies to develop scenarios for the possible uses of the property, including preservation of Providence Academy should they successfully acquire it.

Hidden was no stranger to historic preservation. His father, William Foster Hidden, was instrumental in preserving the Covington House from demolition and relocating it near Kiggins Bowl at 44th and Main Street. And Robert had previously fought to save the 1867 Slocum house successfully (the fancy house, distinguished by its cupola, lacework railings, and octagonal rooms was moved to Esther Short Park and turned into the Old Slocum House Theatre, a center for community productions), and the old Fort Vancouver High School and Auditorium at 26th and Main Streets in 1972, although that attempt failed. Disappointed at the end of the fight, he complained that "in the old days we had an opera house, and people came from Portland for cultural events. Now we have nothing." He was interested in having "the auditorium, two gymnasiums and schoolhouse rooms for community organizations, cultural events and senior citizens." Moreover, Hidden Brothers bricks had been used to build the "Old Fort" high school and its auditorium in 1934 as a part of a Depression make-work program.

"Drive to Save Academy Set" heralded *The Oregon Journal* on January 10, 1968. Three men, brick manufacturer Robert Arthur Hidden (1910-1992), retired architect and former president of the historical society Donald J. Stewart, and property manager Merv Simpson, none of whom were Catholic, launched a fundraising drive with the goal of purchasing the building. The trio may have had vested interests in the campaign's success. Nine days before, Robert

Hidden and his associates, his three sons Oliver M., William F., and Richard M., had obtained an option on the academy property from the provincial superior, valid until February 1, 1968, through the intermediary of the order's real estate consultants. At the time, the Sisters of Providence had a contract out to demolish Providence Academy and had leased the hospital buildings to St. Joseph's Community Hospital for two years, with an additional two-year option. The two parties had agreed on a price of one million dollars, including a two-hundred-thousand-dollar down payment, the terms subject to the sisters' approval.

The religious order had made a difficult decision; they were unflappable in the face of criticism, yet cooperative when citizens began to mobilize to save the structure. By mid-January, a fifty-member preservation committee had been struck with the goal of formulating a preservation strategy. The membership, which included "persons of all ages, including laborers and Catholic nuns," elected Ann King treasurer. Everyone attending the January 17 meeting agreed the building should be converted to save it from the wrecking ball. They examined several economically feasible plans. Hidden's preliminary concept foresaw the construction of two-storey, multiple-family residential housing blocks, offices, shops, and even a three-level department store on the property surrounding Providence Academy. The Academy itself could be converted into a hundred-room motel, although elsewhere in the document he proposed "apartments or offices with community uses for some of the specialized rooms." Elements of this proposal recalled rumors spread in Clark County in May 1966 that "a splendid new shopping center would replace the academy." At the time, a journalist remarked the building needed "at most a new heating system and some electrical rewiring." It was so soundly built, demolition costs alone were estimated to surpass seventy-five thousand dollars.

Hidden envisioned the continued use of the hospital or its renovation into an extended care facility or even a doctors' clinic. In all cases, "parking would surely be in the picture whatever use would be... return to investors." Other projects for the former school were floated in local newspapers, such as a new public auditorium. The Housing Committee of the Health and Welfare Planning Council of Clark County suggested it become "a social service complex for local public and charitable agencies," including the YWCA, Boy Scouts, and Camp Fire Girls. Adaptive-reuse of the sisters' site, Hidden projected, would cost five million dollars, would need commercial investment, and therefore would need to generate income for the investors.

Those at the meeting, according to *The Columbian,* entertained the possibility of "local community buying stock in such a development project." This would require a complex "structure of ownership, financing and operation [to] be set and registered with proper authorities," indicated Robert Harris, chairman of the St. Joseph Community Hospital Association Board of Trustees, a local organization created to lease the hospital for a period of four years. The idea of integrating the former convent into a larger, "international tourist attraction" project that would notably tie together "the Columbia River Indian Village, the partially reconstructed Fort Vancouver on the National Park Service site, Grant House, and the Barracks area" was shot down.

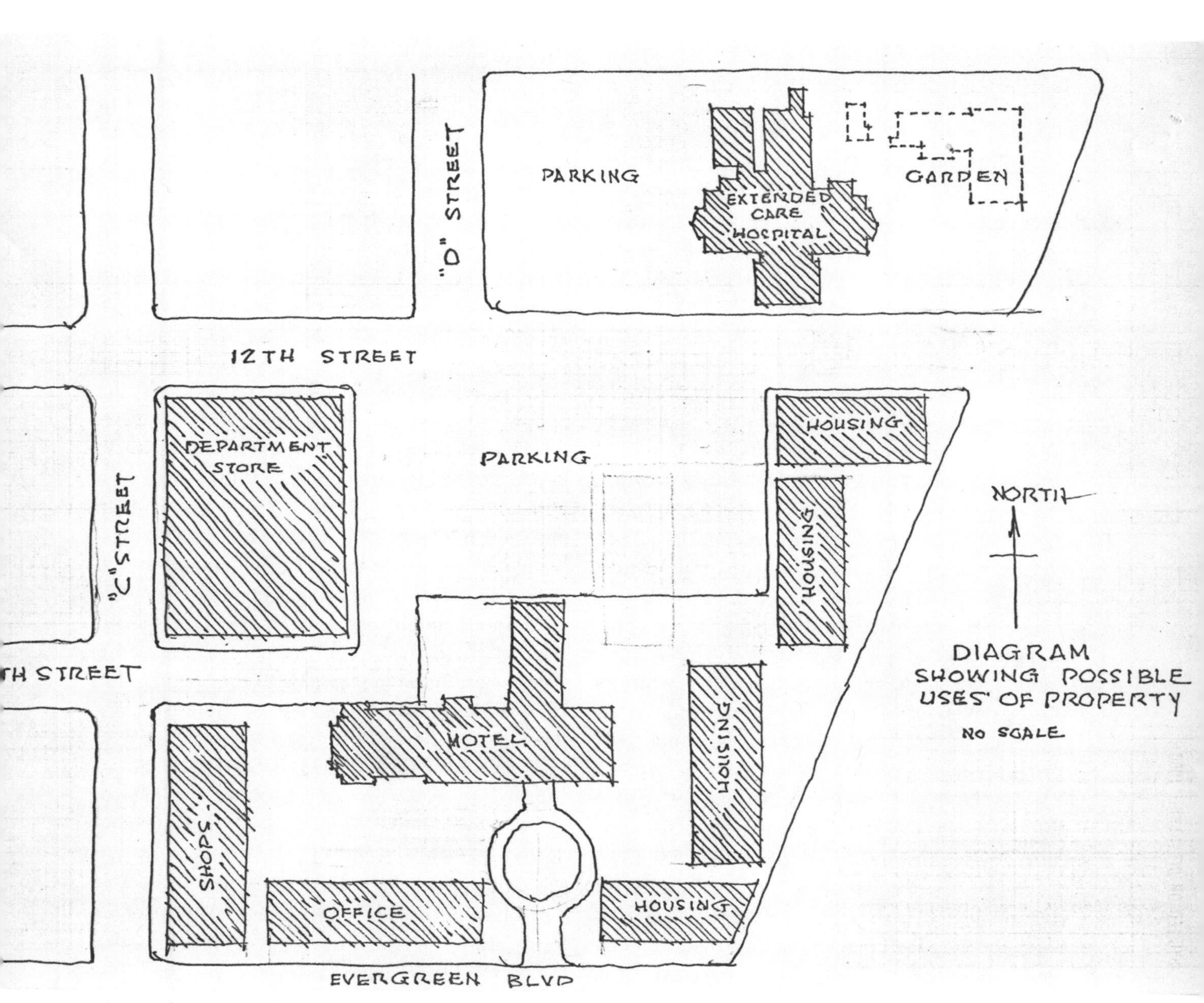

Diagram showing possible uses of property prepared by Robert Hidden, Donald J. Stewart, and Merv Simpson. (Providence Archives, Seattle, Washington.)

Even if it featured Providence Academy in its tourist guides, Fort Vancouver Historical Society realized it could never hope to secure funding, as had Colonial Williamsburg from the Rockefeller Foundation.

Fundraising was the preservation committee's first item of business. It immediately launched a public subscription drive by sending out a communiqué asking residents of the region, "do you want to help preserve this historic building for posterity?" One week before the purchase option on Providence Academy became due, Mrs. Donald J. Stewart, wife of one of the three leaders of the funding drive, rallied Vancouverites "to write letters to the Congressmen and others interested in preserving the historic academy" at the Thursday, January 25, 1968 preservation committee meeting held at Nurses' Hall or Unit 2, St. Joseph's Hospital. Signed by Mr. and Mrs. John Repman, Mrs. Alice Wright, and Miss Lesla E. Scott, mainly women, the letters pleaded potential investors to support their cause, inundated local newspapers, and lobbied the Sister Superior to postpone demolition of Providence Academy and to extend the option's closing date. These efforts to organize a concerted campaign followed classic textbook National Trust for Historic Preservation advice.

A Ms. Harley Mays, "a member of a committee of responsible citizens who are making a supreme effort to save historic Providence Academy from destruction," prophetically argued in a letter addressed to the sisters: "If the building is demolished, the bare land may remain unused for many years, a condition which has occurred with the many square blocks of vacant property in the urban renewal area just a short distance away." Gone were typical nineteenth-century homes captured in a July 1979 photograph taken from the cupola looking southwards. The five and ten-to-twelve-storey apartment and office towers in *The Columbian*'s picture have multiplied since, as have asphalted surfaces.

Mays's thoughts echoed Robert Hidden's observations from the early 1960s, that "urban renewal took away all the residences south of Eighth Street [on Vancouver's lower west side]" and replaced them with offices west of Esther Short Park. "People liked living there, and they used the downtown, and some of the old houses were beautiful." Others, however, remembered the area as an eyesore, the homes run-down and rat-infested. "Moving those people out... changed the whole aspect of town. It, and the new freeway were the things that killed downtown as a retail center." Ironically, Hidden had led an effort to build the Interstate Bridge. Nonetheless, historic preservation seemed to him a good palliative to the ravages of urban renewal.

Margo Kendall, president of the 1966 graduating class, the last to go through the Academy, brought a different perspective to the ongoing discussion in the local newspapers. Quoting from John Dewey, "Piety to the past is not for its own sake nor for the sake of the past, but for the sake of a present so secure and enriched that it will create a better future." She thus pleaded against tearing down Providence Academy, arguing implicitly that the building was as important to the history of Vancouver as the old fort reconstructed by The Fort Vancouver Historical Society in the 1960s based on the archaeological evidence uncovered in the 1940s. "Archaeologists [had] found evidence of the posts outlining the famed old Hudson's Bay post stockade" between twelve and eighteen inches below the surface [in other words, the palisade] as well as an "assortment of metal and china relics of Dr. John McLoughlin's day," reported the *Sunday Oregonian.*

Like many other non-profits across the continent, the preservation committee had used the reconstruction of Williamsburg, Virginia, as a model of historic preservation and as a tourist mecca. As Mrs. Stewart had argued, Vancouver, the cradle of Euro-American settlement in the Oregon Territory, was as precious as Williamsburg in the beginnings of the United States. There, large sums of money had been spent "to dig out the original plans and rebuild all this historic beauty." Together with the Old Fort Vancouver, the intact convent could only bolster Vancouver's burgeoning mass-tourism industry.

As the letter-writing campaign peaked, Robert Hidden traveled to Providence Heights with his wife sometime in late January 1968. They had gone to the provincial administration in order to renew the Hiddens' option on the Sisters' property. Mrs. Virginia Hidden, taking care of the social etiquette on Mr. Hidden's behalf as well as her own, thanked Sister Rita for the community's generous hospitality. She admitted in her letter apprehension in "finding many supporters to help renew our conviction that we must see this effort through to completion," though she assured the Sister Superior that they "have a fine gentleman from Portland working enthusiastically on the land feasibility and now are thinking in the corporate line." Mrs. Hidden's doubt proved well-founded. The preservation committee failed to raise the needed monies, confirmed Sister Scheller.

The Hiddens persevered nonetheless. In October 1968, they asked whether the sisters would be interested in partnering up to build apartments. The sisters declined. The Hiddens asked whether they were willing to sell the properties in several lots, but the sisters again refused. They wanted to sell the tracts in one piece.

Finally, on November 1, 1968, William Foster Hidden and Robert A. Hidden put in a purchase offer for both Providence Academy and St. Joseph's Hospital, which the sisters had also put up for sale. The handwritten document bearing their signatures and conserved in the Sisters of Providence archives set out the following conditions:

1. Hidden Brothers, with the guarantee of Robert A. Hidden, offers to purchase from the Sisters of Charity of the House of Providence in the Territory of Washington the Providence Academy and St. Joseph's Hospital property in Vancouver on the following terms.
2. Sale price, $700,000.
3. Down payment, $100,000 (including $5700 option money paid and $10,000 deposit) payable upon signing of contract.
4. Payments, $45,000 every 6 months.
5. Interest of 6% on unpaid balance.
6. Releases
   a. When principal reduced to $350,000, a deed will be given to 50% of the land area south of 12th street.
   b. When principal reduced to $175,000 all of the property south of 12th street will be released.
   c. All deeds will run to purchasers or assignees
7. $10,000 is delivered to Mr. Andrews to show good faith of purchasers.

Although the sisters would have preferred a cash sale, not less than eight hundred thousand dollars, and considered the six-percent interest too low, they finally settled on seven hundred thousand dollars for both properties, considerably less than the asking price of one million in 1968, as the Hiddens were not backing down. It would take three or four months more to conclude the deal. In the interim, the future owners blocked "holes in the Academy windows to keep the pipes from freezing. The boiler has a hard time to heat the hospital and keep a little heat in the empty [Academy] building. We do not want it to freeze while we are working towards its purchase," informed Robert and Virginia Hidden in the New Year's card they sent the Superior. The two parties finalized the sale in March 1969, but since the sisters had renewed the St. Joseph's Hospital Community Association's lease, it would not officially become the Hiddens' property until the lease expired, or until a new hospital was built.

"As negotiators, the Hiddens can be as unmovable as Mount Rushmore," commented *The Columbian* journalist Bill Dietrich. While the Sisters of Providence had originally set their price at approximately 1.5 million dollars for the two major buildings, a number of minor buildings, and the almost ten-acre property in April 1960, nine years later the Hiddens managed to bargain it down to 718,800 dollars, namely, 494,300 dollars for the Academy and 225,500 dollars for St. Joseph's Hospital and its grounds. No one will deny that Robert Hidden and his sons saved the building from the bulldozer and wrecking ball, yet he was using all of his business acumen and perhaps also his family's long ties with the Sisters of Providence to do so. His proposition was as much a profit-making development venture as a philanthropic gesture. The Hiddens had not only established profitable brickyards, they had also, from generation to generation, built up a considerable fourteen-million-dollar-plus real estate empire.

Hidden family patriarch Lowell Mason, known for "his quiet persistence, his conservatism, his frugality, his singular blend of community philanthropy and tight-fistedness," had acquired generous tracts of land in the 1880s. Both L. M. Hidden and his sons W. F. Hidden *et al.* are listed as owners of riverside property on a 1912 real estate map. Hidden, in partnership with his brothers Arthur and Oliver, had built the four-storey Hotel Columbia at Third and Main Street in 1890, produced bricks for the first Camas paper mill, and established the State School for the Deaf at its present location, on or adjacent to his farm "above Vancouver." That is where he spent a good amount of time, as we can deduce from weekly newspaper notices such as the one that ran on September 27, 1877, telling potential customers: "I will be at my brick yard near Vancouver on the afternoon of Thursdays and Saturdays of each week." He donated the land on which to build the Carnegie Library in 1909, today the Clark County Historical Museum at Sixteenth and Main Street. The building was named after William Foster Harris, and his grandson of the same name sits on the museum board as an emeritus member.

As Vancouver City councilor and historian Pat Jollata remarked, Lowell Mason and William Foster Hidden's houses translated the businessmen's and their families' social positions as "solid, responsible men and women, pillars of the community, to whom many people looked up to." Lowell Hidden had held the post of City Surveyor in the early 1880s (and maybe late 1870s), but he "sent in his resignation" in June 1881, informed *The Vancouver*

Independent that month. The patriarch's two-and-a-half-storey, substantial, brick-clad home was built in 1885, and proudly stood on the corner at 13th Street. Irregular in plan, its multiple ornamented gable roofs and generous porch addressed the street—and the south end of Hidden's brickyards. His son's residence, a rectangular, two-and-a-half-storey, brick-clad, gable-roof house featuring regularly spaced arched dormer windows and fronted by a Grecian porch, was located at 13th Street and Washington Street. Both father and son also owned substantial tracts of property southeast of the U. S. Military Reservation where the New Washington School for the Deaf was built. They also owned a number of lots between 26th and 29th Streets north of Fourth Plain Road, and a few others, labeled as Hidden's additions situated northwest of downtown around 33rd and 34th Streets between Washington and Daniels, are identified on a 1961 Metsker Map.

The Hidden family initially intended to preserve both the Academy and hospital buildings in 1969. Conceived to take advantage of the site's prime real estate potential while also showcasing the original 1873 building, their 14.5-million-dollar Academy Plaza project announced in June 1972 as a joint venture with American Condominium Homes, Inc. and Teeples and Thatcher, Inc. proposed an office, apartment, condominium, and retail store complex. The 1891 west wing was to be demolished, making way for the construction of a five-storey, forty-six-unit condominium apartment house. A seventy-seven-unit, eight-storey apartment house was to be built directly east of the old building. Three shops were to line Evergreen Boulevard in front of the Academy. The construction of a twelve-storey apartment house and a five-storey condominium were slated for a second phase of development. They were to be located to the sides and rear of the site, as was a two-storey parking garage. While St. Joseph's Hospital was to be razed for a motel complex, the original 1873 Academy was to be outfitted with stores and offices and a basement restaurant. The chapel was to be removed, its restoration economically unjustifiable when every square foot of rental space counted. Instead, the developers planned to "set aside a first-floor room with a small courtyard as a memorial to Mother Joseph."

Amputating important additions, bringing back a historic structure to its initial form was common enough practice in the 1970s, despite restoration principles promulgated in international heritage preservation charters. It was all preservationists could do to convince developers to save at least a piece of the historic fabric in their quest to maximize profits. In Montreal, for instance, a Swiss-based firm proposed to tear down all but the chapel of the Mother House of the Grey Nuns in 1972, leaving it as the centerpiece of high-rise towers to be erected on the perimeter of the coveted downtown Montreal location. Since the turn of the twenty-first century, the SSQ life insurance company and financial group has been transforming the site of a former convent of the Sisters of the Good Shepherd in Québec City into a "green neighborhood." The vast E-plan building houses primarily medical offices and clinics on the ground and first floors and condominiums on the second through fourth floors. A piece of the building at the intersection of the three central wings was demolished, as was the barn and other secondary buildings on the site, including a villa, leaving the rest of the site available for the construction of new condominium blocks, an apartment building for low-income renters, and townhouses.

Before locking up and placing Providence Academy under the surveillance of a caretaker on August 4, 1966, the sisters had emptied the building of movable furniture. "Over $6286 was made on the sale of household equipment and supplies. Some articles were sent to [other institutions], some were given to needy families and the rest were donated to the St. Vincent-de-Paul Society of Portland, OR." The sisters had also had the chapel dismantled on June 27, 1966 by Vancouver resident and caretaker of the Vancouver Historical Society Museum Mr. Joseph Pagel, his son Tom, and the Reverend Michael O'Brien. As we learn from the chronicles, "All the parts taken from the chapel, the antiques of the house and pieces of value were sent to the Provincial House at Pine Lake, Issaquah, WA." In contrast, the chapel interior of the Grey Nuns' Rideau Street convent in Ottawa, Ontario, was reconstructed as an architectural period room in the National Art Museum.

Black and white photograph of Providence Academy chapel in 1977, before its restoration. (Providence Archives, Seattle, Washington.)

Earlier in the week of June 27, 1996, Mr. Larry Pratka, his son Steve, and Rev. O'Brien, Assistant to Our Lady of Lourdes Parish, located "the cornerstone [of the wing dedicated to the Sacred Heart of Jesus] Providence Academy... to the right of the main entrance and about two feet off the ground... [and] broke the cement block disclosing a metal box. Sister superior removed the corroded box and found four coins and a medal approximately two inches in diameter of Pope Pius IX, the reigning pontiff at the time," and pieces of disintegrated paper placed there some ninety-three years before. Had the written documents survived, witnesses at the cornerstone removal ceremony would have read:

> This construction is under the auspices of the first founding mother of the missions of the West, Sister Esther Pariseau, in religion Sister Joseph... two of the other founding sisters still living... the building is built with the help of the one we call the "father of the orphans," Mr. Jean-Baptiste Blanchet, our architect, nephew to the Blanchet bishops.

Sister Joseph was among the signatories.

When Sister Hartung, superior of a convent situated in a parish two miles north of Providence Academy, presided over the desacralization ritual of St. Joseph's Hospital in 1970, she found similar contents in the metal box. It was akin to a time capsule placed in the cornerstone of secular buildings. Only after the ceremony did the Hiddens obtain permission to demolish the hospital. In 2013, the cornerstone sat to the west of The Academy, a memento to the adjoining ministry.

Restoration of Providence Academy began in earnest in 1973, one hundred years after it was first built. Academy Plaza developers aimed to provide the necessary "spark... for explosive growth and revitalization of the entire downtown Vancouver area." A planner with the Regional Planning Office considered their plans overly ambitious and expressed his concerns about street congestion, utility loadings, density, and site planning to reporter Ed Mosey in 1974. However, "because of lack of interest on the part of prospective tenants," the Hiddens scrapped the Academy Plaza project.

Mosey summarized Hidden's philosophy: "To save the old, buildings must be made relevant in economic terms." To that end, Robert Hidden raised the capital needed to modernize Providence Academy's electrical system and to add electric heating, by selling the 2.5-acre hospital property as soon as the St. Joseph Community Hospital Association of Clark County Inc. lease expired. The run-down plant's historical significance had been diluted by more recent renovation and additions—a common argument when only the original structure is valued. Moreover, by his estimation, it did not lend itself to new uses. Hidden hoped the Black Angus restaurant and Shiloh Inn that motel developer Dave Christensen built after demolishing the hospital in 1974 would attract people to the area, as envisioned in the Academy Plaza project.

In opening up The Academy (the new name given to the complex), the Hiddens employed a recipe used in similar ventures in Portland, where old industrial structures housed specialty shops; Ghirardelli Square in San Francisco; and "Old Town" of Los Gatos, California, which catered to residents and tourists alike. Robert Hidden told reporter Elisabeth van Nostrand that he envisioned "cozy restaurants in the cellar, outdoor cafes on the balconies and upstairs breezeways, a taste of ol' England in a tea room, shopping arcades featuring imported goods and antiques and specialties—maybe even a museum and maybe even a restored chapel" where Vancouverites and visitors could pause from downtown bustle. Community groups could use the auditorium for their meetings and events.

Three years later, when professionals—architects, marketers, lawyers, and psychologists—started renting spaces in the first floor and basement, the Hiddens had a waiting list and were working to refurbish the second floor. A space in The Academy was rented to a private school for preschool children and the gymnasium to the Vancouver Boxing Club. The laundry-boiler house was to become a media and culture center; however, building officials at the City of Vancouver refused the group's plans.

Bill Dietrich, in his November 8, 1981 article in *The Columbian* about the Hidden family in Vancouver, says some of the people he interviewed "described [Hidden's sons, who were making most of the business decisions by 1981] as shrewd businessmen, others as intelligent but too conservative to take maximum advantage of their holdings." Although The Academy housed a good number of offices, small shops, a restaurant, and two private schools in 1979, the turnover rate was high. Despite charging "less than half the [rate charged for] new office space downtown," they simply could not staunch the tide. Leaseholders failed to succeed; some blamed the family's stingy maintenance, their slowness in answering merchants' problems and lack of promotion of The Academy. Detractors blamed the mediocre, even poor commercial success on the lack of investment on the part of the Hidden family. One former tenant railed that "they are the damndest cheapscrew landlords I have ever rented from," explaining that "except for emergency repairs he had difficulty getting maintenance and improvements" from the Hiddens. Cash-short in taking on such a large project, Monte Hidden was "refinishing the hallway floors on Christmas Eve and New Year's Eve in 1980," mentioned Yvette Payne, former on-site property manager of The Academy, while giving us a tour of the building. It was not the first time the brothers fixed up the building themselves.

The Hiddens felt hindered by the building covenants and preservation easements that restricted development of the site. Yet they were among "the downtown businessmen who refused to agree to pay for a parking garage" that the City wanted to build to attract Telephone Utilities to Vancouver, purportedly because it would have "increased their taxes by $44,000 a year," noted Dietrich. Parking lots typically generate revenue for developers sitting on vacant land and it was a strategy the Hiddens adopted. By giving most of the yards over to the automobile, they maximized the spaces available for lease to downtown workers.

Ultimately, Robert Hidden had spent some "$900,000 to save the building, yet [his] unwillingness to rehabilitate the Academy properly [was] strangling its commercial potential," complained many to *The Columbian*'s Dietrich. Hidden, in his defense, pointed out the family's perceived wealth was misleading: "You can own a lot of property but if you have to pay property tax you do not feel rich. We've always been cash-poor." Because their capital was tied up in land, they had little liquidity.

Robert and his sister, Helene Hidden Van Buren of Portland, had inherited the two-hundred-acre waterfront holdings that had been leased to Kaiser shipyards during World War II. In 1976, they still owned between 112 and 124 acres at Columbia Industrial Park, established on those same lands. In addition to overseeing the Hidden Brick Company until it closed, Robert's three sons, Oliver M., William F., and Richard M. Hidden, commanded the Hidden Bros. Company, a property management firm. Among other buildings, the company had owned an old cinema across town, Payne told us as she pointed out a number of theatre seats stored in the Academy attic.

But as Robert Hidden had astutely observed, changes in building use inevitably require owners to conform to the most up-to-date building and safety codes: "If you want to fix up an old building, you can't just put in the same things you would for a new building. We need changes which the building codes don't allow for." Although they had condemned the chimneys, installed sprinklers and rewired The Academy, it needed additional, costly modifications. Numerous convents and other buildings across North America have been irreparably lost or disfigured because the owners could not obtain approvals for mitigating measures or negotiate creative solutions that respected the spirit of the building code. In many cases it was easier to raze the structure and build anew.

It is illusory to expect a purely commercial retail venue like a mall to function in an institutional structure. Stores in urban settings need to have a street address with people passing by regularly, an advantage The Academy lacks set back on its lot. Arcades, after which the Hiddens' project was modeled, are dependent on the crowds milling the streets and the concomitant activities that a high degree of urban density attracts.

Former institutions characterized by a series of rooms opening off a central corridor do lend themselves to offices for municipal administration or company headquarters; they are also appropriate for rental apartments, though this requires significant transformations to integrate kitchens and bathrooms for every unit. Such programs as museums and destination venues are also suitable. They need not rely on a steady stream of passersby. In exploring these issues with colleagues and students in successive design studios at the Université Laval School of Architecture, we have found mixed-use programs where the building and its site are occupied twenty-four hours a day, seven days a week, yielded the happiest results; similarly, converting the chapels in multifunctional spaces in which worship could still occur, if the number of parishioners warranted it, had positive results.

Mother Joseph Goes to DC, a Landmark is Designated

In 1978, ten years after the Hiddens had started negotiations to purchase Providence Academy, it was listed on the National Register of Historic Places. Robert Hidden may have sought landmark status to qualify for restoration tax credits. He had pointed out in 1976, "Seattle has a landmark and historical buildings ordinance and an historic district ordinance for Pioneer Square and the Pike Place Market. We need this too."

He found an ally in Ann King who had "worked with the Clark County Historical Society in sponsoring a memorial tribute to Mother Joseph," and she appears to have begun building up a case in 1962 for the "pioneering nun's" nomination to the United States National Statuary Hall, established by Congress in 1864. The dossier presented in 1969 was returned. Resubmitted in 1974 by the Historical Society as a bicentennial project, it was endorsed in October 1975, coinciding with the 150th anniversary of the establishment of Fort Vancouver and the return to The Academy of the cupola bell that Mother Joseph purchased in 1887. King enlisted the army's help to hoist the twenty-eight-inch diameter, three-hundred-pound brass bell cast in Troy, New York. Fittingly, the turn to military men echoed the interdependent relationship the sisters had maintained with the soldiers and officers of the adjoining military reserve. Trucked to The Academy from Providence Heights, Issaquah, and installed on February 28, 1975, the sisters had agreed to lend it to the Hiddens "as long as [The Academy] remains a historical building." Although mass had been planned as part of a special program, it was held in the auditorium because restoration of the chapel had not been completed.

The "Mother Joseph Statue Committee," co-chaired by Ann King and Donna Schmaltz, lobbied hard to have the Catholic sister inducted to the U.S. National Statuary Hall, where statues were displayed "in marble or bronze... of deceased persons who have been citizens [of that State], and illustrious for their historic renown or for distinguished civic or military services, such as each State may deem to be worthy of this national commemoration." The Senate Bill 2431 passed in April 1977 and female Governor Dixy Lee Ray signed the legislation on May 4, 1977, completing the first step of ensuring state support.

Formed in spring 1978, the Mother Joseph Foundation began fundraising "to pay for a... statue and pedestal and the dedication ceremony." Committee members launched a full-scale education campaign to place Mother Joseph in the spotlight. "If we weren't taught by the Sisters of Providence, we missed out on the works of Mother Joseph, who seems, even according to the secular press, to have been one of the most influential pioneer architects, administrators and social workers that the state of Washington has ever seen," one person admitted to *The Progress* reporter Diane Gianelli on November 16, 1979. Vancouver children attending parochial schools nary saw her name mentioned in their Clark County history lessons, inciting "activist... Milton Bona, editor of the Fort Vancouver Historical Society, [to begin lecturing] on the life and works of Mother Joseph to historical societies and other groups." But even Sister Hartung had only the basic outlines of her order's history. It was not until she incorporated a pilgrimage to the heritage site as part of the formation of executives and leaders into Providence that she could fully appreciate the details and the extent of Mother Joseph's accomplishments. Since 2000, she had brought over three thousand leaders through the Academy to experience firsthand the works of Mother Joseph.

Statue of Mother Joseph of the Sacred Heart by Felix de Weldon, 1980. (Providence Archives, Seattle, Washington.)

The ninety-sixth Congress of the United States of America approved and published Senate

Concurrent Resolution No. 48 on April 1, 1980, thereby recognizing Mother Joseph's and the Sisters of Providence's active roles "in building the Pacific Northwest from 1856 when she first arrived at Fort Vancouver" from Montreal, Quebec, Canada. The Foundation then commissioned world-renowned Viennese sculptor Felix de Weldon to represent the fifth woman and first Catholic sister, and the 92nd American to be admitted into its "official gallery of 'first citizens.'" She was to join Marcus Whitman as Washington's second representative in the Capitol, because she had made "monumental contributions to health care, education and social works throughout the Northwest," as the inscription under her statue states.

Oddly enough, a French-Canadian woman who had taken religious vows was treated as a U.S. citizen and as an architect. When she landed at Fort Vancouver, Washington had barely been established as a Territory. Although she was forty-six years a resident of Washington State, except for travels related to her fundraising and architectural work for the Sisters of Providence, Mother Joseph never became a U.S. citizen and never really learned English. According to Kathleen Crosman, an archivist at the National Archives Pacific Alaska Region:

> Citizenship was not automatically conferred on anyone when a territory became a state. Citizenship had to be applied for and involved several steps over a period of five years. While it was not unheard of for women to apply for citizenship, it was very rare because one of the main reasons for becoming a citizen was to be able to vote. Since women didn't acquire the right to vote until the twentieth century [1910 in the state of Washington] most women either did not naturalize or naturalized by derivation through their husbands/fathers.

When sculptor Felix de Weldon, creator of the U.S. Marine War Memorial "Flag Raising on Iwo Jima," was asked "why he created a kneeling statue [in contrast to the more usual upright figures in the Capitol]... [he] answered 'Because Mother Joseph could never have done all she did without prayer.'" Crucifix around her neck, scapular around her shoulders, rosary in hand, she personifies Catholic sisterhood. A female version of "her holy Patron... a very good Architect," De Weldon's portrayal of the French-Canadian pioneer in a submissive posture, clothed in her habit and kneeling face upturned towards the heavens, the hands of a laborer clasped in prayer, greatly contrasts with the way Sister Mary Veronica remembered her: "[She] had her own ideas on how certain things should be done, and if anyone took issue... she could tell any man off when the occasion called for it." Weldon says:

> [He] attempted to portray [Mother Joseph's] brilliance and creativity of mind, as well as her simplicity and charm of manner, her deep faith and the love of the humanity she served. If you look at her face, one side will show her strength, will power and determination. The other side expresses sweetness, love and compassion. The hands are strong working hands, which built brick walls. At her knees are the tools she used to make architectural drawings for the construction of hospitals and schools. Her works of love for the humanity are works of peace.

Canadian-born Esther Pariseau, who took the name Joseph in religion, continues to be a model

Interior of restored chapel, looking towards the choir lofts, August 2013. (Photo, Tania Martin.)

Interior of restored chapel, looking towards the sanctuary, August 2013. (Photo, Tania Martin.)

for Washington's youth. Vancouver sixth-graders lobbied to have April 16 recognized by the State as a non-legal holiday to commemorate this extraordinary humanitarian, pioneer, artist, and administrator. Senate bill 5734 was passed on March 9, 1999. It was a worthy tribute to one who "especially loved children, orphans, boys and girls, rewarded them for their help on the farm or the garden premises, and trained the older boys as bakers, engineers, gave outings to larger groups, and freely praised their work with courteous treatment." Even on her deathbed, Mother Joseph invited orphans to sing and recite the rosary with her, rewarding them with sweets.

Restoration of the Chapel

The work of promoting Mother Joseph and Providence Academy paid dividends in the long term. The return of the historic bell and the two nominations certainly drew attention to the importance of the building. But in order to function as a commercial venue, The Academy needed an anchor, a destination that could generate visibility and activity. Sensing renewed public interest in the heritage site, William Hidden perhaps found the solution when he set about restoring the chapel to function as "an interdenominational sanctuary for weddings, concerts and plays." No overtly religious symbols appeared in the restored chapel's décor. Payne says the building lent itself nicely to such events, as wedding parties typically also rented the auditorium for receptions. It was baptized the Blanchet ballroom in honor of the two early missionary brothers, knighted Bishops, and their nephew, Jean-Baptiste Blanchet, erstwhile architect and aid to Mother Joseph.

The three-storey volume had been stripped; everything in the chapel, renovated by the sisters in 1923, needed to be reconstructed. Bill Hidden and his wife "actually went to Seattle and brought [pieces of the dismantled chapel that been placed into storage] back on a truck," said Payne. Although the sisters had removed most of the furnishings and fixtures, souvenir hunters and vandals stripped the Academy during the years it stood empty so that "even all of the stain glass windows, the railings, everything on the altar, all of it was gone. The building was abandoned for over two years," Payne added. Hidden had asked the public to return items they had bought from the sisters. Before starting on the restoration, he asked the Sisters of Providence for copies of the four-by-five-foot architectural blueprints as well as old photographs and prints in February 1973 so that he could bring it back to its former glory.

Some one hundred years after its original inauguration, the restored chapel opened to the public on Friday, September 17, 1982. The Hiddens had spent a year restoring the three-storey arches fashioned from Portland cedar, the curved paneling of the balconies, doors, and window frames. They had the maple floors sanded and varnished and the altars' carvings and moldings hand-painted in gold-metallic paint to highlight intricate details. These "structural items" and "heirlooms," as the provincial superior reminded Mr. Robert Hidden when she heard rumors that the building was for sale in 1984, were placed in his custody to contribute to the authenticity of the restoration, along with the hand-hewn chapel pews built of fir and beautified with cherry-wood arm rests.

The Academy for Sale

The Hiddens placed The Academy on the real estate market in 1984. "It's been a lot of hard work, like any other commercial project. But we're not going to keep it just because we like it," confided Robert Hidden to *The Oregonian* reporter Don Hamilton. The seventy-four-year-old knew "the property needs to be developed, and the building needs to be improved… All we're doing is looking for a way to do that." The three sons bought out their father, since deceased. Vancouverites have little conception of the financial burden the Hidden family carried to buy and keep The Academy open.

Fast forward to 2009: the Hidden brothers, aged between mid-sixties and mid-seventies, are ready to retire. Building maintenance is more than they can handle; they no longer have the capital to undertake needed major repairs to continue preserving the 140-year old structure, even with ninety-five percent occupation. Their children and grandchildren have no interest in continuing the family business. The Academy is still a money-loser (Hidden had taken out a mortgage to finance the purchase) so they put the property up for sale a second time. Tenants learned of it through the newspapers and started looking for space elsewhere.

At the time of our August 2013 visit, The Academy was still for sale. Elson Strahan, President and Chief Executive Officer of the Fort Vancouver National Trust (FVNT), was in the process of negotiating its acquisition from the current owners, Monte, Bill, and Oliver Hidden. As he explained to Carla and me:

> Hidden Brothers run as a jointly held LLC, so all decisions must be agreeable to all three brothers.

> The Hidden brothers are anxious to get this property sold. Why? Because they have held it for over forty years and it's time to sell but also it creates estate complications if something happens to one of them... as you would guess with family businesses... So, they preserved it for more than forty years, really to their credit. But it's possible, that if we don't make the acquisition, for a developer to acquire it and let the Academy fall into such disrepair, then it is no longer eligible [as a historic landmark]... So then [a developer] can come in with bulldozers and knock the entire thing down and scrape the property clean.

"Which is probably more valuable to them," added Alishia Topper, Director of Development at the Fort Vancouver National Trust in charge of fundraising initiatives, capital campaigns, and community outreach from 2009 to the end of May 2014.

But the Hiddens, too, worried that another purchaser less concerned with historic preservation would let the building deteriorate, leading to its demolition by neglect. They were willing to sell their property for two million dollars less than the 12.5-million-dollar listed price, already reduced from the initial sixteen million dollars asked, acknowledging the seriousness with which the Trust would treat the building and the capacity of the Trust in applying for preservation grants unavailable to conventional businesses.

Enacted by Congress in 1996 as a 501(c)(3) nonprofit organization, the Trust currently manages and interprets over 150,000 square feet of residential, office, and public space on the 366-acre historic site and will add another 32,000 square feet with the renovation of the West Barracks planned for 2015. Its recently revised mission, as explained on its website, is to "achieve national recognition of Fort Vancouver National Site as a premier historic destination. The Trust is a nonprofit organization formed to advance the preservation and education purposes of Fort Vancouver National Site. The Trust supports Fort Vancouver partners in a collective effort to preserve, enhance and operate Fort Vancouver for public benefit through education, resource development, advocacy, community identity, programs and cultural tourism." The Trust is funded by private donations and grants, and the net revenues it generates as acting property manager of the West Barracks and Officers Row, which average 500,000 dollars yearly, are used for capital improvements and development and to leverage government grants and other funding for the continued capital investment in the historic buildings. The non-profit had dreamed of adding the historic convent to their building portfolio. As stated on the *academycampaign.org* website, "acquisition [of The Academy] will strengthen and diversify the revenue streams of the Trust, further ensuring the development of programs and operations of the Fort Vancouver National Site and enhancing the Trust's goal as a self-sustaining nonprofit" as well as "preserve this important piece of Northwest history for all." Unlike the properties it leases and manages at the Fort Vancouver National Historic Site (FVNHS), ultimately owned by the City of Vancouver, The Academy property would belong solely to the Trust.

Both buyers and sellers are motivated to complete the transaction and they have enlisted Sister of Providence Sister Hartung for help. She effectively completes a trio of actors spearheading a new cycle in the historic preservation story of Providence Academy.

Providence Academy, Vancouver, Washington, ca. 1901. (Providence Archives, Seattle, Washington.)

Mother Joseph's Signature Building

Walking along 10th Street from St. James Catholic Church, the former Cathedral located at 12th and Washington Streets, Carla and I approached Providence Academy from the west. We had just enjoyed a thorough tour of the 1884-1885 house of worship and seat of Nisqually diocese until 1907. The 145-by-60-foot structure could accommodate some eight hundred people. Its exterior was clad in red brick made by the local Hidden Brick Company, as were the parish hall and the parish rectory and administration building (formerly the bishop's residence). The original 1854 bell was showcased in a lovely garden in the block's interior.

At first, Carla did not notice the redbrick, three-and-a-half storey edifice obscured from our view by a gaudy, hand-painted sign announcing "First Friday at the Academy: Local Vendors, Featured Art and Refreshments" and a single-storey, Mexican-food diner that occupied the southwest corner of the property. It was only when I pointed out the cupola peeking above the giant, thirty-foot-tall cedar and

Avant-corps of Providence Academy, August 2013. (Photo, Tania Martin.)

locust trees that she excitedly pulled out her camera. Had we taken 12th Street instead and been walking in the 1920s we would have been on the same route the sisters and their orphaned charges, aligned in double rows, would have taken from the Cathedral back to the House of Providence, where a six-foot-tall wooden board fence enclosed the entire property. It was taken down in 1930 and replaced by a hedge of donated shrubbery.

We had arrived early for our meeting with Yvette Payne, former on-site property manager of The Academy, which gave us a chance to explore our surroundings. Walking east, we quickly found ourselves on an overpass bridging Interstate 5. Formerly a country road, then the Old Reserve Highway, the deep channel cut off the Sisters of Providence from the military reserve, today the Fort Vancouver National Historic Site, where they had first established their works near the north bank of the Columbia River. Looking southeast, I was intrigued by another formidable institutional building, the Post Hospital. One wing of the T-plan structure had been displaced to one end to make way for the widening of the highway in the 1950s. Built in 1904, the brick edifice was considered one of the most modern and efficient military hospitals of the nation until the end of the Great War (1914-1918).

Turning west, back towards downtown Vancouver, we noticed a resolutely modern library standing across the street from The Academy, its reddish metal siding a nod to the redbrick historic building. The designers of the flat-roofed, glass-and-steel cubic forms opted for contrast rather than imitation of the "French colonial flavor," characterized by "narrow, floor-to-ceiling windows that open onto three stories of columned, balustrade galleries," the Georgian-styled "pedimented central pavilion… giant pilaster order," and the "symmetry and axiality of [Providence House's] original plan," as Providence Academy is described in the National Register of Historic Places Nomination Form.

After taking a few pictures of The Academy's façade, Carla and I trekked through the sea of

Photo looking across Interstate 5 towards The Academy from the interior of the Post Hospital, Fort Vancouver National Historic Site. (Photo, Tania Martin.)

parking around to the west side and back of the former convent. The three-storey structure, plus attic, rested on three-foot-thick rough-basalt stone, laid in broken courses, and brick foundation walls of the substantial basement (although the floor of the basement was only two feet under soil grade). We could see where balconies on the west end of the west wing addition of 1891 had been removed and, at rear, the joint between the original building and later construction. A couple of service wings, housing restrooms, had been added to the building, as well as a single-storey kitchen extension off the north wing. We guessed the chapel lay behind second-storey lancet windows of the north wing,

Photo looking towards the Post Hospital, Fort Vancouver National Historic Site, and the Columbia River from the cupola of The Academy. (Photo, Tania Martin.)

as they differed from the segmental-arch openings of all the other doors and windows in the building. That was when a tall, blond woman, who was striding in our direction, hailed us. Payne had seen us and come to fetch us. Our official tour was to begin... in the attic.

Payne led us in through the back to a service elevator, the only elevator in the building. It was as if we had stepped back in time. She opened the wood and glass door, slid the metal grille aside to let us enter the tiny cubicle and then closed the grille again before pressing the button that would activate the hoisting mechanism. It made me think of the scene in *The King's Speech* when Queen Elizabeth goes to scope out the offices of London speech therapist Lionel Logue and has to figure out how to get into and then operate the elevator.

Graffiti in the Cupola... (Photo, Tania Martin.)

Once we got out at the third-floor landing, we continued up a stairway to the fourth floor, under the gently pitched gable roof. There we could appreciate the hefty twelve-inch-wide, eight-inch-deep chevrons supporting the two-inch-deep circular-sawn roof boards, and the four-inch-wide attic floorboards. Usable living space had been enclosed with painted plaster and lath walls and ceilings. Beautiful wood panel doors, standard for the time, surrounded by simple wood moldings, gave access to the sisters' quarters, one of the girls' dormitories, and built-in, numbered storage lockers. Some of these were finished in cedar, probably to protect clothing from moths. When originally built, the attic had been wide open except for closets outfitted between the dormers and tiny rooms in the shallow projecting *avant-corps*.

I climbed out of one of the numerous dormer windows which lighted these spaces onto a platform that led to the outside of the elevator shaft, much to Carla's consternation. From this vantage point, I could see that the red-painted, standing seam metal roof had been patched in places and covered over in others. The paint was peeling in many areas. Red asphalt rolls had been screwed to the old roofs of the main building; new, red-asphalt shingles finished the north service wing. The original roofing material might have been cedar shingles, however, metal roofs were quite com-

Bird's-eye view of the laundry building, powerhouse, and the sea of parking. St. Joseph's Hospital once stood in the place of the Comfort Inn. (Photo, Tania Martin.)

mon for similar monumental buildings in French Canada. The shiny zinc would reflect the sunlight; the building would be seen from afar.

At the crossing of the two original wings of the 1873 structure, we climbed up the narrow stair into the octagonal bell tower. From its four-over-four windows we had a panoramic view of the city, the Columbia River, the military reserve and the interstate highway I-5. Towards the north, we looked down on the L-shaped laundry-boiler building comprised of a two-storey structure connected to a tall, single-storey structure joined by a passage, the prominent chimney, a huge parking lot, and the Comfort Inn beyond, where the five-storey, brick St. Joseph's hospital once stood. On the inside of the cupola's frame structure we could read graffiti left by tourists and Vancouver residents. As one tag read, "Mother Joseph was here before any of you!"

An unsupported, winding, wooden, central staircase under the bell tower connects the first through fourth floors. This elegant space is lit with large, arched windows framed by Doric columns

Central staircase. (Photo, Tania Martin.)

that support an entablature decorated with dentils, rectangular blocks resembling teeth, and a polygonal dome, which is in turn surmounted by a lantern having many of the same features and is topped by a cross. Visitors would ascend to the second floor chapel by climbing this formal vertical circulation route, which was punctuated with sculpture niches. Before descending to the third floor by way of the northeast stairwell, we had a peek of the curved topside of the chapel ceiling, suspended by two-inch-diameter rods from the massive roof structure. Similar to the other stairs in the building with their more than five-foot-wide, thick-board steps, the sturdy handrail started at a turned wooden post at the ground floor and wound upwards through the four storeys. The honey-colored wood wainscoting, grained to mimic nobler essences, contrasted with the light-colored, painted plaster walls.

The second and third storeys were similarly organized: a series of rooms off of a double-loaded, eleven-foot-high, central corridor was lit at both ends by generous windows. Impost windows over the doors let additional light into the corridor, especially important before the installation of the electric ceiling lamps that marched down the center of the hallway. We could tell when we were passing from the 1873 construction to the 1891 wing from the two-and-a-half-foot-thick opening, created by the construction of two independent, loadbearing, brick walls. This was further signaled on the third floor by a slight change in floor height. Carpeting covered the original wood floors.

The Sisters of Providence Archives have a set of plans presumably dating to when steam heating was introduced, as they show the piping of the 1873 convent's basement, first, and second floors. Many of the rooms are labeled, giving us an indication of the layout of the building when Mother Joseph lived there. Each of the three wings of Providence House accommodated different populations. The central part of the building was reserved for the sisters; one wing for the day pupils and boarders; another for the orphan girls; and, in the tail of the T, the orphan boys. The community room was located west of the central stairs on the second floor. Across the hall, next to the chapel, was the infirmary where Mother Joseph spent her last days. She had asked that an opening be made in the wall so that she, and any other convalescent sister, could hear the mass from their bed. In the days before speakers and television screens transmitted devotional services live into infirmary rooms, this was a common arrangement. The opening was probably walled over at some point. The patients and their nurses could go outside onto the gallery directly from the infirmary, or to the adjoining bathroom or office. Also on the second floor were two recreation rooms across the hall from each other in the west end of the building. On the north half of the east end were the orphan boys and tucked in a room behind the staircase was a class for small infants. A mirror image, the south half of the east end was given over to orphan girls.

At each storey, Payne led Carla and me into the chapel. From the fourth floor (attic) we entered through a simple, wood-paneled, double door featuring a lancet motif repeated in all of the doors and windows of the sacred space, and stepped onto a small balcony from where we had a bird's-eye view of the ornate, restored interior. The third and second-floor doorways were lancet-shaped, the transom window subdivided into three lobes. Like tour groups before us, Carla and I rang the bell before entering under the roof-loft. Looking towards the apse, the five altars had been reconstructed, although none of the statuary adorned the niches. As was the tradition prior to the Second Vatican Council, a low, forged-iron railing and two steps separated the sanctuary from the nave.

The chapel remained an empty shell until Mother Joseph, thanks to a few donations, could have a first coat of plaster applied to the sanctuary, and the three altars and the niches above them covered with tapestry. In her letters respectively dated April 12 and August 2, 1875, she twice indicated to Mgr. Bourget that it resembled the motherhouse chapel in Montreal. Although the two-and-a-half-storey chapel had been dedicated on March 18, 1875, it was not until 1883 that it assumed "its intended Gothic aspect," conforming to a widespread architectural trend in Canada and the U.S., particularly for religious architecture in the second half of the nineteenth century. Lancet windows lit the interior; the slender, bunched columnettes and window tracery highlighting the chapel's underlying structure; the wainscoting complementing the red-oak floor. Pointed arches, trilobate (three-lobed) motifs, and quatrefoils (four-leafs) were repeated in the balcony balustrade, doors, altars, and their corresponding retables (frames enclosing painted or decorated panels raised above the back of an altar). Vaults sprung from column capitals and brackets in the shape of acanthus scrolls.

Design of the chapel is readily credited to Mother Joseph. Yet in early 1882, *The Vancouver Independent* reported the finishing touches were "under the skillful care of Mr. [Donald] McKay, the architect who planned the so-loudly-praised church of Rev. Father Duffy in Walla Walla." Mother Joseph was to let the bids for plastering, painting, and other work soon after the article appeared. She had previously collaborated with the architect on the design of St. James Cathedral, erected in 1884, which would explain the strong resemblances between the two houses of worship.

A 1948 black-and-white photograph of the interior of the Providence Academy chapel. Photographer, Wescott Studio, Vancouver, Washington. (Providence Archives, Seattle, Washington.)

Father Louis Schram, pastor and vicar general of the diocese, and J. B. Blanchet, Mother Joseph's right-hand man, also had a hand in overseeing the Cathedral's construction.

Mother Joseph is said to have carved the five wooden altars, some of the statues that adorned the apse and flanking niches, as well as pews, such as the dark ones up front in the choir loft that Payne pointed out to us in August 2013. She also would have carved much of the Gothic ornament, as indicated in the 1978 National Register of Historic Places, Inventory Nomination Form. It is said she sculpted the pieces in her basement workshop. This has some basis in the Sisters of Providence chronicles' description of the elegant, simple, and beautiful sacred space: "The workmanship of the altar is delicate; all of the moldings and the columns are the work of Mother Joseph and of her companion, Sister Alexandre." A life-sized statue made by Mother Joseph graced the altar to St. Vincent de Paul on the right and that of St. Joseph on the left. Two other altars furnished the chapel, one to St. Anne in a gallery and the other to the Sacred Heart.

A number of paintings hung on the walls. Those of the Sisters of Providence's holy patron saints, Elizabeth and Geneviève, on either side of the choir, and the Sacred Heart, in its oval frame, above the main altar. Mother Joseph had made the picture frame of the *Garde d'honneur.* "Everywhere we look," all of the statues and paintings spoke "to the heart and tell us to become better persons," concluded the sister chronicler.

Nonetheless, it is unclear from readings of archival sources (almost all in French through to the 1910s, and some contradictory) how much Mother Joseph carved. She appeared to have acquired ready-made statuary, sacred linens, and other objects on her trips east in Montreal and New York, and may have been integrating them into her vision for the chapel. She had also started fabricating plaster statues in 1865, having received lessons from Mr. Dauphin, a Montreal sculptor and statue maker. Earlier in that year, she had brought back molds for statues and crucifixes from Montreal, the New York of Canada in the nineteenth century, for the various chapels and houses of the Sisters of Providence, in addition to the first statue of Our Lady of Seven Sorrows that she had made with Sister Martin, her blood sister, using one at the motherhouse as a model. A letter to Superior

General Mother Amable, dated March 6, 1882, however, makes mention of the purchase of such a statue. It was placed above the main altar in 1883.

Mother Joseph promised in founding the Vancouver mission to erect and dedicate an altar to the Sacred Heart "following the plan that had emerged in her spirit and that she had not yet executed until twenty-seven years later... She still had to complete the ornamentation of her altar, to install nine choirs of angels, nine little angel heads that would make an aureole around the golden heart that is in the vault above the altar to the Sacred Heart." The devotion of the Sacred Heart of Jesus was part of the obedience given to the missionaries who left in 1856, one Mother Joseph strived to practice throughout her life. She "was [finally] able to complete the totality of her altar" in 1890, related the chronicles. Again, it is unclear whether the angel heads were carved out of wood or made of plaster or had been bought. Nonetheless, Mother Joseph's statues were greatly admired and were considered the most beautiful throughout the dioceses of Oregon and Nisqually. As we exited the chapel, I pointed out to Carla the ghost marks of the confessionals on the back wall of the narthex under the balconies where they had stood on either side of the main door.

Auditorium, from the stage, August 2013. We see the double-loaded corridor in the background. (Photo, Tania Martin)

Continuing our tour, Payne led us through the central east-west corridor of the 1873 building to a vast shoebox auditorium in the west addition. Two double truss beams spanned the twenty-three-foot length of the music room. They transferred structural loads from the upper storeys through the columns, spaced ten feet two inches apart, which marched down an eight-foot-wide center aisle to the exterior end wall where the stage was built, and down to the load-bearing walls in the basement. We then retraced our steps towards the main first-floor entrance and turned left into another double-loaded corridor that led northwards, under the chapel. A restaurant used to operate there, Payne informed us, which explained the secondary entrance. It occupied the former kitchen, which had been expanded over the years. As related in the chronicles in 1888, "a new [eighteen-by-forty-four-foot] brick kitchen... offers all of the conveniences and solves many problems in the layout [of the old one]." Three years later, it was widened by seven-and-a-half feet, making space for a range and small storage room, and lengthened by eighteen feet across the full width of the newly-enlarged wing for a pantry, a back stair, passage, and storeroom.

We exited the first floor at this point in the tour in order to explore the second through fourth storeys of the north-south wing, inaccessible except

View of the 1873 east wing and chapel exterior from the yard. (Photo, Tania Martin.)

through the sacristy of the chapel. We re-entered The Academy by the north entrance. Contrary to many of the spaces in the east-west wing, those in this portion of the building remained undivided. Otherwise, the painted plaster ceilings and walls, the wooden floors, the generous stairs had become familiar.

To get to the basement, we used a service entrance on the east end of the convent located just south of the east portico. We descended narrow stairs set into a steep ramp, which facilitated deliveries. Again, we traversed a central corridor, the painted thick brick walls pierced by oculi near the low, seven-foot ceilings for ventilation of the kitchens, storage rooms, and workshops. At key areas, massive twelve-inch square columns supported deep beams overhead. A couple of service stairs led up to the first storey. Only in the north wing were spaces on either side of the corridor rented out.

It was in the basement that Carla and I could appreciate the thickness of the foundation walls: minimum one-foot-five-inch brick masonry, rest-ing on stepped stone foundations, as illustrated in plans dated 1891. When first built in 1873, wood stoves heated Providence House and there were not enough of them to keep everyone warm. Steam heating was later installed. Brick walls separated basement rooms, probably to prevent the spread of fire from one room to the next rather than as load-bearing structures.

After having thoroughly toured The Academy, we continued with a visit of the property and secondary buildings, all of which were in various states of disrepair. Looking through a laundry-room door that Payne succeeded in pushing open, we saw a rusting, rolling ironing press amidst junk and debris from fallen plaster and peeling paint. Clearly the building had not been heated for some time. It was unsafe to venture inside, let alone go upstairs. Approximately one hundred feet from the convent, the two-storey, redbrick structure built around 1875 once contained "all the newest labor-saving machinery" powered by a steam engine. The laundry's rounded arch openings resembled those of the convent, enhancing the reading of the site as a single complex.

The powerhouse was in worse shape, the roof having caved in and the smashed window boarded up. Weeds and ivy were growing around the massive iron furnace installed for the House of Providence in 1910 by Swanby & Scheider Heating Contractors, as imprinted across the top of the hulking machine. Yet both of these redbrick structures had once been carefully detailed. The powerhouse sported a corbelled crenelated cornice; several rows of brick projected outwards from the face of the wall to create a series of indentations. The space between this decorative feature and the arched window openings below it had been stuccoed. Within the upper portion of the arch, the bricks were laid in a herringbone pattern framed with a handsome brick reveal.

The polygonal smokestack was set on a square base, the junction and the corbelled mouth at the top adding visual interest to an otherwise utilitarian structure. Down the south face of the stack, white letters spell out A C A D E M Y to inform the passerby about the property. Walking towards Evergreen Boulevard from the powerhouse, we looked at the outside of a single-storey, pitched-roof building known as the gymnasium. Rather than the redbrick used at all other existing buildings on site, it was built using red-clay blocks. Pilasters expressing the structural bays were the only notable detail of this freestanding building.

The redbrick powerhouse. Note architectural details such as the corbelled crenelated cornice, the herringbone brick pattern, and the rounded arches echoing those of the laundry building and Providence Academy. (Photo, Tania Martin.)

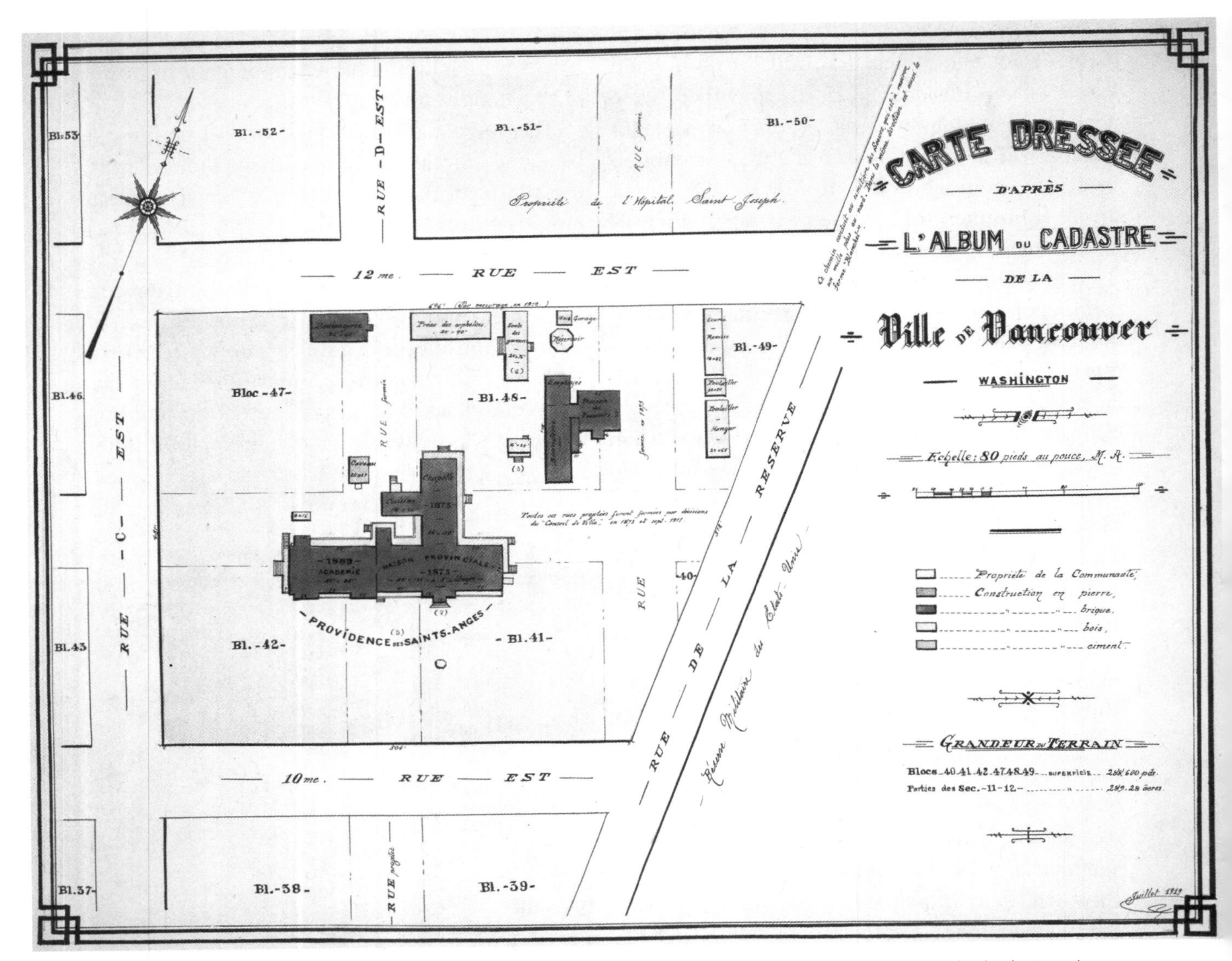

Cadastral map of Providence Academy, Vancouver, Washington, July 1919, drawn by Sister Anatolie (Mary Elizabeth Eugenie Desroches, 1861-1940) of Montreal, showing the buildings that comprised the complex. The Abstract of Title gives the property boundaries as "Beginning at a point on the North line of Tenth Street, Eighty (80) feet East of the Southeast corner of Block 43 in that part of the City of Vancouver, Washington, lying East of Main Street; running thence North 480 feet to the South line of Twelfth Street; thence East along the South line of 12th Street, 672 feet and 10 inches, to the West line of Reserve Street; thence Southwesterly along the West line of Reserve Street to the North line of 10th Street, 479 feet 3 inches to the place of beginning." (Providence Archives, Seattle, Washington.)

The sea of asphalt makes the property look relatively empty, but as a 1919 cadastral map drawn by a sister shows, a host of secondary buildings populated the grounds. A thirty-six-by-sixty-foot bakery had been built just south of 12th Street around 1910. It likely produced bread for the patients housed in St. Joseph's hospital, built in 1909 across the street, as well as for the resident population of the House of Providence. A covered playground had been erected near the thirty-four-by-ninety-foot boys' school, a wooden building the sisters had undoubtedly recuperated from St. James Mission, as probably was a sixteen-by-thirty-four-foot house. The structures were demolished in 1930 and 1959. Additional structures included a thirteen-by-twelve-foot garage, an eighteen-by-thirty-two-foot stable and shed, a twenty-four-by-sixty-five-foot henhouse and shed, a twenty-by-twenty-foot henhouse, and a twenty-by-twenty-seven-foot stone root cellar, built in 1873, to store surplus vegetables. The grounds were planted with an orchard, which would eventually be turned into a baseball field for the boys, and a kitchen garden. It was a productive landscape, an ancestor to twenty-first-century urban agriculture.

We ended our tour in the front of Providence Academy, where a garden and driveway take the shape of a heart, an indentation at the center of the circular drop-off, reminding visitors of "the sanctity of the purpose of [Mother Joseph of the Sacred Heart's] work." We cannot say for certain whether this is exactly how Mother Joseph had landscaped the grounds, although it does respect the underlying motif of her 1875 plans. To execute them, she had mustered a contingent of Catholic soldiers from the adjacent military reserve to prepare the soil. Her design included three concentric parterres, probably radiating out from the building. The one in the center was dedicated to the Sacred Heart and was planted with lilies and red flowers. The second parterre, dedicated to the Virgin Mary, surrounded the first. There she had planted a variety of flowers with which to decorate the altars. Finally, the third, dedicated to St. Joseph, she devoted to fruit trees, whose roots would be protected by green grass. Vines climbed each side of the fence and additional fruit trees were planted here and there. A number of the locust, cedar, and holly trees as well as flowering bushes, shrubs, and vines survived in 1978, noted the author of the *National Register of Historic Places Inventory Nomination Form*. Our ending point is the starting point of Sister Susanne Hartung's tours of the cradle of the Sisters of Providence in the Pacific Northwest.

Holy Trinity of Development

Monte Hidden introduced Elson Strahan to Sister Susanne Hartung after one of her tours in 2009. At the time she had started organizing tours of the former convent and the sites of the first ministries as part of the three-year formation program she developed to introduce and cultivate Sisters of Providence values to new managers, directors, and executives of the Providence Health and Services, all of whom are laypeople, the Academy offered no public tours. Hartung determinedly obtained the number of the Hidden brickyard and asked whether she could tour the building with her executive team. Since then, Monte accompanies Sister Hartung; she brings groups of thirty to forty people to visit the site about ten times a year. The tour has since expanded to include a visit of the fort, where Mother Joseph first opened the orphanage, and to St. James' cemetery, where she has eulogies of the sisters read. Since 2010, she also takes groups to visit Mother Joseph's birthplace, located north of Montreal, when they go to the Sisters of Providence's Mother House in Canada.

Sister Hartung and her team want those who will replace the Sisters of Providence:

> [T]o know they are continuing the legacy of Mother Joseph, that's the important thing. So when I get to the Academy, and they see the pictures of the orphans and Mother Joseph building... the schools and orphanages, the health institutions, they get it. It is so powerful to see the location and that building and to know that house started this ministry... And by the way, I am a teacher, that's my background, I taught for twenty-five years.

As with most Catholic religious communities in the Western World, the Sisters of Providence have declined in numbers. In 2013, of the five thousand Sisters of Providence there once were, they were only five hundred worldwide, including two hundred in the infirmary. There are 138 Sisters of Providence in the Northwest. Of these, only ten are under the age of fifty. Their ministry will only continue through like-minded lay people, those "who have some spiritual sense that drives you to the greater good," regardless of their personal faith, and who can subscribe to Mother Joseph's parting words: "Whatever concerns the poor is always our affair."

Sister Hartung quickly sensed the Trust was a promising buyer, especially after Strahan showed her the restoration and renovation of the grand houses on Officer's Row and the historic fort. It was plain to her if an organization like the Trust did not step up to the challenge, Vancouver risked losing Providence Academy. She addressed the Board in the hopes of convincing them to purchase The Academy site by telling them the story of Mother Joseph and the convent using the same pictures she uses on her tours. Soon after that autumn 2011 presentation, the Trust began negotiations with the Hidden Brothers.

After it signed an agreement with the Hidden family, the Trust announced their plans to purchase the Vancouver landmark for 10.6-million dollars at a press conference held on May 1, 2012, in the chapel. Some sixty to seventy people, including significant civic leaders, attended. The same day it launched a sixteen-million-dollar capital campaign towards the acquisition and initial restoration work. Ed Lynch, co-chair of the twenty-four-member Trust board, personally pledged two million dollars.

"The Hiddens, understandably, wanted to have a short time frame to make sure that we were serious about moving the campaign forward," explained Strahan, so the Trust decided to bypass the three to four-year silent campaign phase of advance fundraising to compress the process into twelve to eighteen months. "This is something we have never done before,' Elson said to Sister Hartung, 'we usually do capital campaigns over years but we're going to do this and we're going to get it done, and I had never done it before, but we were going to get it done. Will you help us?' [Hartung] said, 'Of course I'll help you.'" She agreed to sit on the steering committee in December 2011 and has since been involved in the financing campaign. The Hiddens agreed to "carry the note out for eight years," leaving the Trust to annually pay seven hundred thousand dollars "to retire the balance of the debt." The Trust succeeded in creating a "partnership" with the previous and current owners of Providence Academy.

The Trust was simultaneously applying for grants to cover the costs of capital improvements, particularly for repair and rehabilitation work, and working to take advantage of historic preservation tax credits. The Trust would have qualified for new market tax credits had the property been located in a low-income census tract. With this two-pronged approach, Strahan and Topper hoped to amass the five-million-dollar down payment by December 2013, but anticipated, at time of interview, a six-month extension, as the Hiddens were satisfied with the progress they were making. Strahan confirmed in October 2014 the purchase and sale agreement is to be executed in January 2015, and the closing of the contract within ninety days afterwards. He added, "The charitable interest in the campaign is really linked to the acquisition of the Academy itself for approximately half of the $10.6 million total, with the remaining half to be funded through development agreements of the excess property."

Hartung helps the Trust educate the population and potential donors, much as Ann King had done in the 1970s, to create a visceral connection with the site. Once the campaign was launched, "I started going down [to Fort Vancouver] and having dinners with all the wealthy people at the Grant House. I probably had ten different dinners with three or four different couples," recalled Hartung. She would tell them "about what an iconic building this [was], what a treasure for the community, and of course this was a treasure for this city to embrace... And I would say, 'It would really be good if you could just write a check—for a million dollars or half a million or whatever.'" She started asking one to two-hundred-dollar donations from those touring Providence Academy.

In August 2013, Alishia Topper estimated that they had secured 4.1 million dollars in pledges and 2.5 million dollars in pending proposals, and a challenge grant of 650,000 dollars from the Vancouver-based M. J. Murdock Charitable Trust. Because of the deadlines involved, a one million dollar grant announced in the Senate's April 2013 capital budget plan and received from the State of Washington was put towards converting the Fort Vancouver Historical Site's Infantry Barracks into apartments, Strahan informed us in October 2014, adding "will be seeking an additional capital appropriation of $1 million in the next legislative session for the Academy renovation."

The Trust also needed to approach smaller donors. In March 2013, Columbia Credit Union kicked off the Trust's two-month P2 (purchase/preserve) drive with a matching gift of one hundred thousand dollars. The goal of this campaign was to recruit fifty community leaders, especially in the business community, to convince forty of their peers to donate one hundred dollars or more, and thus involve two thousand community members. The Ken and Dean Kirn Matching Gift Challenge promised to match all pledges and gifts that would be made between August and December 2013. The announcements of these fundraising campaigns made for good press in the local newspaper, as did endorsements from the City of Vancouver and the Archbishop of Seattle, Peter Sartain.

Providence Health System, towards the end of 2012, asked its sixty-five thousand employees to help raise money for the restoration and for the privilege of naming the bell tower "The Providence Bell." As Hartung explained to journalists in January 2013, "The bell is very significant in the life of religious women. It's a call to prayer; it's a call to solemnity. It's the sacred tone of the community." By August 2013, "We probably had about six hundred people contribute and the corporation is going to match that contribution. We're probably in for… $400,000 at this point, but not enough. In the definitive agreement, when it is purchased, the Sisters of Providence will always have access to the building. But it has been a hard pull. Alishia has been great. We are hoping we can contribute $1,000,000." Typical of such campaigns, donor names are to be displayed in the Academy on a donor recognition wall.

The Trust adopted this strategy in offering naming rights to the chapel, the ballroom, and other areas in the Academy. Four of seven corridors were reserved by the end of February 2014, each netting one hundred thousand dollars. Every donor who gave one thousand dollars would have his or her name inscribed on an art installation specially created for the building.

In contrast, we will never know the names of those who gave monies towards the Sisters of Providence's works, although some of the major benefactors were listed in their records. As recounted to us by Topper:

> Hartung… tells a story that Mother Joseph would go on horseback begging tours, and she would go to the mines [and lumber camps], even as far as Montana. She always made sure she arrived on payday and she always brought the prettiest sister along with her. So she was telling the story to a group of foundation directors and one said, 'That is manipulative' and a fundraiser said, 'That's not manipulative. That's very strategic.'

One such tour, retold in the chronicles, brought Mother Joseph, accompanied by Reverend M. St. Onge, into the Idaho territories and Montana mines. From St. Ignace, Idaho, they traveled by horse to Missoula, sleeping out-of-doors eighteen nights. On their journey, they had encountered wolves, a wildfire, rain, native warriors, and a grey bear: the stuff of an exciting adventure, to be sure, and of hard-earned cash. They netted three thousand dollars thanks to the introductions priests had given them to the families of Idaho City and other settlements, where they could hope to receive support from "Protestants and infidels" as well as Catholics.

The sisters also put on charity bazars as well as music and drama benefits. They sold "*billets de messe*" (literally, tickets to mass) in the form of cards, which on one side was printed an image of the Sacred Heart of Jesus and on the other a prayer to the Sacred Heart. These were sold especially in areas where outright begging was forbidden. Depending on the price paid, the sisters would include the purchaser in their monthly intentions (prayers) for five, ten, or twenty-five years, or in perpetuity. Buying a "Providence ticket" for ten dollars a year guaranteed full hospital coverage. Some say this was a pioneering form of medical insurance. The Mother General made a subscription drive among the missions to raise twenty-seven thousand dollars towards construction of the 1891 wing of Providence Academy. Mother Joseph amassed two thousand dollars in less than two months by asking people to "purchase" a window or door of the 1873 construction. Their names were inscribed on a list, not on a piece of the building.

At last count on October 15, 2014, the http://www.academycampaign.org/ website stated that the Trust had raised just over four and a half million dollars of the 10.6-dollar purchase and just over 310,000 dollars of the 5.4 million dollars needed for capital improvements, thanks to more than eight hundred donors.

A Bridge Across Time, and Interstate 5

Professionals and public alike cited Providence Academy as an important landmark in the City of Vancouver. Among readers' top choices in August 2007 were Officers Row (mid-1800s); St. James Catholic Church; The Academy; Hidden House (1885) at 100 W 13th St.; Fort Vancouver (reproduction built in 1966); and Clark County Historical Museum and former Carnegie Library building.

> To MulvannyG2 Architecture associate Kalina Kunert, The Academy represents both the bright and dark aspects of Clark County's architecture… [The building] is her favorite… structure not only because it possesses landmark status, but also because it was designed by the first female architect in Washington. Yet The Academy troubles Kunert as well. 'It's in terrible shape… I think it's very sad that it doesn't have a suitable purpose right now… There was a proposal to put City Hall in there, and I think that would be amazing, to have the city seat be this architecturally significant landmark building.'

Another architect ranked the Academy high "because the Catholic nun 'was really the first architect in the sense that we think of architects to design a major building in the county—it was a tremendously major endeavor at the time it was built.'"

Further, "The Trust's interest in purchasing the Academy has to do with the historic ties to [the Fort Vancouver] site, the fact that Mother Joseph had her first orphanage here," says Alishia Topper. Once the Trust succeeds in acquiring the property, it hopes to re-establish, conceptually and physically, the relationship between the U.S. military reserve, the old Hudson's Bay fort, St. James Mission, and Providence Academy. All of the sites will be managed and interpreted, in part, by the same umbrella organization.

The neighborhood has been slated for revitalization, but only the new Vancouver Community Library across the street from The Academy was built. A downturn in the economy, Strahan informed us, put the construction of condominiums, projected in the 2008 plan, on hold. "The local economic development council for the past two years [has been working] with a significantly updated recruitment plan [to] bring in new employers and hundreds of jobs to the community by attracting businesses involved in the 'creative economy' to add to current industries in the community… Nautilus is here and SEH [a wafer manufacturing company] and certain high tech jobs," he explained. "Heavy industry like lumber and aluminum processing had been the mainstays of Vancouver's economy," says Strahan. He further pointed out:

> Boise Cascade employed a portion of the 2500 employed in the wood products industry in 1979…

> Alcoa, the smelter, an aluminum plant, [was the] second largest employer with 1,200 employees... Del Monte, Frito-Lay employed 2300. Then the high tech companies started coming in, Hewlett Packard built a plant here [they sold their property to SEH], Techtronics, built a big plant here [but is now gone].

Many of these old heavy industries were located along the Vancouver riverfront, blocking access to the waterfront. However, "Now... waterfront development [is] literally cutting holes into the [railway] berm and creating a flow of people between the waterfront and the uptown." The reuse of old heavy industry sites, such as the Alcoa Aluminum plant, will change the waterfront. "They're going to build an entire...project with housing, retail, new roads, sewage and an interconnected rail system with Main Street."

Redevelopment of The Academy property has been discussed as part of the Columbia River Crossing Project to build a wide, pedestrian, park-like connector bridging the I-5 next to the existing overpass, between the rear of the old Post Hospital to the new library. Construction of this bridge would re-establish a strong link between downtown and The Academy with the military reserve, where there are up to seventy-three thousand square feet of space yet to be renovated and leased. The library and The Academy, located on the west side of the bridge crossing the interstate, would reinforce the primary entrance to the Fort Vancouver National Site. But before going to press, Strahan informed us the Columbia River Crossing project was not moving forward due to lack of funding.

For the Columbia River Economic Development Council, "the focus for now is on the creative economy and in fact [the Fort Vancouver] site is one that they are really trying to bring people to because they like the historic buildings more, they like the open architecture. They don't mind exposed brick and ductwork and all of that." So FVNT's proposal is to convert the Post Hospital (built in 1905 and superseded by Barnes General Hospital in the 1940s) into an arts and education building tied into an overall development plan for that part of the city that wishes to attract businesses like "Google [which] has put a huge installation up the river... [or] Amazon [which] has located a big operation in Seattle." Despite a weak economy, Strahan estimates that demand remains high for niche-market space, unique locations in which to live and work, and boutique hotels.

The Trust points to Colonial Williamsburg's Merchants Square as a model, one where historic preservation is used as a magnet and where amenities are provided by private commercial development around the landmark. In Strahan's analysis, mixed-use office space, retail space, restaurants, and residential development should complement tourism while meeting the different needs of local residents. Strahan has strived for such a synergy for the Fort Vancouver National Historic Site and that he hopes to generate at the Providence Academy site.

The Trust has the General O. O. Howard House as their administration building. Along Officers Row, the Grant House restaurant serves up fine fare and the George C. Marshall House is a popular wedding venue. Families and non-profit organizations have taken up residence in a number of other historic dwellings. The 1919 Red Cross Building is now used as a reception hall, with upstairs offices and basement classroom space. It was the first restoration project of the sixteen historic buildings in the West Barracks section. The Artillery Barracks have been partially renovated to offer ground-floor reception and conference space, and it is projected the former Infantry Barracks will be redeveloped as studio and one-bedroom apartments.

Though it has high community value, Strahan believes that The Academy site is underutilized. Acquisition of the property would give the Trust opportunities to supplement amenities that it cannot offer the local community or tourists within its precinct. He would like to see additional restaurants, or a bookstore and shops that would appeal to future residents of the sector. He imagines a trolley dropping people off or picking them up, shuttling to and fro between the two sites. At The Academy, they could get an overview of the site and stop in the gift shop before continuing to the Fort Vancouver National Historic Site. Although the Fort has periodic demonstrations and costumed interpreters, Strahan believes this needs to be enhanced. He feels there is equilibrium to achieve in serving the local community and tourism.

The Trust worked with architect Bing Sheldon, a former co-chair of the Trust's Board. He was one of the founders of Portland-based firm SERA Architects, specialized in urban revitalization, adaptive reuse, and sustainable design. Among other projects, his firm oversaw the historic preservation of the federal courthouse in downtown Portland, the very same building that had inspired Mother Joseph. Strahan asked Sheldon to help the Trust with a "visioning process" for the development of the property, which included meetings with various stakeholders. However, even before doing so, Sheldon and the Trust awarded Venerable Properties, a private Portland, Oregon, real estate redevelopment consultant, a contract in June 2012 to assess the actual physical state of The Academy and the grounds and to submit a *pro forma* budget weighing costs and benefits of alternative development scenarios. The resulting due diligence report evaluated the property in terms of environment studies, electrical systems, plumbing systems, seismic work, and all of the architecture engineering studies to Level 1 and Level 2 criteria. It also estimated probable expenses and identified possible revenue streams.

President of Venerable Properties Art DeMuro, now deceased, believed The Academy is one of the most important restoration projects in the Portland-Vancouver area. As a commercial property, it could break even or make a modest profit, but not as a museum. His team determined the building was generally in good shape, structurally; even if it was built with non-reinforced brick he found no seismic issues. They identified several maintenance problems. The former convent needed repairs—the roof particularly required new covering—and the Trust would have to complete fire and life safety upgrades, and modify entry and egress to conform to universal accessibility standards. The Mexican restaurant is considered recent enough that it can be demolished without compromising the integrity of the site. The 1940s gymnasium, however, does qualify as historical fabric. Constructed out of unreinforced clay block, it does not, however, meet current seismic safety codes.

DeMuro's team concluded that the sea of parking that currently surrounds the Academy, although generating one hundred thousand dollars in revenue annually, is in fact out of compliance with city ordinance. Besides, from an urban design perspective, it contributes little to "life on the street."

It is one of the reasons the Trust's program seeks to intensify development of the site in partnership with the private sector. For example, since June 2014, Clark College Center for Restaurant and Fermentation Sciences is exploring acquiring the laundry and boiler buildings to house a student-run restaurant and brewery-distillery as part of a new training program, reports David Suffia of the *Vancouver Business Journal*. Venerable Properties also reminded the Trust that because the entirety of the property is listed as a National Historic Site, plans must respect Secretary of the Interior's Standards for Historic Preservation, which suggest the types of materials to be used in restoration and in new construction, for example. The Trust proposes, then, to harmonize new construction with old by using red bricks, hence reinforcing Vancouver's identity as a city of bricks. At the time I reacted to their approach with the question, "Can't you do something with background buildings?... Why not go for something contemporary, maybe still have them working in brick [if absolutely necessary but avoid mimicry], maybe get a conversation going... Let them be audacious enough, keeping the height restrictions and the view corridors and everything, have a natural interface, there seems to be a lot of green space and so forth," thus letting the crown jewel, Providence Academy, shine.

While there will inevitably be new construction, the Trust is committed to preserving the House of Providence. The artistic renditions Strahan and Topper showed us call for uses such as mixed-use commercial, retail, and residential development on the property, notably in the southwest corner, in place of the Mexican restaurant, El Presidente, and northward. Buildings taller than the convent will ring the northern boundary of the property, although there is a height restriction. People will have views of the city from all angles of the property as well as onto the Academy, as new construction closest to the Academy will have a single storey and they will step up in height the further they are from it, thus framing the Academy, rather than overpowering it as in previous plans conceived by other developers. In those plans, the historic convent was lost in a sea of glass and steel structures.

The Academy building, however, is to remain an "incubator space" for business start-ups, health counselors and practitioners, and the marketing representatives that "need a place for a desk and a phone and a computer." The continuity in function makes sense, as "some tenants of the building have been there for twenty years or more." They are a sure source of revenue, so the renovation work will be phased such as to create the least disruption possible. In providing such spaces, the building "serves a need in the marketplace," and in terms of the overall project as proposed as a magnet, it is the hub for the surrounding development. Residential units will bring life to the place and the site will be occupied twenty-four hours a day, seven days a week, just as at the Fort where up to "a third of the houses on Officers Row are leased to residential tenants."

Since the property is currently privately owned, there is little community access, which is a major weakness the Trust wishes to rectify by opening space on the ground floor to the public. Plans include a small museum "where people can learn more about Mother Joseph and the Sisters of Providence" through rotating exhibits and passive education elements such as panels and interpretive paths complete with self-guided audio-tours highlighting the breadth and impact of Mother Joseph in the northwest. Sister Hartung approves, though she hopes that one day Mother Joseph's presence at the trading post site and early mission will also be acknowledged *in situ*. Carla and I, too, were surprised that neither she nor the early works of the Sisters of Providence were interpreted at the historic site. They had, after all, lived and worked at St. James Mission from 1856 to 1873, almost twenty years, and had developed a special relationship with the military officers and soldiers. They could call upon the men stationed at Fort Vancouver in time of need, even once they had moved to the House of Providence. The army donated old metal bedsteads and let the sisters maintain their unique privilege to beg in the military reserve on payday. As Hartung loves to point out in a historic photograph, one officer led the orphans and students in calisthenics.

The Trust also plans to restore the prayer and reflection garden located on the east side of the property. The woodworkers union would like to rebuild the now-disappeared water tower located between the Academy and the Hospital, to the north, since demolished. The Sisters of Providence have plans of it in their archives. Hartung also hopes that a clinic can be incorporated on site so that downtown Vancouver's aged and downtrodden can find refuge, warmth, and care. It would be a way of replicating their mission in the twenty-first century.

Mother Joseph's biography and her signature building, Providence House Vancouver, later named Providence Academy and today known simply as The Academy, are regularly pressed into service of the Providence Healthcare and Services spiritual pilgrimages as a way to transmit the wider mission of the Sisters of Providence. It is a testament to their ministry of social justice in the Pacific Northwest and an important teaching tool to train those who are hired to administer the works they instituted. In 2013, Providence Health operated thirty-two hospitals and schools between Alaska and California. The Sisters of Providence opened and, in its new incarnation as Providence Health, continue to extend services into the communities where there is the greatest need. In the Renton (Washington) Office, where the system offices are located, the employees work in the Tukwila School District where twenty-five percent of the students are homeless. At the Des Moines (Washington) food bank, they fill weekend backpacks so the impoverished children have food to eat over the weekend. Employees also serve in local low-income housing units and the Providence Regina food bank and clothing center in Seattle. It is in these ways that Sister Hartung and the teams that work with her feel they are continuing the work of Mother Joseph, caring for the poor in their own backyard.

De Weldon's statue, now installed in the U.S. National Statuary Hall, embodies the ways the Sisters of Providence wish to remember the leader of their community in the Pacific Northwest. Her story, captured in bronze, is meant to inspire emulation; she was the Émilie Gamelin, the first superior, of the western missions.

On September 24, 1911, the Sisters of Providence moved from the aging hospital, designed by Mother Joseph in 1876, to their new, state-of-the-art building at 17th and Jefferson Streets on Seattle's Renton Hill. This process was repeated at all of the institutions credited to Mother Joseph, leaving the House of Providence, Vancouver, as the only extant example of her work.

PART II

Saving a Grand Old Lady

Carla Blank

You have requested me to speak upon 'Women in Architecture.' The subject might, from a masculine standpoint, at least, be disposed of with the brevity which characterized the famous chapter upon the 'Snakes of Ireland.' In fact, in order to have any topic at all, we must talk of women and architecture, assuming a connection which it is hardly safe to assert.

Louise Bethune's opening remarks to her 1891 address, "Women and Architecture"

Jennie Louise Blanchard Bethune (1856 – 1913)

It was Louise Blanchard Bethune who opened the door through which generations of women architects have walked. Her model of success through hard work, discipline, and adaptability, underlined by her observations that women should not expect "special favors," or even to be welcomed into this society, remain relevant today as women continue to fight for an equal playing field with men, in the profession of architecture in particular.

Much about Louise Blanchard Bethune's life is elusive, and subject to conjecture. Her history lacks the level of evidence Tania and I found preserved in the Providence Archives, which hold the letters, yearly reports (called 'chronicles'), and newspaper articles written by or about Mother Joseph during her lifetime.

For example, the program commemorating the tribute ceremony by the Western New York Chapter of the American Institute of Architects, inducting Bethune into the Western New York Women's Hall of Fame in 2006, states that "building permits filed with the City of Buffalo are recorded since 1892, but the architect's name and descriptive building data appear after 1896." Therefore, since she began working as an architect in 1881, a definitive and complete listing of Louise Bethune's building sites may never be assembled. Still another factor compounds the difficulties in verifying her work.

Louise Blanchard Bethune, circa 1889. (Buffalo History Museum, used by permission.)

Although Bethune is widely acknowledged as the principal architect of her landmark and best known project, the Lafayette Hotel, the name on the plans for the hotel's original design, submitted in 1902 and preserved in Buffalo's City Hall, is that of her firm, Bethune, Bethune and Fuchs.

The Sources of Buffalo's Heyday

Christened "Queen City of the Lakes," Buffalo has a prime location next to Lake Erie, a great water resource, which is largely responsible for its becoming a boomtown during the nineteenth century and a gateway to the western frontier. Today, Buffalo's growth is something like 2.5 percent, and while many still consider the city to be on life support, every time it approaches the flatline, it gets a new heartbeat. This time the economic engines are the healthcare and education industries; the linchpin, the University of Buffalo, is bringing its medical campuses to the downtown area. The success of the renovation of Bethune's still-existing masterwork, now called Hotel @ The Lafayette, coupled with the expected influx of people working and living in the downtown area, promises to spur further historic preservation of what remains of the downtown core.

In comparison to a Buffalo on the decline, Louise Bethune's Buffalo was one of prosperity. The city was a thriving lake-port metropolis with a soaring economy based on grains, steel, railways, and an important water system, the Erie Canal. William Fargo, its mayor from 1862 to 1866, the year the Blanchard family arrived in Buffalo, was a founder of Wells Fargo & Company of Pony Express fame, who then became a founder of American Express Company and was its president at the time of his death in 1881. In 1825, the Erie Canal opened up 454 miles of engineered water channels, making Buffalo the central transfer point between Albany and New York City and the Atlantic Ocean via the Hudson River, and between Chicago and points west via the Great Lakes. When connected to Canada's Lachine Canal, which also opened in 1825, and the Welland Canal, which opened in 1829, the three canals connected Lake Ontario to Lake Erie, making it possible to move manufactured goods and raw materials to Montreal and on to the Atlantic Ocean. Because these canals made it possible to transport goods cheaply and rapidly, the resulting development of the shipping industry jump-started Buffalo's economic success. In 1835, Buffalo could process 112,000 bushels of grain a year. After Buffalo grain merchant Joseph Dart invented grain elevators in 1842, the city became the world's busiest transfer point for grain storage and processing. By 1855, 22,400 bushels of grain could be loaded onto ships per hour.

The canals' worksites employed thousands of the five-million-plus immigrants who would enter the two countries between 1829 and 1860. Of the 74,214 people living in Buffalo by 1855, only forty percent were born in the United States. Buffalo's population tripled during the last three decades of the nineteenth century, when Bethune was in training and practicing as an architect. In 1880, Buffalo's population was 155,134; by 1900, it ranked as eighth largest city in the United States with a population of 352,387. In 1910, Buffalo made its last appearance in the top ten U.S. cities, holding tenth position, with a population of 423,715. The city's growth was largely because more workers were needed to service the burgeoning transportation business, as Buffalo became a railroad hub in addition to being a port.

The railroads would prove to be both a blessing and a curse. As early as 1852, five local rail lines had been set in place; by 1869, when the transcontinental system of railroads started operations, railroad technology began to overshadow the Erie Canal's success as a means to transport freight. Compounding this, by the 1890s, proposals were floated to expand this system of locks, canals, and channels into a bi-national deep waterway, through cooperative agreements between the United States and Canada, finally resulting in the opening of the Saint Lawrence Seaway in 1959. From 1964, when it became possible for ocean-going vessels to travel between Lake Ontario and the Atlantic Ocean from the port of Montreal (officially known as the Eastern inlet to the Seaway) through the Welland and Erie canals and on to Detroit, Chicago, Duluth, or Thunder Bay, Ontario, shipping was diverted around Buffalo, whose port could not accommodate the larger-sized, ocean-going vessels. This triggered Buffalo's era of economic decline.

However, back in 1888, Buffalo's prospects were excellent. George Westinghouse won a key victory in the "War of Currents," the fight to establish electrical standards waged against Thomas Edison's direct current system, when Westinghouse Electric Company was awarded an international Niagara Falls Commission contract to harness the energy of Niagara Falls. By 1896, using a polyphase induction motor and transformer (an AC system invented and patented by Nikola Tesla), and with three hydroelectric generators built and functioning, Buffalo could boast that it was the first U.S. city whose streets were lit with electric lighting. The inexpensive hydroelectric power source was also available for Buffalo's emerging industries, and this unique opportunity encouraged more industries, including aluminum and chemical companies, to construct plants in the area. That year, Louise Bethune, ever quick to incorporate new technologies into her designs, collaborated with Tesla on the Cataract Power & Conduit Company's terminal (1898), a still-standing transformer building at 2280-2286 Niagara Street, which housed the nation's first alternating current, twenty-two-thousand-volt power line. Besides supplying manufacturing companies at a lower cost, it fed electrical power to run the city's trolley lines.

Electrical Power Station, 1898, 2280-2286 Niagara Street. Photo from *History of the Germans in Buffalo and Erie County, NY.* (Buffalo History Museum, used by permission.)

As one member of the 1901 Pan-American Exposition's Board of Woman Managers opined, the "sublime spectacle" created by approximately two hundred thousand eight-watt light bulbs outlining the fairground's buildings every night, crowned by the 405-foot Electric Tower ablaze in an unimaginable play of colors, caused many to feel they were witnessing the spiritual beginnings of a new age. By 1904, the Lafayette became the first Buffalo hotel featuring electrical wiring and telephones in every room. These were heady times, full of unknown possibilities, when it felt like dreams could come true.

The Making of an Architect

> "The qualities which would be required to make a woman a successful architect? Why they are very much the same as those demanded to achieve in any direction, persistent industry, the power of intense application, and great patience."
>
> Louise Bethune, as delivered in her 1884 speech, "Women as Architects"

Louise Blanchard Bethune is the name by which America's first professional woman architect is most commonly known. A woman with deep roots in America's colonial past, she was born Jennie Louise Blanchard in 1856, in the upstate New York rural town of Waterloo, located in the Finger Lakes region of Seneca County, between the Cayuga and Seneca Lakes.

Dalson Wallace Blanchard, her father, was a teacher and descendant of French Huguenots known to have emigrated to New England in 1639 after their flight from France, by way of England, when, as members of the Protestant Reformed Church of France, their lives were endangered during the religious wars of the sixteenth and seventeenth centuries in France. The family name was originally Blanchet, a word whose root in French means "white," but was changed in England.

Jennie Louise Blanchard's mother, Emma Melona Williams Blanchard, was also a teacher, whose Welsh ancestors arrived in the Massachusetts colony in 1640. She was the great-granddaughter of Sarah Stedman and Ebenezer Williams (1749-1847), who was born in Lebanon, Connecticut. He enlisted in 1775 as a Minute Man from Richmond, Berkshire County, Massachusetts, served in the Revolutionary War, and died in Central Bridge, New York.

This western New York farmland, once part of the Iroquois Confederacy of Six Nations' territorial lands and home to forts established by France in the seventeenth century, was ceded by force to the U.S. federal government after American army troops sacked villages and farmlands in retaliation for dissentions among Iroquois Nations during the American Revolution (1775-1783). When the

Mohawk and Seneca chose to support the British Crown, the Cayuga and Onondaga remained neutral, and the Oneida and Tuscarora supported the colonies. In 1794, a delegation of fifty leaders of the Iroquois nation, led by the Seneca orator, Red Jacket (Sagoyewatha), negotiated the Treaty of Canandaigua with President Washington, in which they set the boundaries of the ceded lands in exchange for peace with the U.S. government. Many Seneca and Mohawk resettled in Ontario, Canada, at the Six Nations Reservation. Soldiers who fought on the side of the former British colonies were eligible to receive allotments of these former Iroquois lands.

This is how Jennie Louise Blanchard's maternal ancestors came to live in upstate New York in 1807. One of these ancestors, lawyer and banker Elisha Williams (1773-1833), secured one of Waterloo's original land grants of 640 acres for his Revolutionary War service. He created a town plan, named New Hudson, after having laid the groundwork for the town's future in 1791, when as a member of the New York state legislature he introduced the first bill to build a canal. In 1815, Williams' plan was built as the Seneca Canal, which later became a feeder into the Erie Canal known as the Cayuga-Seneca Canal. By this waterway, Waterloo was just three miles north of Seneca Falls, where Elizabeth Cady Stanton and Lucretia Mott famously organized the first Women's Rights Convention in 1848. As many convention participants continued to reside in this area while Jennie Louise Blanchard was growing up, their proximity has led researchers to postulate on the extent to which these proto-feminists influenced her development as an independent thinker. One who pioneered as a woman in architecture, who diligently worked to develop that profession's standards, pointed out, "The open sesame to the favor of our compeers and the respect of the public is 'Equal remuneration for Equal Service,' and a strict observance of all the honorable traditions of our profession and its amenities of practice."

Woodrow Wilson, Sigmund Freud, Oscar Wilde, George Bernard Shaw, Booker T. Washington, Louis Sullivan, Nikola Tesla, zoologist Edmund Wilson, and engineer Frederick Winslow Taylor, who would create the first time-and-motion studies of workers, were also born in 1856, the year of Jennie Louise Blanchard's birth. Eighteen fifty-six was the year Mother Joseph of the Sacred Heart arrived at Fort Vancouver, in the Oregon Territory, as a missionary for the Sisters of Providence. For U.S. and world events, 1856 was part of a volatile transitional period, with many forces shaking up old orders. One in every seven Americans lived in cities that year, with Buffalo ranking as tenth among ten American cities whose population exceeded fifty thousand. Just two years after the pro-abolitionist Republican Party was formed, this was the year the Nativists' Know-Nothing Party, with its anti-Catholic and anti-immigration platform calling for limits on immigration and promoting Protestantism as the country's democratic model, lost to the Democrats' nominee, James Buchanan. They nonetheless won one of the highest percentages of the popular vote ever for their third-party presidential nominee, ex-president Milliard Fillmore of Buffalo. During the same year, Abolitionist John Brown and his followers killed five pro-slavery men at the Massacre of Potawatomie Creek, Kansas, in retaliation for pro-slavery guerilla forces destroying Lawrence, Kansas, a stronghold of abolitionists.

In a decade in which the nation established its first public elementary schools, open to both boys and girls, the University of Iowa, in Iowa City, became the first public college to accept women students. Furthermore, the first U.S. kindergarten was founded in Watertown, Wisconsin, by a recent immigrant from Germany, Margarethe Schurz, with her husband Carl.

In a particularly bold demonstration of the United States' promotion of expansion and imperialism, President Franklin Pierce recognized the Nicaraguan government headed by U.S.-born adventurer William Walker, who had appointed himself its president in 1855, following the capture of Granada by his private army. The Western Union Company was founded and a printing telegraph patented by David Hughes, which by the following year made it possible to spread word of a financial panic across the country within one day, a feat that formerly would have taken months.

An inexpensive steel-making process, called the Bessemer converter, was invented and patented by metallurgist Henry Bessemer (England, 1813-1898). Architects, including Louise Bethune, would be quick to understand steel's strong and pliant structural underpinnings provided the most fireproof building material to date; steel would make it safe to realize such "modern" forms as skyscrapers.

In 1857, the year following her birth, the American Institute of Architects (AIA) was founded. The AIA would remain exclusively male until 1888, when they voted to include Louise Bethune as their first and only woman member.

Jenny Louise Blanchard was raised as an only child, following the death of a younger brother. Described as "a delicate child," her school-teacher parents chose to home-school her until the age of eleven, which at the time was a relatively common choice for educating elementary-school-age children. Their undivided attention resulted in her developing strong mathematical skills, good study habits, and unwavering self-confidence and self-reliance. These four attributes would serve her well, as throughout her adult life she would be the first and, in most situations, only woman in a career that, until she hung out her shingle, was almost exclusively chosen by men: the professional world of architecture.

Some historians suggest the Blanchards' major reason for relocating to Buffalo in 1866, shortly after the end of the Civil War, was to provide their daughter with a better, more intensive and extensive high school education than was available in Waterloo. Others say they were motivated to secure better teaching jobs with higher pay in Buffalo's public school system, even though Dalson Blanchard was already employed as both the principal and mathematics teacher of Waterloo Union School. As remains true for most school teachers today, the Blanchards had to manage on a modest income, and once relocated to Buffalo, both Emma and Dalson Blanchard taught school. Dalson Blanchard's excellence as a mathematics teacher again led to his appointment as principal at Public School No. 3, where he continued to work until his death in 1891.

Gifted at drawing and mathematics, and said to have shown an early interest in designing houses and other buildings, an 1893 *Women of the Century* entry on Louise Bethune reported her decision to become an architect was sealed the day someone's "caustic remark turned her attention in the direction of architecture, and an investigation, which was begun in a spirit of playful self-defense, soon became an absorbing interest." (My guess, the remark was something like, "Girls can't be architects!")

In 1874, at age eighteen, Jennie Louise Blanchard, known as Lulu at the time, graduated from Buffalo High School, where she selected its classics curriculum, the most rigorous choice. Her course of study was heavy on language arts courses offering texts taught in their original Latin and Greek, as well as the sciences of botany, geology, chemistry, physics, astronomy, and physiology, besides mathematics, including algebra, geometry, and trigonometry. Among the electives she could choose were moral philosophy, rhetoric, bookkeeping, drawing, and courses in French and German. The beginning of her 1891 address, "Women and Architecture," reflects her classical foundation:

> When Cain built Eros architecture began; but its authentic history dates from the two great river courses of ancient civilization where Menes laid the foundations for Memphis and the architect King Urukh, fell heir to the throne of Nimrod. Its earliest records are Egyptian hieroglyphics and brick inscription tablets built into the foundations of Ur, home of Abraham.

Concomitantly, another pioneer latched on to the Egyptology trend that was popular during this period. The year Bethune's Lafayette Hotel opened, 1904, was also the year Ruthie Dennis, soon to become famous as the dancer and choreographer Ruth St. Denis, arrived in Buffalo with impresario David Belasco's touring production of *Du Barry*, a melodrama in which she had a small role. St. Denis experienced a mystical, life-changing moment upon seeing an Egyptian Deities' cigarette poster in a downtown Buffalo drugstore window, depicting a bare-breasted goddess, Isis, seated in a temple niche framed by lotus blossoms and two pillars similar to those crowning the Lafayette' lobby. She later recalled:

> Here was an external image which stirred into instant consciousness all that latent capacity for wonder, that still and meditative love of beauty which lay at the deepest center of my spirit... I identified in a flash with the figure of Isis. She became the expression of all the somber mystery and beauty of Egypt, and I knew that my destiny as a dancer had sprung from that moment... I had never known such an inward shock of rapture."

From 1874-1876, when the then-unmarried Louise Blanchard was poised between high school graduation and the beginning of her apprenticeship with the architect Richard A. Waite, she is known to have attended Buffalo Central High School for an additional postgraduate year, where her concentration on math and drawing courses plausibly indicate that she was working toward the goal of becoming an architect. She is also known to have traveled and secured employment as a teacher.

However, there are conflicting versions in this part of her story. Some accounts mention she considered the academic route at Cornell University's school of architecture, which had just opened in 1874. The only land-grant university in the state of New York, Cornell was the first co-ed school among what became known as the Ivy League. It had begun admitting women in 1872. Cornell was closer to Buffalo and was also the most affordable school that offered architectural training to women.

These were serious considerations if she and her family were struggling with financial constraints.

It is quite possible that this two-year delay in pursuing her professional goals was simply related to the fact that the United States and the rest of the world were in the midst of an economic crisis. It lasted five years, starting with the Panic of 1873 and continuing into the spring of 1879. In the United States, Depression hit with the September 18 failure of the banking house, Jay Cooke and Company, triggered by the collapse of their one-hundred-million-dollar speculative financing scheme to secure use of public lands in the West for the Northern Pacific Railroad. On September 20, the New York Stock Exchange closed for ten days. Before the Depression ended, thousands of unemployed marched through the streets of New York and Chicago. Owners responded by bringing in immigrant strikebreakers and fought strikers with militias, as hundreds of banks, eighteen thousand businesses, and ten states went bankrupt. So Bethune could have been using this time as conscientiously as possible, learning and working to save money for tuition, because in this period when many wages were cut, even the reduced cost of Cornell University's education, compared to the fees at private universities or colleges, might have been beyond the Blanchards' reach.

It is also possible that by working as a teacher during this time, Bethune may have been prudently preparing a back-up option. Teaching was one of the few professions that respected and welcomed educated women by early in the nineteenth century, when women began to outnumber men as primary and secondary school teachers. Some historians estimate that by the 1830s to 1860s, about one-quarter of all American-born white women had some teaching experience, and from 1870 to 1880 the number of women teachers increased by eighty percent. Her early teaching experience may have first brought home to Bethune the practice of unequal "remuneration for equal service," which she later famously spoke against, since women teachers were routinely paid considerably less than men for the same professional services. Or perhaps teaching was just the most available and dignified means to gain income, because there was always a steady turnover in teaching jobs as most public school districts did not allow single women to continue teaching after they had married, a practice which continued until school districts experienced severe labor shortages during World War II.

There is no evidence of exactly where Blanchard traveled during this time, but it was probably not too far from home. It is unlikely she ever managed to afford a Grand Tour of Europe, as was the height of fashion in her day, although it would have been useful considering how many of her future works were inspired by European architectural traditions. Since train trips out of Buffalo to sites around New York State, New England, and the eastern coast of the United States were easily arranged, an excellent alternative could have been a tour of monumental homegrown Beaux-Arts beauties, including the miniature Beaux-Arts city created at Philadelphia's Centennial Exhibition, the first official world's fair to occur in the United States. President Grant kicked off the Centennial's opening May 10, 1876, and it had become a national sensation by its November 10 closing.

It is quite likely that Bethune at least heard the news of how nearly nine million people, comprising about one-sixth of the entire U.S. population, celebrated the nation's "century of progress" since the signing of the Declaration of Independence. She also probably knew about the exhibitions from all thirty-eight states and thirty-seven foreign countries that were assembled in 260 separate Beaux-Arts-style pavilions on the 285-acre Fairmont Park grounds, mainly designed by a twenty-seven-year-old German immigrant, Chief Engineer and Architect-in-Chief Hermann J. Schwarzmann (1846-1891). She might have heard about Machinery Hall's fourteen acres of technological innovations in American and European engineering, science, and manufacturing, including the featured displays of Otis's steam passenger elevator; Russian inventor M. Alissoff's typewriter; Thomas Edison's telegraph; and Alexander Graham Bell's early telephone. Furthermore, she probably would have known how the 1,400-horsepower Corliss Centennial steam engine, spanning thirty-nine feet from floor to the top of a walking beam at the highest pitch in the roof, reliably powered all this machinery from the beginning to the end of the fair.

Bethune might have been inspired to learn of the significant presence of artworks by women exhibited in the granite, iron, and brick Renaissance-style Art Gallery, where hundreds of European and American-born artists' works were displayed. This gallery "represented a milestone in women's struggles to achieve public visibility in American cultural life," according to art historian Whitney Chadwick in *Women, Art & Society*, because "approximately one tenth of the works of art in the United States section were by women, more than any other country's display." She might also have been impressed how another forty-thousand-square-foot space, the Women's Pavilion, "was devoted to the work of almost 1500 women from at least 13 countries," in photography, painting, sculpture, engravings, weaving, and embroidery, as well as furniture, laundry appliances, and educational and scientific exhibitions. Paid for by a women's thirty-thousand-dollar fundraising drive organized by Mrs. Elizabeth Duane Gillespie (the President of the Women's Centennial Executive Committee and descendant of Benjamin Franklin), the pavilion was designed by Schwarzmann. However, Mrs. Gillespie later wrote in *A Book of Remembrance* (1901), "Weary and longing for rest, we never thought of employing a woman architect! And thus made our first *great* mistake… To this hour I feel pained, because I fear we hindered this legitimate branch of women's work instead of helping it," explaining she had discovered a woman architect too late, a "Miss Kimball of Lowell," listed as Emma F. Kimball, "draftist," in the Lowell, Massachusetts directory from 1874-1876.

This separate facility for women's works might have provided a cautionary tale when similar controversies would surround the planning and execution of the Woman's Building for the 1893 World's Columbian Exposition in Chicago, in which Bethune herself would play a significant part. Happening at a time when women already comprised one-fifth of the nation's labor force, one of the nation's leading feminists, Elizabeth Cady Stanton, believed "the [1876] Pavilion was not a true exhibit of women's art," since the hall did not include works made by women in factories owned by men. As Chadwick commented, "Ironically, the building became both the most powerful and conspicuous symbol of the women's movement for equal rights and the most visible indication of woman's separate status."

There was another, slightly ironic side effect, given the Centennial's extravagantly Beaux-Arts surroundings. In an annex to the Women's building, Mrs. William Wright of Weymouth, Massachusetts, viewed a Froebel kindergarten organized by the Women's Committee to demonstrate the benefits of that pre-school educational philosophy, utilizing a teacher from Boston and a group of sixteen students from the Northern Home for Friendless Children in Philadelphia. Mrs. Wright purchased one set of Froebel Kindergarten wooden blocks, called "Gifts," for her nine-year-old son, Frank Lloyd Wright. In his *Autobiography*, Wright recalled the importance of his mother's find:

> [A] small interior world of color and form now came within grasp of small fingers. Color and pattern. [*sic*] in the flat, in the round. Shapes that lay hidden behind the appearances all about. Here was something for invention to seize, and use to create. These 'Gifts' came into the gray house in drab old Weymouth… [and] made something live there that had never lived there before.

This was but one of thousands of spin-offs from the Centennial's conduit of ideas that viewers were said to have carried away and replicated throughout the country, arguably a major factor generating the Second Industrial Revolution in the U.S.

What is well documented is that in 1876, Jennie Louise Blanchard fortuitously managed to secure another completely respectable and more direct route to her goal of becoming an architect, by undertaking the era's traditional training method of apprenticeship in the office of a professional architect. Even had she graduated from Cornell University's architecture department, in this time before licensing had been standardized, an apprenticeship would have been required to be considered a professional architect. The invitation she could not refuse came from Richard Alfred Waite (1848-1911), then head of one of Buffalo's most prominent architectural offices. When Blanchard joined Waite's firm, she was nineteen and Waite was twenty-seven.

It makes sense that Waite's offer would appeal to Blanchard, as his recently finished German Insurance Building (built 1874-1875 on Main Street and Lafayette Square, demolished 1957), was probably the talk of the town. The six-storey brick structure was Buffalo's largest office building to date, already becoming a popular address for architects' offices, including the out-of-town luminaries of the day. When Blanchard joined Waite and his small staff in 1876, they were established in Office #13, where Waite's firm would remain for twenty years.

Featuring a decorative cast-iron and glass façade, a mansard roof, and dormer windows projecting outward from the building's roof, the German Insurance Building was said to have introduced Buffalo to French Second Empire style (sometimes called Second Empire Baroque), an eclectic mix from the Italian High Renaissance, Louis XIV, and Napoleon I periods. The "official" style in Napoleon III's reign, between 1852 and 1870, it dominated the designs of the grand apartment hotels of Paris, the *hôtels particuliers* lining Baron Georges-Eugéne Haussmann's recently laid out boulevards and residential squares. By the 1870s,

"Modern French," as American interpretations of Second Empire style are also identified, was already fashionable in major cities of the Eastern seaboard and in Canada. Bethune was to create her most ambitious project on another side of this same square, the Hotel Lafayette.

Waite first arrived in Buffalo, New York, as a nine-year-old, when he and his family emigrated from London. After moving to New York City by 1866, he apprenticed to become a mechanical engineer with Swedish-American engineer and inventor John Ericsson. The latter was already famous as the designer of the Union Navy's ironclad steamship, *USS Monitor*, which in the first naval battle between two ironclad warships, the 1862 Battle of Hampton Roads during the American Civil War, achieved a strategic victory for the North. Although it did not sink, the Confederate's ironclad *Virginia* (the former steam frigate *USS Merrimack*, previously captured by the South), Ericsson's mastless design, with its revolving turret that allowed cannons to shoot any direction without turning the ship around, proved so effective that they were also adopted by other nations. From Ericsson, Waite learned the advantages of using iron, information he was soon to adapt to architectural applications, as from mid-nineteenth century it had become fashionable for ornamental uses, as cladding, or a facing material. Engineers and architects recognized that in many situations iron's strength, durability, and fire-resistant properties, especially when turned into steel, made it more utilitarian than wood, the most popular building material of the time.

The first structural use of iron façades had appeared in New York in the 1830s. A complete iron building was patented in 1850 by engineer/builder James Bogardus, although never built. Described in *Historical Building Construction* by Donald Friedman:

> [It was] composed of individual columns, beams, and infill panels. The columns and façade were all cast iron. The floor beams were wrought iron and the girders were cast iron with wrought-iron tie rods... Cast iron construction became popular between 1850 and 1870 through Bogardus, [Daniel] Badger [owner of his foundry, Architectural Iron Works] and other backers emphasizing three points: speed of erection, entry of additional light into the building interior, and safety during fires.

By using iron structural frameworks in a building he actually constructed, Bogardus is credited as being the first American to prove that thick masonry load-bearing walls were not the only way to support large or tall buildings. Cooper Union's Foundation Building (constructed 1853-1859, architect, Frederick A. Peterson) was one of New York's first buildings to be supported by rolled wrought-iron beams, which Peter Cooper developed and produced at his own New Jersey ironworks.

By the late 1860s, Waite decided to become an architect, starting in the office of John Kellum, one of New York City's prominent architects. Waite's experience fitting ships with iron skins found useful applications, as Kellum was fitting brick buildings with iron-front shells, painted to look like stonework. Waite returned to Buffalo in 1868, and in 1869 married Sarah Holloway, the daughter of Isaac Holloway, a prominent contractor. By 1874, he had managed to secure enough significant contracts to open his own Buffalo practice.

An advertisement in the Buffalo City Directory of 1877 presents:

> Richard A. Waite, Architect
> Sketches, Designs, Elevations, Plans, Sections, Specifications, Details, Working Drawings, General Draughts for Churches, Public Buildings, City and Suburban Residences, promptly furnished.

During her five apprenticeship years, Louise Blanchard also managed to find time to work for another well-respected local architect, Frank Wellington (aka F. W.) Caulkins (1855-1940). Caulkins established his Buffalo practice in 1878, and was listed in the 1879 city directory as an "Architect and Superintendent," with an office on the southwest corner of Main and Swan Streets. Around the time she worked with Caulkins, he was designing the John F. Kamman Building, a commercial structure still standing at 755 Seneca Street, and recently undergoing renovation. Caulkins was praised in the 1886 *Real Estate and Builders' Monthly* for having "made a specialty of that important incident of art, for of seventeen churches which he designed, not one has failed to be acoustically perfect."

During her five years as apprentice and assistant to Waite and Caulkins, Jennie Louise Blanchard's day went from 8 a.m. to 6 p.m. She was given full access to Waite's library, and under his training mastered the skills of technical drafting, construction detailing, and architectural design. The workload was so intense, Bethune advised in her first recorded speech, "Woman as Architect" (reprinted in the July 13, 1884 *Buffalo Daily Courier*), that to become an architect a woman needed:

> [A]s a special endowment great physical strength in order to be able to stand on her feet a good many hours a day without tiring, especially while a student. Three-fourths of the drawings of the young draftsman must be done standing. It is no exaggeration to say that during the first three years of my office studying I did not sit fifteen minutes consecutively out of the day.

Waite's steady stream of commissions was to fully equip Jennie Louise Blanchard with the expertise necessary to design and execute buildings suitable for various functions, just as his city directory ad promised. Waite soon entrusted Blanchard with drafting the firm's initial plan for Buffalo's 174th Armory, and her apprenticing years coincided with the firm's engagement on one of their most elaborate projects, Pierce's Palace Hotel, erected between 1876 and 1877 or 1878. Waite's Victorian confection of a structure was similar in style to the Chautauqua Institution's Athenaeum Hotel (built in 1881), which continues to function as a hotel.

Pierce's Palace Hotel became the site of D'Youville College when it was founded by the Catholic religious order commonly known as the Grey Nuns of Montreal in 1908, after fire demolished the hotel in 1881. Its quick disappearance must have given Louise Blanchard a dramatic demonstration of the need to seek better fire-proofing solutions, should she have needed one, as devastating city fires were occurring with alarming frequency around this mid-nineteenth-century period. There was the 1862 fire in Troy, New York, when sparks from a train's engine ignited flames on a covered wooden bridge that high winds spread, causing 671 wooden and brick buildings to be destroyed and about eight people's deaths; and the 1871 Chicago fire, when

Mrs. O'Leary's famous cow got the blame for a fire that started in her barn. Due to a prolonged drought and widely ignored fire codes and construction regulations, thousands of buildings were destroyed and some three hundred people killed. Chicago's fire was shortly followed by the 1872 Boston fire that started in the business district. It destroyed 776 buildings, killed thirty people, and cost seventy-five million dollars, the equivalent of today's 3.5 billion dollars in reconstruction.

The definition of a fireproof building continued to evolve as the need for better protection remained a major factor pushing research for new materials and construction technologies. Steel began to be favored from the late 1870s, with stone, brick, and terra cotta façades preferred for residential and office buildings, although builders used wrought iron through the 1880s. There is also engineer and architect Ernest L. Ransome's 1884 patent for a system of ferro-concrete, today known as reinforced concrete, using "rods of iron, steel or other suitable metal, which extend through the material and are twisted... and a rigid bond is thus formed throughout the entire length, the tendency of the iron to stretch or draw being resisted at every point in its length." When exposed to catastrophic fires' extreme heat, reinforced concrete proved superior to steel and iron-framed structures. Bethune had a close-by example in Carlton T. Strong and Ransome's Berkeley Apartments (1894-1897, 24 Johnson Park, Buffalo), a multi-storey Italian Renaissance-style apartment hotel built of reinforced concrete. As Bethune's design for the Iroquois Door and Lumber plant (1904) "was strong enough to survive a major fire that took the top two floors off the plant in the early 1920s," according to architectural historian Reyner Banham in *A Concrete Atlantis*, she evidently learned this lesson well. However, non-combustible materials were not enough, and other effective fire-safety practices were introduced by the nineteenth century's end, such as regulations defining easy exit access, the development of automatic sprinklers, and more effective firefighting techniques.

Soon after Jennie Louise Blanchard completed her apprenticeship with Waite, he gained international fame for design commissions from Scotland and Canada. Canadian architectural historian Kelly Crossman believes that "Waite was not an original architect, but he was an enterprising one." This assessment is similar to one frequently made about his most famous apprentice, Louise Blanchard Bethune, who evidently watched his business model and made it her own.

How Buffalo Became an Architectural Museum

Louise Blanchard Bethune was lucky to be in the right place at the right time. When she chose to focus on an architectural career, Buffalo provided a front-row seat to developments in many technological innovations, which, when applied to construction materials and design, gave architects new solutions that could make buildings and cities safer, more hygienic, comfortable, and convenient to live and work in—in other words—to be "modern."

Buffalo's ability to offer great examples of how the country's architects responded to challenges began with its first village plan in 1804, when the city fathers commissioned Joseph Ellicott (1760-1826), then a Holland Land Company agent, to devise an urban plan. The design Ellicott offered was based upon Washington, D.C.'s geometric grid of radiating avenues punctuated by circular park hubs, originally proposed in 1790-1791 by its first architect, French-born Pierre Charles L'Enfant (1754-1825). L'Enfant evolved the capital's plan from the similar design of radiating boulevards, which he first developed for Paris.

Joseph Ellicott was well acquainted with both the federal city's plan and western New York's township tracts. He had served as assistant to his brother, Andrew Ellicott, during the latter months of his work as L'Enfant's head surveyor of the federal city site, and when Andrew Ellicott inherited L'Enfant's job as the federal city's architect as well. Joseph Ellicott spent two years, from 1798-1800, surveying the tract of land known as The Holland Purchase, which included the township of Buffalo.

Buffalo was booming after the Civil War. Its population had grown from a count of 81,189 in the 1860 census to 116,463 by the 1870 census. During the last half of the nineteenth century and beginning of the twentieth century, when it could claim more millionaires per capita than any other city in the nation, Buffalo was able to support the work of various local architects in addition to becoming host to many of the major architects working in the United States. Besides Bethune's firm, among the busiest local firms were the partnerships of Milton E. Beebe and Son, Edward B. Green and Williams S. Wicks, and August Carl Esenwein and James A. Johnson. Nationally recognized architects of the day—Richard Upjohn, Henry Hobson Richardson, Daniel Burnham, John M. Root, Louis H. Sullivan, Frank Lloyd Wright, and the firm of Charles McKim, William Mead, and Stanford White—all won important design commissions for civic and commercial projects, homes, and later, Pan-American Exposition buildings. Many established offices in town, often, as noted, in the German Insurance Building. Their completed buildings soon contributed to the heady mixture of elegant and conspicuous consumption that earned the last three decades of the nineteenth century through the first two decades of the twentieth century their name, "The Gilded Age." This name was inspired by the title of an 1873 satirical novel co-authored by journalist Charles Dudley Warner and Mark Twain, who from 1869 to 1871 was editor and part-owner of the *Buffalo Express*.

With her developing interest in architecture, Louise was sure to have observed the many buildings going up in Buffalo's downtown. Her high school years coincided with the years the cast iron and brick commercial buildings were starting to be built between 76 and 92 Pearl Street. She could easily see the 268-foot clock tower rising on the Gothic Revival-styled granite City and County Hall, called "Norman" by its designer, the Rochester architect Andrew Jackson Warner. Perhaps Bethune's fascination with French Renaissance Revival styles began with two homes built on Delaware Avenue. One of the town's grandest mansions was built in Second Empire style by Stephen Van Rensselaer Watson, the founder of the Erie County Savings Bank (now Buffalo Club, 388 Delaware Avenue, 1870). The other French Renaissance-inspired home, the William E. Dorsheimer House (434-438 Delaware Avenue, 1868-1871), was one of Henry Hobson Richardson's earliest projects. Completed three years after his return to America from his studies at École des Beaux-Arts, it employed the

Louis XIII style currently popular in Parisian suburbs. This well-connected lawyer's mansard-roofed home was the setting for the first meetings between landscape architect Frederick Law Olmsted and the Buffalo parks commissioners concerning his ideas to expand upon Ellicott's original radial street plan with a park and parkway system, interconnecting all parts of the city and providing pastoral spaces for the public to enjoy without having to leave town.

From 1870 to 1898, Olmsted and his associate, Calvert Vaux, were in and out of Buffalo, overlapping with a considerable portion of the years when Bethune trained and practiced as an architect (from 1876 through at least 1905) in Buffalo and surrounding areas of Western New York. When they started work on their Buffalo plan, Olmsted and Vaux were still involved in realizing their great park design for New York City known as Central Park. That project was begun in 1856, the year Bethune was born, and finished in 1876, the year she began her apprenticeship. Simultaneously, in 1876 Olmsted was planning a design for Mont Royal Park, the highest elevation in Montreal, which was only partially realized, though it still functions today as a popular green space and delightful vantage point from which to view that city.

Some parts of Olmsted and Vaux's Buffalo park and parkway plan still remain, although some parts never got past the drawing board stage, and some that were constructed were later cut apart by freeway construction. Today the plan is most clearly seen in the layout of Delaware Park and the development of grand mansions now distinguished as the Delaware Avenue National Historic District. Its West Side neighborhood included 133 acres of the 350 acres devoted to the Buffalo 1901 Pan-American Exposition, a legacy that continues to be symbolized by the neoclassical Buffalo Historical Museum. Designed by local architect George Cary to first serve as the New York state pavilion, it was built out of Vermont marble rather than the plaster used to construct other fair buildings, and was the only Expo building intended to remain as a permanent structure. Largely undeveloped until implementation of the Olmsted/Vaux plan, this area would prove beneficial to Bethune herself, both because she would remodel five houses in the area for her family in 1891, including an office for R. A. & L. Bethune on the corner of Franklin and Huron (now demolished), and because she would secure commissions to design homes in the now-fashionable area for her middle class and more affluent clients as well.

On April 12, 2014, on what locals agreed was the first day to feel like spring in Buffalo, I observed a steady stream of people enjoying the park, fulfilling Olmsted and Vaux's vision.

The Architectural Practice of Louise Blanchard Bethune

> Architecture is seldom satisfactorily defined, perhaps never briefly and well. It is not construction in any of its various branches, nor is it arrangement of interior nor exterior, nor coloring, nor carving, nor profiling of moldings; neither is it acoustics, not fenestration, nor sanitation, nor any one of a hundred other things. It is the arranging and adjuncting, harmonizing and contrasting of all these and many other elements into a suitable and satisfactory whole.
>
> From Louise Blanchard Bethune's address to the Women's Educational and Industrial Union, Buffalo, March 6, 1891

In the 1880 United States Federal Census Record, Jennie Blanchard, whose occupation was recorded as "Works For Architect," was listed as a twenty-four-year-old, single, white, female household member in her parents' rented Buffalo home at 325 Porter Avenue. The 1880 Census also listed a boarder living in the Blanchard's home as Robt. Betheun [*sic*], age 25. Known as Robert Armour Bethune, he was born to Donald and Mary Telfer (Gay) Bethune on June 7, 1855, in Bowmanville, Ontario, Canada. He came to the United States in 1865, receiving his education in the Detroit public schools, and from 1873 to 1876 apprenticed in the Detroit office of British-born architect Gordon W. Lloyd (1832-1904). Considered an authority on classical and gothic architecture, Lloyd was well known in the Midwest for his Gothic and Romanesque Revival churches, especially Episcopal, and his expertise in masonry construction.

Robert Bethune also worked with L. A. Pratt of Bay City, Michigan, before he moved to Buffalo in 1877. He became a draftsman and colleague of Jennie Louise Blanchard at R. A. Waite's office, which would soon lead to the two becoming partners in their personal lives and their work. Except for a short time working on a Niagara Railroad suspension bridge for the bridge contractors and engineers Morrison, Field & Co., Bethune continued working for Waite at least through 1879, when the Buffalo City Directory listed him on his own, as a "draughtsman," at 383 Oak Street.

On October 19 to 21, 1881, women from throughout the United States gathered in Buffalo for the Ninth Annual Congress of the Association for the Advancement of Women. Among others who addressed the Congress in speeches related to their mission, to promote philanthropy and advances in science, art, education, and legal reforms, especially those concerning women, was Mrs. Belva D. Lockwood, who would become the first woman to argue a case before the Supreme Court, and the second woman to run for president of the United States.

Jennie Louise Blanchard had already begun to fulfill the challenges inherent in the address by their president, Julia Ward Howe: "We meet as workers and thinkers, and that in all economies, ideals and methods, woman have an equal interest with men." That same month of October 1881, at the age of twenty-five, Blanchard opened her own Buffalo architectural office at 531 Main Street. One of the first researchers of this architect's life, retired Fellow of the American Institute of Architects Adriana Barbasch, who for fifty-one years worked as a registered architect both in her native country of Romania and the United States, states this "marked what is considered the entry into the field of the first professional woman architect in the United States."

Shortly thereafter, Robert Bethune joined Jennie Louise Blanchard's practice. They married on December 10, 1881. Ever a careful businesswoman, they formed a partnership, legally naming the firm as R. A. & L. Bethune. Among other historians, Martin Wachadlo and Frank Kowsky, on their co-authored successful 2010 application for the Lafayette Hotel's listing on the National Register of Historic Site Places, postulated that Bethune recognized that in order for her office to succeed in the extremely competitive environment of the time, she needed a male partner. It may also be that the Bethunes chose to use their initials to obscure the fact that one of the partners was a woman, similarly to how pen names devised by women writers, such as George Eliot (born Mary Ann Evans, 1819-1880) and the Imagist H. D. (born Hilda Doolittle, 1886-1961), were used to obscure their gender. Wachadlo and Kowsky also suggest the ordering of the firm's initials, with Robert's first, was "analogous to those of the members of the Chicago firms of Burnham & Root and Adler & Sullivan, where the first-named partner got the work and dealt with the clients and contractors and the second-named partner did most of the designing in the office."

Louise Bethune was steadfastly focused on succeeding in her profession. In 1883, during the year of her pregnancy and the birth of her only child, son Charles William, she maintained an intensive work schedule, juggling at least seven projects. That year she designed and supervised the building of three seven-to-twelve-thousand-dollar private homes, a seven-thousand-dollar store for R. K. Smither; a six-thousand-dollar brick stable; a twelve-thousand-dollar building for the "Guard of Honor," and began work on Public School No. 16, completed in 1884, for forty-five thousand dollars, according to a "Partial List of Known Works" compiled by Wachadlo in 1996.

This volume of work was not enough of an achievement for Bethune. She sought her colleagues' validation and the strength in numbers that an architects' association could offer to pursue her goals for the entire profession. In 1885, just four years after her office opened, Bethune applied for membership in the Western Association of Architects (WAA), shortly following its formation. At their Second Annual Convention, held in St. Louis, November 18 to 20, 1885, four of the WAA's and United States' leading architects—Chairman Daniel Burnham, Secretary John M. Root, President Charles E. Illsley, and Louis H. Sullivan, a member of their Board of Directors—served on the membership review committee that unanimously accepted Bethune's professional credentials. This is documented in their "Official Report," reprinted in the profession's journal, *The Inland Architect and Builder,* Vol. VI, No. 5. First, however, they agreed to "the principle of admitting women as members of this Association." During the vetting process a member stated, "If the lady is practicing architecture and is in good standing, there is no reason why she should not be one of us." That motion was adopted, after which President Illsley made it clear that "Mrs. Louise Bethune is the applicant. Her husband was an applicant but withdrew. She has done work by herself, and been very successful. She is unanimously elected a member." A loud cheer was recorded to have followed this announcement.

Acceptance as a WAA Fellow, the classification given to all WAA members, meant Louise Bethune had achieved another "first," by becoming the first woman to be approved as a member of a professional architecture association. Wearing this mantle with modesty, grace, and purpose, she expressed in a handwritten letter to Mr. John A. Root that can be found in the AIA archives:

> My sincere thanks are certainly due to you and thro' you to all members of your society for the cordiality of the welcome you have accorded me, and also for the extreme delicacy and adroitness with which the nomination and election were managed.
>
> I am particularly sensible of the kindness the association has rendered me, and the honor it has

done itself in preserving my admission from any taint of ridicule or notoriety. If the society's new member is no great acquisition, its new measure is certainly creditable and progressive.

Louise Bethune remained the WAA's first and only woman Fellow through 1889. Immediately appointed to their Committee on Formation of State Associations, she made good on her assignment, reporting at the Third Annual Convention of the WAA in November 1886 that the Buffalo Society of Architects had been formed with fourteen charter members, under the rules of the WAA. In 1887, she followed this success with the formation of the Western New York Association of Architects, with thirty-one charter members, which became the Buffalo Society of Architects by 1888, to then become the New York State Association of Architects by 1891, known today as the Buffalo/Western New York chapter of the AIA.

In 1888, Bethune again became the first woman to apply and be unanimously elected an associate member of the American Institute of Architects. One requirement for admittance was that the architect had been principal of a firm for at least three years; by 1888, she had accumulated seven years' experience. The Board of Directors, chaired by Richard Morris Hunt, with A. J. Bloor as Secretary, based their votes upon her already impressive body of work, which by that year totaled about fifty structures. A typed letter in the AIA archives from Mr. Bloor to Mrs. Bethune, dated April 6, 1888, informed her that:

> Notice of your election to Associateship was forwarded yesterday. I send today, by American Express, as per within duplicate receipt, 1 package containing the illustrations and documents you forwarded for inspection, as follows: Yours respectfully, A. J. Bloor
>
> 3 Specifications for P. Hoffman's Millinery House.
>
> Hoffman's Millinery House ______ 1 blue print
> Police Station No. 2 ______ 1 " "
> Dwelling for Wm. Mitchell ______ 1 " "
> " " Spencer Helleg ______ 1 " "
> " " H.G. Brooks ______ 2 " "
> Residence for A.J. Meyer, 1 set of tracings and one pen and ink drawing
> Frame House for Geo. Waterman _ 1 blue print."

When the WAA merged with the AIA in 1889, as a condition of the merger, every current member of the WAA was allowed to maintain their title of Fellow in exchange for the WAA agreeing to give up its name and use the AIA's name for the unified body. As Bethune was a member of both organizations, this is how she also came to be the first woman Fellow of the AIA in 1889. She continued to carry the FAIA distinction for fifteen years, until she terminated her AIA membership in 1904.

Although the exact year William L. Fuchs began his apprenticeship with the Bethunes is in question, consistent with the then-customary practice of training an apprentice for five years, it is most frequently stated that Fuchs started to work for the Bethunes around 1884. It would make sense that their heavy workload, combined with the pregnancy, persuaded the Bethunes of the need to hire an apprentice. Fuchs was made the firm's third partner in 1890, when the firm formally changed its name to Bethune, Bethune & Fuchs. An October 7, 1893 article, titled "SOME DISTINGUISHED WOMEN OF BUFFALO," in *American Woman's Illustrated World*, which provided biographical sketches of

Members of the firm, Bethune, Bethune & Fuchs, circa 1889. From left to right: unknown intern, Louise Blanchard Bethune, Robert A. Bethune, and William L. Fuchs. (Nancy Herlan Brady, used by permission.)

Buffalo's women artists, executives, or professionals, confirms that Louise Bethune acted as principal partner in her firm:

> Mrs. Louise Bethune, an architect of the firm 'Bethune, Bethune and Fuchs,' has been in business sixteen years. Before her marriage, she was in business for herself. After she married, the firm to which she belonged was formed. Mrs. Bethune has for some years taken entire charge of the office work, and complete superintendence of one-third of the outside work. She has been the architect of many pretty dwellings, but gives her attention now to public buildings. She prepared the plans for the 74th Regiment Armory, a number of the Police Stations, and the Niagara Storage House. Several of the public schools are her designs. School houses are Mrs. Bethune's favorite line of work, due possibly to her being one of a family of teachers.

Small in stature, Louise Bethune was known for her graceful and pleasant manner, while at the same time managing to be a forceful presence. Clearly she was not one to take offense easily, as when then WAA President Dankmar Adler continued to address the 1886 convention delegates as "Gentlemen and Brother Architects," even though she was among those present. Bethune chose instead to become instrumental in making Buffalo the site of the 1887 WAA convention. Her strong will was a quality she shared with both Mother Joseph and Mary Colter. However, she must have had a quiet way of going about her business, unlike the communication styles of Mother Joseph, who was probably more volatile as she was constantly asking forgiveness for her gruff ways of interacting with the Sisters in her charge, and Colter, who was said to have inspired her male workers to wish she would not show up on their construction sites.

In the two known existing studio portraits that have become Louise Bethune's signature images, she appears somber, solid. Probably taken during the same sitting, circa 1889, one portrait is a head shot of Louise Bethune in profile. In the other she is joined by her office partners, Robert Bethune and William Fuchs, and an unknown young man, assumed to be an intern in their office, all framed in an upper torso shot. The men are dressed in suits, of whom the most formal is Robert, wearing a jacket with wide, pointed lapels and a cravat affixed with a five-pointed, star-shaped pin centered at the collar line. She is dressed in simply-tailored office attire, showing an unpatterned bodice of a dress or shirtwaist, fitted close to her body, with little adornment other than six overlapping, cloth-covered buttons centered at the front of a high collar rising to just under her chin, a white interior collar peeking out at the back of her neck, and a bit of ruched trimming circling at the neckline. Her head is uncovered, her hair neatly tucked into a bun with short bangs across her forehead. In the shot with her partners, she presents with a direct, open gaze, perhaps appearing sterner than usual because of the long moments of stillness necessarily required by cameras used for formal photographs in those days. Ishmael Reed commented, "She is dressed like a West Point cadet."

As one of Buffalo's most successful architectural offices, the practice was seemingly unaffected by the fact that Louise Bethune was the only woman practicing architecture in town. Buffalo's architectural historians agree that her office maintained a high volume of commercial, industrial, residential, and municipal clients in Western New York during its years of business. At least twice in her life Bethune gave full and public expression of her beliefs and principles on how to be an excellent architect and "businesswoman." She practiced what she preached, as her office earned its steady stream of commissions through her reputation for completing jobs on schedule, and finding efficient, frugal solutions that remained within or under budgetary limits without sacrificing functionality or safety, while still including at least a bit of artistic flair. The business was so solid they managed to secure enough jobs to keep going in spite of the depressed economy resulting from the Panic of 1893 which continued until 1897, while some other architecture offices in Buffalo did not survive.

Bethune rarely benefited from circles of women clients. In that she differed from Julia Morgan, whose practice was in large part brought to prominence by commissions for large institutional projects from philanthropist Phoebe Hearst, who introduced Morgan to her son William Randolph Hearst, as well as many commissions from wealthy women for private homes, and commercial and institutional settings. Perhaps this had to do with the differences in the times during the major portion of each woman's practice. Common to the Eastern establishments, Buffalo's male-dominated ruling society networks were firmly in place during the late-nineteenth-century decades of the Gilded Age, when most of Bethune's career unfolded. Whereas in the West's San Francisco Bay Area, where society leaders' commitment to bettering their communities largely developed around the turn of the twentieth century or later, networks of clubwomen, often wealthy, socially-conscious widows of those Gilded Age capitalists had become a significant power base, to which Morgan gained access through her UC Berkeley sorority connections as well as Mrs. Hearst. Or perhaps it had something to do with how Bethune's firm divided the workload. Similarly to earlier suggestions of how the Bethunes assigned responsibilities when there were two partners, Robert Bethune and William Fuchs appear to have functioned as the more active business contacts in the firm of Bethune, Bethune & Fuchs. Whatever the reasons, the Bethunes' clientele was predominately male. Among them were successful businessmen and professional men such as druggist Robert Smither (three-storey frame flats and store at 396 Niagara), and businessmen John C. Jewett (three-storey brick factory/warehouse at 37 Chandler), Walter J. Wilson (Iroquois Door Building at 659 Exchange Street), and chemist and philanthropist Spencer Kellogg (211-15 Summer Street family residence; and Kellogg-McDougall Linseed Oil Works, his factory, both built in 1885).

Iroquois Door Company, 659 Exchange Street, 1904. (Buffalo History Museum, used by permission.)

As was common practice for many architects of that day and today, Louise Bethune was comfortable creating designs based on various existing architectural styles and believed in following clients' requests rather than imposing her preferences. Bethune, Bethune & Fuchs consistently incorporated the latest technological developments as they became available. Their building designs were all about efficient use of space, providing electricity, good natural ventilation and light, central heating, sanitary engineering, and fireproofing, besides incorporating the technology to support modern conveniences of telephones, elevators as needed, and even an early solution for air conditioning. Although their wealthier clients may have already been aware of what was going to deliver the most up-to-date, fashionable home, store, or office, the firm also must have been very good at convincing less savvy clients of the need for these innovations.

One justification seriously put forth by those who questioned Bethune's ability to practice architecture was that because she was a woman, she could not possibly supervise construction sites for the reason that the attire then considered proper for women could easily turn inappropriate or even hazardous. Specifically, it would be a blouse or jacket covering everything up to the chin and a heavy skirt covering everything down to the ankles, with crinolines and corsetry adding weight and rigidity to the costume. Criticism of this kind, rather than holding Bethune back, probably inspired her to do more, just as someone's comment to her as a young girl, about women not being suited to architecture, had sparked her interest.

Because more than one account attests to Bethune climbing around construction sites and supervising the work, it is likely she adopted a similar costume to Julia Morgan, who was known to have solved this same problem by wearing pants under her long skirts. She could even have maintained her modesty fashionably, protected by "bloomers" hidden underneath her skirts. Bloomers, first seen in the 1850s, were a kind of Turkish-style loose trouser gathered at the ankles. As an early bicycling enthusiast, Bethune might have adopted the more up-to-date, revised, knee-length version, called "rationals" or "knickerbockers," fashionable by the 1890s, which some women took to wearing with a jacket and blouse, gaiters, and boots for leisure activities like cycling and walking.

Similar to today, when bicycles have become symbols of protest against fossil fuels, bicycles in Bethune's time were symbols of women's emancipation. Bicycling was such a national rage that Susan B. Anthony famously commented:

> I think [bicycling] has done more to emancipate women than anything else in the world. It gives women a feeling of freedom and self-reliance. I stand and rejoice every time I see a woman ride by on a wheel... the picture of free, untrammeled womanhood.

Pioneering Feats

Bethune felt "women who are pioneers in any profession should be proficient in every department." Between 1881 and 1904, her "departments" of architectural design eventually included at least fifteen commercial buildings, eight industrial buildings, five police stations, two grandstands, eighteen schools, and two hotels, in addition to her single and multiple residential projects, according to research compiled by Ms. Barbasch in the 1980s.

In addition to the designs submitted to the AIA in 1888, by that point in her career Bethune had completed various other private residency projects along with the construction of four schools (P.S. No. 8 [formerly No. 16] and P.S. No. 39 [formerly No. 24] in 1884, P.S. No. 40 in 1886, and P.S. No. 4 in 1887); the 74th Regiment Armory (1885, Virginia Street and corner of Fremont Place, which became the Elmwood Music Hall in 1900); and a three-storey lithography and printing factory for Cosack & Co. Lithography (1885). The latter was one of the first industrial buildings designed with an open floor plan, which predated the conventionally cited "firsts" for open-plan factory designs and perhaps influenced them, as they were both also built in Buffalo. One was for the George H. Pierce Company, where Pierce Arrow automobiles were produced (completed 1906-1907 with design by Albert Kahn with Lockwood and Greene, engineers, currently undergoing renovation), and the other was an extant part of the Larkin Company Complex (designed by Frank Lloyd Wright, 1896-1913, currently owned and maintained by Graphic Controls).

The 74th Regiment Armory Building, 285 Elmwood and Virginia Streets. Built in 1886, in 1900 its function was changed into a cultural center known as The Music Hall. (Buffalo History Museum, used by permission.)

This rendering documents the open-plan that Bethune provided for the interior work space of Cosack & Koerner Company's lithography plant, which appeared in *The Industries of Buffalo [N.Y.]: A Resume of the Mercantile and Manufacturing Progress of the Queen City of the Lakes*, Elstner Publishing Company, 1887. (Buffalo History Museum, used by permission.)

A rendering of Bethune's design for the Livestock Exchange, which appeared in *Illustrated Buffalo*, NY: Acme, 1890. (Buffalo History Museum, used by permission.)

The majority of Bethune's most famous projects were completed after her induction into the AIA, including the Lockport Union High School (1889, demolished), built in Western New York's Niagara County seat for ninety thousand dollars and the biggest school project with the largest budget of those designed by Bethune, Bethune & Fuchs; the East Buffalo Livestock Exchange (1890); an extension to the Women's Prison at the Erie County Penitentiary (1890-1891, Root Street); the four-storey Metropolitan Hotel (1897); the Cataract Power & Conduit Company (1898), which was the Tesla collaboration that provided the first power line to bring electricity from Niagara Falls to Buffalo, and was used for operating the city's electric trolley system; the still standing industrial buildings, Buffalo Weaving Company (1903, 234 Chandler Street complex) and the Iroquois Door Plant Company warehouse (1904, 659 Exchange Street, corner of Larkin); and her largest and most luxurious project, the 425,000-dollar, seven-storey Lafayette Hotel (1902-1911).

As one 1893 biographical sketch stated, Bethune preferred commercial and municipal commissions, with school buildings said to be a favorite. Designing private residences was not a primary interest of hers, although she is credited with numerous single and multiple residential projects. In her 1891 speech "Women as Architects," she acknowledged that clients might find residential projects a natural fit for a woman architect because they were more likely to understand the importance of many small details that a male architect might not consider, such as:

> Women are not likely to forget either that the kitchen closet should not be far away from the sink, and that there must be a wide space provided for the bedstead in the bedroom. Women are also particularly alive to the importance of sanitary draining. I make sanitary drainage my special department in our office. All the plumbing is left to me to plan. You see women as a rule have more patience than men in studying to perfect all the little details of domestic architecture.

This stance was curiously similar to that presented by Catherine Beecher in her best-selling book, *The American Woman's Home: Or, Principles of Domestic Science: Being a Guide to the Formation and Maintenance of Economical, Healthful, Beautiful, and Christian Homes*, co-authored with Harriet Beecher Stowe. First published in 1869, Beecher's pragmatic text promoted in minute detail the latest technological solutions to achieve a clean, convenient, comfortable, and ecological environment. Her essential requirements were adequate light, ventilation, heating and running water, efficiently operating kitchen, and in a most passionate discussion, construction of "earth closets," rather than water closets, as the most ecological way to recycle human wastes.

Later in her career, Bethune evidently did not want clients to assume that because she was a woman, her practice would specialize in designing private homes. In her "Women and Architecture" speech, she explained that she had come to avoid private home projects because an architect "must strive to gratify the conflicting desires of an entire household, who dig up every hatchet for his benefit and hold daily powwows in his anteroom, and because he knows he loses money nearly every time. Dwelling house architecture, as a special branch for women, should be, at the present rate of remuneration, quite out of the question." However, the firm continued to accept designs for private homes at least until 1900. Some of those residential commissions came from clients who engaged them to design commercial projects that combined the functions of both a store and residence within one structure or building complex.

Perhaps because she was the daughter of teachers and had grown up hearing discussions of what was needed to create a healthy and pleasant environment for learning, and perhaps because she was a mother and a believer in actively contributing to the betterment of her community, Bethune was ahead of the curve in promoting good architectural principles when designing schools. According to historian Kathleen D. McCarthy in *Women's Culture: American Philanthropy and Art, 1830-1930*, it was not until the 1910s that women's clubs actively worked for beautification of school buildings to deliver "the salvation of our country from the sin of ugliness." It was not only the appearance of learning environments that motivated their involvement. Partly driven by the rapid growth of urban populations that rendered existing buildings inadequate, and partly by widespread belief that children could not be expected to learn where there was inadequate light and lack of heat or fresh air, educators and concerned citizens pushed for a school building boom. They feared overcrowding in unsanitary conditions, especially due to poor ventilation in existing facilities, could even lead to increased mortality rates among the school-age population.

Bethune had received training in school-building design while an apprentice in Waite's office, so she was well prepared to benefit from Buffalo's population explosion, which had resulted in school "accommodations" becoming "in arrears of our needs," as Superintendent of Schools James F. Crooker explained in his 1887-1888 Report. Between 1881 and 1904, after the district system of taxation was abolished, which made it possible to budget building costs under the general city tax coffers, the city commissioned fifty-four new school buildings and twelve additions to existing buildings. The office of R. A. & L. Bethune was chosen to design eighteen of those schools, which were executed between 1883 and 1889. They worked closely with Superintendent Crooker, supplying designs that fit his conviction that smaller schools, of no more than two storeys, created the most supportive learning environments.

In his Report of the Superintendent of Education of the City of Buffalo for 1885-86, Superintendent Crooker called two schools that the Bethune firm

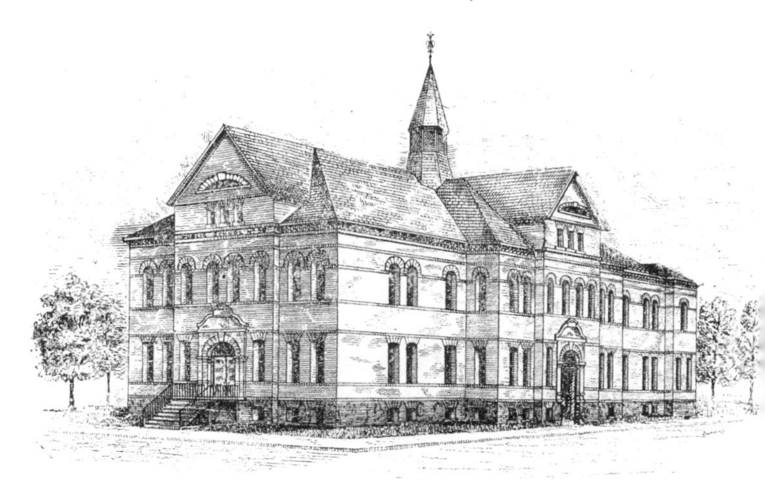

Public School No. 39, High Street, as published in "Report of the Superintendent of Education of the City of Buffalo, 1883-4." (Buffalo History Museum, used by permission.)

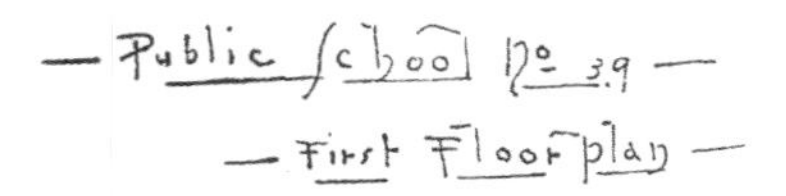

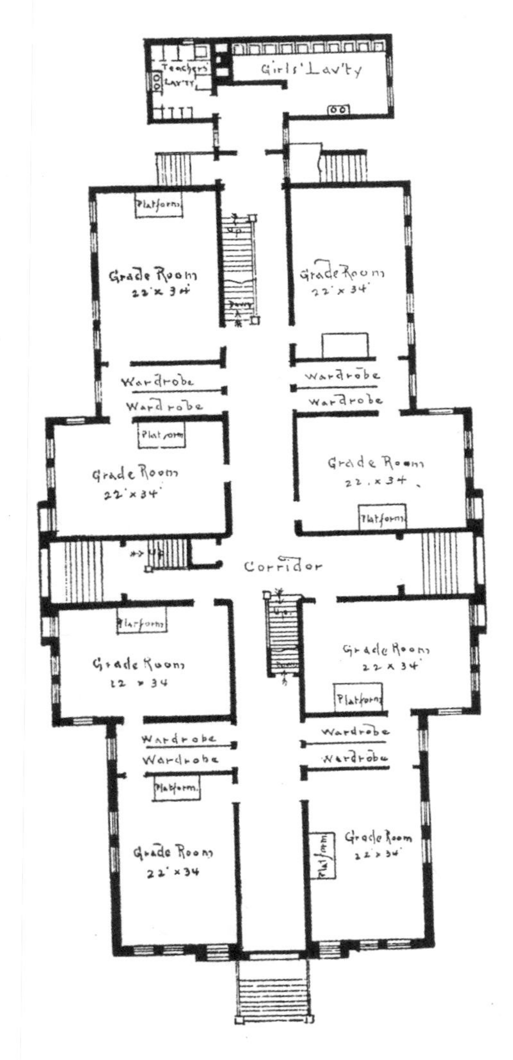

First Floor Plan, Public School No. 39, High Street, as published in "Report of the Superintendent of Education of the City of Buffalo, 1883-4." (Buffalo History Museum, used by permission.)

designed "models of their kind and to rank with the very best in the State." He quotes R. A. & L. Bethune's description of these projects, P.S. No. 38 on Vermont Street and P.S. No. 39 on High Street, respectively:

> #38: The limited size of the lot, 150 feet by 156 feet, compelled a decided departure from the conventional plan in order to accommodate 600 pupils, both indoors and out. The charming, almost suburban, location of the site on two quiet streets, made it allowable to face each grade room directly on the street while the corridors, wardrobes and lavatories occupy the rear portion of the building.
>
> The girls' yard opens upon Vermont street and the boys' yard upon Hodge street, and each floor has a separate entrance from each yard, so that the smaller and larger children are kept as much apart as possible...
>
> The basement is given up wholly to furnace, coal and playrooms. The first floor contains six grade rooms, 22 by 34 feet each, lighted wholly from one side, and with the seating so arranged that the pupils receive the light on the left side. The two wardrobes for each room are just across the hall, and face the yard.
>
> The girls' lavatory is at the end of the girls' hall in close connection with the teachers', and while under the same roof as the main building, they are completely isolated from it by a thoroughly ventilated corridor. The arrangement of the boys' lavatory is similar. The most approved plumbing appliances have been used, and the work made as simple and as nearly self-cleansing as possible...
>
> The general interior effect of the building is bright and pleasing, the maple floor, oak stair-cases and cherry furniture giving a clean, wholesome and substantial appearance to the rooms and halls; and the general air of comfort is enhanced by cheerful-colored woodwork and the softened light of the stained-glass window-heads.

The building is heated by steam, both direct and indirect, and it is expected that when the ventilating apparatus is completed, the warm, fresh air will flow in the grade rooms at the rate of eighteen cubic feet per pupil per minute.

The exterior of the building is executed in local brick and dark-red sandstone, and the roofs are black Bangor slate.

#39: [I]n its way, [it] is quite perfect a building. Being located in the center of a large open lot, with unobstructed light in all directions, the result was a plan somewhat more compact...

The wardrobes are located in pairs between the rooms, and the plumbing is all in the rear annex, with the boys' lavatory in the basement, the girls' lavatory in the first story and the teachers' lavatories in the first and second stories. Each floor of the annex is isolated from the main building by a thoroughly ventilated corridor...

In all other essentials and particulars No. 39 is similar to No. 38, having eight grade rooms on each floor (sixteen in all) each 22 by 34 feet, with commodious wardrobes in close connection.

In his Department of Education Report for the years 1887-1888, Crooker wrote:

> The new school houses that have been erected are of a superior order... The department has been successful in having the most improved methods of school architecture carried into effect... I firmly believe Buffalo possesses some of the best structures of the kind to be found anywhere in the United States.

Crooker went on to become head of the Department of Public Education for the entire state of New York. Serving in that position from 1892 to 1895, he continued to encourage architects to apply ideas that R. A. & L. Bethune had developed with him to schools throughout the state, including the early designs of Charles B. J. Snyder, the celebrated architect of over four hundred New York City schools between 1891 and 1922.

In 1897, editor Frances Willard's *American Women: Fifteen Hundred Biographies* states, "During the ten years of its existence the [Bethune] firm has erected fifteen public buildings and several hundred miscellaneous buildings, mostly in Buffalo and its immediate neighborhood." On Wachadlo's "partial list" of known works by Louise Bethune and her office, he includes 122 projects, mostly of complete buildings, but also alterations and additions. Johanna Hays, author of the first doctoral thesis on Bethune, completed in 2007, credits her with 125 building designs, remodels, or additions, but believes this estimate still only represents a portion of her work. Both scholars located their documentation in architectural, engineering, and real estate periodicals of the time, and "The Proceedings of the Common Council of the City of Buffalo." The exact number of projects will never be known because few building records and architectural drawings made by the Bethune office survived its closing, as it was common practice at that time to destroy company files when a firm closed its doors. Julia Morgan is another woman architect for whom no complete record of projects can ever be completely established because Morgan had her office files, blueprints, and most records destroyed when she closed her office in San Francisco's Merchant Exchange Building in 1951. This action was not an indication she no longer cared about her legacy, because in that same year she requested and was honored with emeritus status by the AIA. However, because Morgan was sole head of her office for most of her career, there are no questions as to who did what, which does come up regarding Louise Bethune's role in the firm of Bethune, Bethune & Fuchs, where jobs were routinely not documented as the work of a particular partner, but rather by the firm's name.

Searching Bethune's Buildings

On our August 2013 trip, Tania and I rented a car and, accompanied by my daughter Tennessee and partner Ishmael, spent one morning and one afternoon seeking what Bethune buildings other than the Lafayette remain extant. Not knowing our way around town, even with a GPS we found ourselves driving back and forth through various Buffalo neighborhoods, following a checklist of possibilities. Sometimes we found empty lots, parking lots, or newer buildings where reports compiled earlier than 2013 had listed a Bethune work would be standing. The ones we found, all undoubtedly more or less altered, were:

An example of one of Bethune's solid, utilitarian residential projects, at 35 Richmond Avenue (1883). (Photo, Tennessee Reed.)

- Mrs. E. H. Noye's fifteen-thousand-dollar brick, shingle, and wood siding home at 35 Richmond Avenue (1883)
- William W. Tyler's eight-thousand-dollar home at 39 Richmond Avenue (1883)
- Edward E. Webster's three-storey frame home at 430 Prospect, also had a stable (1885)
- Davidson's three-storey shingle and wood siding home at 354 Ashland (1885)
- George Thorn's three-storey, brick, 3500-dollar building at 40 Bidwell (Thorn & Angell Real Estate, 1885)
- Roger Graves' two-and-half-storey, 4500-dollar frame home at 310 W. Utica Street (1885)
- Spencer Kellogg's red brick home at 211 Summer Street, a fifteen-thousand-dollar project (1885). Now an apartment building; most substantial Bethune residence we saw.
- Nathan G. Benedict's seven-thousand-dollar, three-storey frame apartments at 319-321 14th Street (1889)
- Bald Meat Market, a 6,500-dollar, two-storey building at 1762 Main Street, whose street front has been sheathed in a modernist skin so we were not sure about this one, but from the looks of its painted brick side, it could remain from the original attached dwelling (1899).
- Robert K. Smither's multi-use row of flats and stores. Two of three remain at 590-592 Niagara, now an African market and nail and spa salon.

On a trip in 2012, I saw two commercial buildings: the Iroquois Door Company warehouse, now the Artcraft Building (1904); and the Fred Jehle store at 309 Bryant Street, corner of Ashland (1899), now Just Pasta. In 2013, we ran out of time so were

Spencer Kellogg's family residence at 211-15 Summer Street, presently converted into an apartment building. (Photo, Tania Martin.)

not able to check out the Cataract Power & Conduit Company's terminal (1898), or addresses mentioned in the 2010 National Register of Historic Places application, including residential designs at 436 Franklin Street (1891), 193 Ashland Avenue (1895), and 165 Lexington Avenue (1899); a former stable at 177-179 Elm Street (1891); and a commercial building at 621-623 Main Street (1908). There may be others, but most of Bethune's buildings, including all the schools, met the wrecking ball by the 1960s or 1970s.

While driving around with us, Ishmael realized that when he was growing up in Buffalo, in the 1940s and 1950s, he never visited the residential neighborhoods where Bethune houses were located. While none of Bethune's designs we saw, with the possible exception of 211 Summer Street, could be described as mansions, his experience of exclusion seemed particularly true in North Buffalo. As we entered streets close to its Delaware Avenue district, around Richmond Avenue, variously lined with substantial upper-middle-class homes to truly grand mansions, we could feel the era's competitive energy, to be more impressive than the rest. He now realized to what extent the town had been divided into two Buffalos—one white and one black. Although a couple of the remaining Bethune-designed buildings are

Niagara at Jersey Street. Flats and stores for Robert K. Smither, 1889-1890. (Photo, Tennessee Reed.)

located in what has obviously changed into predominately poorer, mixed-race neighborhoods, Bethune's Buffalo became the white Buffalo; Ishmael knew the black Buffalo, whose borders were Main Street, West Ferry Street, Humboldt Parkway, and Eagle Street.

The Business of a Dedicated Professional Woman

> The objects of the business woman are quite distinct from those of the professional agitator. Her aims are conservative rather than aggressive; her strength lies in adaptability, not in reform, and her desire is to conciliate rather than to antagonize.
>
> From "Women and Architecture," Louise Bethune's talk before the Women's Educational and Industrial Union, Buffalo, March 6, 1891

Acting on her own adage that "the future of woman in the architectural profession is what she sees fit to make it," Louise Bethune furthered her reputation by refusing out of principle to enter the 1891 national competition to select a woman architect to design the Woman's Pavilion for the 1893 World's Columbian Exposition in Chicago.

Susan B. Anthony is credited for initiating the campaign to include a Woman's Building in the Columbian Exposition plan. An appointed Board of Lady Managers functioned as its official governing committee, authorized and funded by an Act of Congress, April 25, 1890, to oversee all aspects of the Fair involving women. The Board included 117 members, two from each state, territory, and the District of Columbia, with alternates and nine prominent society women from the city of Chicago. The woman architect was to be selected by a board of men, including Chief of Construction Daniel Burnham, the same architect who had championed Bethune's application for WAA membership. Once the woman was chosen, the terms of the design plan and further decisions pertaining to the Woman's Building were overseen by the Board of Lady Managers, presided over by Chicago's reigning society matron, Mrs. Bertha Palmer. Her husband, Potter Palmer, had built "The Palmer" (as the first Palmer House hotel was known) as her wedding present. The Palmer burned down in the Great Chicago fire thirteen days after it opened in 1871 in Chicago's Loop. As a gauge of his power, Potter Palmer was able to immediately obtain a 1.7-million-dollar loan, said to be the largest loan secured at that time, and the hotel reopened in 1875.

Mrs. Palmer's leadership of Chicago society had also been achieved by becoming one of the city's most powerful art patrons. She maintained this was the first time a women's organization had been established as "official, acting under government authority and sustained by government funds." Even though an ardent suffragette, Mrs. Palmer expressed "astonishment" that women applicants could come up with adequate designs for the Woman's Building, confiding, "It was not generally known in this country that there were many women architects until the design for the building was called for."

Consistent with the Classical Revival design motif dominating Chicago's White City, Sophia Hayden's winning design in Italian Renaissance style for the Woman's Building was said to resemble her MIT thesis project, a design for a "Renaissance Museum of Fine Arts." Just a year earlier, in 1890, Hayden (1868-1953) had established her own "first," as the first woman graduate of MIT's four-year architecture program. Hayden might have been better prepared for what lay ahead had she consulted Louise Bethune. For starters, Hayden could have hardly been encouraged to hear Mrs. Palmer describe her as "a Boston architect, only 22 years old, and a modest girl of such retiring appearance that architecture is the last thing one would think her guilty of."

This commission would prove to be the first and last building design Sophia Hayden is known to have ever executed. The difficulties she encountered throughout the experience were widely reported to have caused a nervous breakdown. Although the completed building was considered a success, especially considering the smaller budget Hayden was allowed in comparison to the budgets for buildings architected by men, many critics continued to make Hayden an example, as living "proof" that women were constitutionally unfit to work as architects. At the opening ceremonies for the Woman's Building, even though Mrs. Palmer at last publicly lauded Hayden's work in her formal address, saying, "We rejoice in the possession of this beautiful building, in which we meet to-day, in its delicacy, symmetry and strength. We honor this architect...," such loud and sustained applause was said to follow these words we will most kindly guess that is why Mrs. Palmer never managed to mention the architect's name.

Bethune, who had been practicing architecture for ten years when the call went out for the Woman's Building competition, made no secret of her negative stance on competitions in general, which she considered the source of Hayden's problem. Bethune's opposition was basically connected to her drive to establish guidelines for the best professional business practices. She was in agreement with the AIA's position at the time, which actively opposed design competitions (whose results were often fraught with abuses of power), although they did develop guidelines.

For one not known to be confrontational, especially as a business practice, Bethune picked two worthy fights on the occasion of her public talk on "Women and Architecture" before the Women's Educational and Industrial Union of Buffalo on May 6, 1891. When reprinted in *The Inland Architect and News Record* [Vol. XVII, No. 2, March 1891], Bethune's statements on the Woman's Building and income equity received a national platform.

First, Bethune called competitions "an evil against which the entire profession has strived for years, and has now nearly vanquished; it is unfortunate that it should be revived in its most objectionable form on this occasion, by women, and for women." Detailing her reasons to boycott the Chicago competition, Bethune was adamant, "Such a building is talked of, but the idea of a separate Women's Board Exhibit, etc., expresses a sense of inferiority that business women are far from feeling."

Second, Bethune used "the competition's" highly visible platform to go on the record with her belief that women should receive "Equal remuneration for Equal Service." Wyoming had passed a law in 1869 guaranteeing equal pay in government employment for women, but it would take almost another hundred years for the Equal Pay Act of 1963 to make this a more general practice. In 2014, 123 years after Bethune spoke out, continued legislation and presidential directives in the United State have yet to achieve equality in all instances. Statistics show that, on average, women earn seventy-seven cents to each dollar earned by men, a wage gap measured to cost a woman 443,000 dollars over the course of her career—enough to pay off a mortgage, send three children to college, or provide some security after retirement.

Some historians have used Bethune's statement to prove she was a feminist, and she was, if feminism means men and women should have equal economic opportunity; fair play for all in the professional workplace was a position her public statements clearly make. However, I have found no evidence that she ever commented publicly on other equal-rights issues affecting women, such as giving women the right to vote (a primary issue of her day), let alone, as was common in the sixties and seventies, singling out women as the superior sex at the expense or downplay of men.

Mrs. Bethune was rankled by the Woman's Building competition's obvious hiring and payment inequities:

> The building will cost about $200,000, and the prize offer to the successful competitor is $1,000. This is all she is to receive. That is, she renders 'personal artistic service' and also prepares her competitive drawings, all for one-tenth of the regular rate for full professional service. The extremely equitable arrangement made with the appointed architects for the ten large buildings is that each renders his personal artistic service for $10,000, all his drawings to be made at the expense of the commission. The sum total to be expended for the ten principal buildings is in the neighborhood of $6,000,000, making an average of $600,000 each. Thus each architect receives about one-third his regular full commission, for which he renders about one-third his full professional service.
>
> The proportion of remuneration to the architect of the Women's Building is about three-tenths of the average rate paid the already appointed architects for nearly similar service. It is an unfortunate precedent to establish just now, and it may take years to live down its effects.

Bethune's business concerns about the lasting effects of Chicago World's Fair parallel Louis Sullivan's aesthetic concerns, as he describes in *The Autobiography of an Idea*:

> Meanwhile the virus of the World's Fair, after a period of incubation... began to show unmistakable signs of the nature of the contagion. There came a violent outbreak of the Classic and the Renaissance in the East, which slowly spread Westward, contaminating all that it touched, both at its source and outward... By the time the market had been saturated, all sense of reality was gone. In its place, had come deep seated illusions, hallucinations, absence of pupillary reaction to light, absence of knee-reaction-symptoms all of progressive cerebral meningitis; the blanketing of the brain. Thus Architecture died in the land of the free and the home of the brave... The damage wrought by the World's Fair will last for half a century from its date, if not longer.

Bethune chose to fight long and hard in a different battle: the future of architecture as a profession. As a measure of her belief in the need for architecture to be worthy of respect and ensure confidence in its professional standards, Bethune gave generously of her time to her professional organizations. Clearly the firm of Bethune, Bethune & Fuchs had won the respect and trust of their hometown colleagues, as shown on the AIA Buffalo/Western New York website's list of known executive committee officers of these organizations. Louise Bethune served as first vice president of Buffalo's Architect's Association in 1887 and treasurer of Buffalo's AIA Chapter from 1895-1896. Her husband, Robert, held the office of the Architect's Association's treasurer from 1886 through 1893, and the office of Buffalo's AIA Chapter's first vice president in 1896. Their partner, William Fuchs, also was a member and held offices in Buffalo's AIA chapter, including the positions of treasurer (1894), secretary (1903), and second vice president (1905).

Bethune worked vigilantly to move both male and female architects toward ever higher standards of professionalism. Over her nineteen years of membership in professional associations, she actively promoted an Architects' Licensing Bill, because she believed it was necessary to promote a "law to enforce rigid preliminary examinations," to credential all who called themselves architects, as there were no official standards in place either at a state or national level for granting licenses to practice architecture. In 1915, two years after Louise Bethune died, New York State became the tenth state to pass a licensing law.

She expressed her concerns and interest in women's future in the profession in her "Women and Architecture" address before the Women's Educational and Industrial Union, opining that women architects "meet no serious opposition from the profession nor the public. Neither are they warmly welcomed. They minister to no special needs of women, and receive no special favors from them." Having researched the current situation for women architects, she was critical of women who did not fight for their places in the profession after receiving training:

> The total number of women graduates can hardly exceed a dozen, and most of these seem to have renounced ambition with the attainment of a degree, but there are among them a few brilliant and energetic women for whom the future holds great possibilities.

Bethune must have been an optimist, or else was being diplomatic. It has taken until the twenty-first century for the profession to bestow a major honor on any woman architect. Fifty-six years after her death, the AIA designated Julia Morgan its 2014 Gold Medal winner, the highest award an American architect can receive. She was the first woman to receive the AIA award, albeit posthumously, since 1907, which was the year this honor was inaugurated. According to the *Architectural Record* website, a campaign to retroactively acknowledge the work of Denise Scott Brown, whose collaborator and husband, Robert Venturi, received a 1991 Pritzker Prize, brought attention to how few women architects have received architecture prizes. The Pritzker Prize, established as architecture's international equivalent to a Nobel Prize since 1979, awarded its first woman laureate, Zaha Hadid, in 2004, and its second, Kazuyo Sejima, who shared it with her collaborator, Ryue Nishizawa, in 2010.

However, even when well-meaning, as the AIA undoubtedly was in conferring this award, their official press release revealed how art critics' old habits still prevail, of only allowing one-at-a-time tokens, whether they be minority men, or white, black, yellow, or brown women. To put it more generously, this may be another instance where all architects are judged by contemporary qualifications of what constitutes an architect, regardless of the accepted standards of the time when the architect practiced, which is still the measure for some. Because in the closing paragraph of its press release, the AIA quoted architectural historian Mark Anthony Wilson referring to Julia Morgan: "She was America's first truly independent, fulltime woman architect..." In his book *Julia Morgan: Architect of Beauty*, Wilson's only mention of Louise Bethune appears in an endnote to the introduction, where he crucially amended his quoted text used in the press release. The note, citing the *Encyclopedia Britannica*, states that because Bethune "did not have a license, and she learned architecture as a draftsman in the firm of Waite and Caulkings [*sic*]... it seems safe to say that Julia Morgan became the first *licensed*, independent woman architect in America when she opened her own office in San Francisco in 1904 *without a partner*." [Italics added. The second phrase in italics refers to Wilson's finding that Bethune opened her first office in partnership with Robert Bethune, although other scholars agree that she founded the firm on her own, changing it to a partnership three months later, after the two were married.]

The AIA's press release is especially puzzling, as Louise Bethune's importance to the AIA can easily be confirmed on its website. Luckily, at the 2014 AIA convention where Morgan's award was presented, architect Beverly Willis was more generous in her statement during the final keynote event. She said, noting her ignorance of women who practiced architecture early in the twentieth century, that "women in the '50s, '60s, '70s and '80s were denied the incredible role model of a successful practitioner... As recently as 1978, the president of the AIA declared to the press that he would never hire a woman architect... On behalf of these women architects, I express our collective and respectful anger."

Private Life

So what did Louise Bethune do to relax? The evidence suggests that Bethune very consciously maintained decorum then considered "proper" for a lady, perhaps because of the controversial position she held, being a pioneer in her professional work. This was the era when many middle-class and upper-class women created acceptable ways to participate in the world outside of their responsibilities to home and family. Volunteering time to club work was considered an especially respectable social outlet. Some women organized clubs to develop civic reform agendas as a means of helping those less fortunate, through establishment of Settlement Houses, benevolent societies, or other community-based support services. Book clubs thrived and became a major resource to achieve literacy. Others sought to preserve and encourage the cultural life of the nation, as in the "village improvement movement." Society women took on fundraising drives, and communities came to depend upon their support to build and administer civic monuments such as art and science museums, libraries, schools, and theaters, and to preserve and maintain historic sites and buildings. Many women also simply sought individual pleasures outside of the home, be it shopping in one of the popular covered arcades or department stores, gathering in the company of others in approved restaurants and theaters, or exercising for health benefits.

While Bethune mostly kept her nose to the grindstone, she embraced the latter hobby when, in 1888, she became a founding member of the Women's Wheel Club, a club whose grounds for expulsion included "unbecoming conduct," or violation of their eleven By-Laws and Rules. Known as the first

Buffalo woman to purchase the first women's bicycle to go on sale in Buffalo, an article about "Ladies of the Wheel" in the *Buffalo Morning Express* (August 14, 1892) described Bethune as "one of the most tireless and persevering riders in the club. No morning is too dark and threatening, no road too hilly, or too sandy, or too muddy, to daunt her courage." This group booked itself into an eighteen-mile run to Big Tree Corners one week after six members had bicycled to Niagara Falls (although on that excursion they allowed themselves to take a train back to Buffalo). These cyclists did not use three wheelers, but paid about 150 dollars for the two-wheeled Swift, Dart, or Psycho brands. By 1891, four divisions of the Women's Wheel and Athletic Club of Buffalo had been organized: wheeling, pedestrian, bowling, and billiards, with programs of speakers during the winter's off season.

The women were so highly organized in all regards that their constitution, names of officers, and minutes of meetings were professionally printed in an elegant, gray, soft-cover chapbook. In 1894, when membership had grown to forty-five, their annual report featured formal Articles of Incorporation, listing members, officers, and directors, including Mrs. Bethune. The *Buffalo Morning Express* quoted the club's Wheeling Captain, Miss Emma L. Villiaume, regarding the required cycling uniform in 1892, which "should be as nearly like a riding habit as is possible, close fitting and inconspicuous," of "navy blue storm serge with some three yards of material in the skirt; the waist fastening diagonally at the side, and cut with a postilion back. The hat we wear is a small, soft felt, which is comfortable and does not blow off easily." The same *Morning Express* article interviewed another club member, just returned from a Western trip. She observed even more women cyclists were active in Chicago and St. Paul, and found their favored riding habit, a "wide-pleated skirt," looked better.

Louise Bethune also served as treasurer of the Society of New England Women, was an active member of the Buffalo chapter of the Daughters of the American Revolution (founded in 1890), and was a member of the Buffalo Historical Society. In 1904, she was noted in the *National Cyclopaedia of American Biography* as being a registrar of the Buffalo Genealogical Society and served a term as its president. She clearly devoted much time to researching and creating a document detailing the genealogical history of eleven generations of her Blanchard family tree, copies of which can be found in both Buffalo's Public Library and the Historical Museum archives.

The Closing Days

There is some question as to exactly when Louise Bethune ended her active practice as an architect. Her December 19, 1913 obituary in the *Buffalo Evening News* is in agreement with a January 11, 1914 obituary in Buffalo's *Express* that states: "Up to two years ago Mrs. Bethune was an active member of the firm Bethune, Bethune & Fuchs." This dating matches listings in the Buffalo city directory, where through 1911 the firm's name appears as Bethune, Bethune & Fuchs, changing in 1912 to Bethune & Fuchs.

Louise Bethune ended her AIA membership in 1904, giving credence to some historians' calculations that around 1905, at the age of forty-nine, she appeared to withdraw from active practice. In addition, they cite signatures on some building permits registered in the city records, which changed from "Bethune, Bethune & Fuchs" to "Bethune & Fuchs." That would mean her career in architecture ended, at the earliest, twenty-four years after she opened her first office, in the same year her son graduated from the University of Buffalo School of Medicine.

However, it was not necessary to hold membership in a professional society such as the AIA in order to practice architecture during Louise Bethune's years of practice, as continues to be true today. Robert Bethune, for instance, was only a member of the WAA from 1887 to 1889, using projects independent of his wife's for his application. Although he was a founding member of the Architect's Association in Buffalo, he did not immediately join the national AIA when it merged with the WAA. He sent a letter to the AIA requesting consideration for membership in 1901, in his name and that of the firm's third partner, William Fuchs. Both men were elected associate members in 1902; their status remained active until the year of Robert Bethune's death in 1915.

While it does appear Louise Bethune did not take on any new projects after the Lafayette's opening, I found four existing documents to support the idea that she managed to see the Lafayette addition project through, in spite of illness, for five or six more years (or, two to three years before her death). Buffalo's Department of Economic Development, Permit & Inspection Services in City Hall retains Louise Bethune's signature on both a 1909 City Building Permit (#29241) for a fireproof, 250,000-dollar, seven-storey hotel addition at 236 Ellicott Street, and a 1910 Building Permit (#32241) for a 17,000-dollar brick Boiler House, a stand-alone building to house the heating and electrical plant. These permits coincide with two work orders for the first addition, now in possession of the Buffalo Historical Museum, where the name "Bethune, Bethune & Fuchs, Architects" appears under the title "Specifications of Cooking Apparatus and Equipment for the Lafayette Hotel." The first bid was dated March 15, 1910, and the revised bid April 12, 1910.

Because, as the *Express* stated, "Mrs. Bethune took special pride in the work she did for the Lafayette Hotel company," it is consistent that she would want to ensure the Lafayette's first addition worked seamlessly with her original plans. In process from 1906 to May 1912, there is widespread consensus that it did. These four documents could also explain why Louise Bethune's name was not legally removed from the partnership until 1912, a date that coincides with the presentation in the *Express* obituary.

However she managed her professional commitments, she did not completely withdraw from the world during her last years, as she kept active memberships in the historical and genealogical-related societies and organizations mentioned above.

It is most likely Bethune's incremental retirement was initiated due to poor health, probably related to a kidney ailment. Although the exact nature of her illness is unknown, as one newspaper describes her as "stout," this condition could have been complicated by diabetes. It is also possible she managed a chronic condition throughout her life. By 1907 she was listed in the Buffalo City Directory as living at 904 Tonawanda with her son, Dr. Charles William Bethune, who became a specialist in urology after completing his post-graduate work in urology at Harvard Medical School in

1908, perhaps inspired by the nature of his mother's illness.

Meticulously consistent, Louise Bethune prepared for an orderly exit from her work and this world. On November 28, 1906, she signed her typed will as Jennie Louise Bethune, leaving 881 Tonawanda Street and lot to her mother and 904 Tonawanda Street to her husband and son. She otherwise divided up her personal property and effects between her mother, her appointed "Executrix, " her husband, and her son. She bequeathed "all the money that I may have in Banks or elsewhere at the time of my death; all my personal property… and all my clothing and jewelry wherever situated," to her mother. She left her husband the "office furniture and office library, books and papers, and all my interest in all uncollected office accounts and claims." To her son she bequeathed "all my remaining books and library." She counseled them to "share and share alike" all of her remaining "residue."

Bethune's Signature Legacy: The Lafayette Hotel

There is general agreement that as principal architect of the firm Bethune, Bethune & Fuchs, Louise Bethune was the primary designer of the Lafayette Hotel. This assumption is based upon biographies written contemporaneously with her professional career and a similar expression in her *Express* obituary concerning her "special pride" in the Lafayette Hotel company work. There is also general agreement that the Lafayette is her most significant achievement in existence.

The Lafayette's Neighbors

Located in the heart of Buffalo's downtown at 391 Washington Street, the hotel boasts façades on Washington, Clinton, and Ellicott Streets, where it sits on the southeast corner of Lafayette Square. Originally a public park the size of one city block called Courthouse Square, it was part of Joseph Ellicott's 1804 Buffalo street plan. Officially renamed Lafayette Park in 1879, it featured a Civil War Soldiers and Sailors Monument at its center designed by George Keller with sculptures by Caspar Buberl. Dedicated in 1884, it is flanked by eight Civil War cannons facing outward on opposite sides of the four diagonal crosswalks that radiate from the monument's base and are separated by grass plots (In October 2014, no cannons were present in the park.)

The hotel's location was wisely chosen because Lafayette Square was and continues to be one of Buffalo's two main downtown squares, and is adjacent to Main Street—the commercial center of downtown. For out-of-towners, the hotel was a short ride by horse-drawn carriage or taxi, and even at walkable distance from downtown railroad terminals at the corner of Exchange and Michigan Streets or the foot of Main Street, as well as the Erie Canal terminal. In addition, since 1977, the Metropolitan Transportation Center's bus terminal is even closer. Trolley lines on Main Street made it easy to travel to and from Buffalo neighborhoods beyond the downtown area. At the turn of the twentieth century, rimming Lafayette Square or within easy walking distance, guests could conduct business at many banks and offices or enjoy both small shops and department stores, including Adam Meldrun & Anderson's and tradesmen's

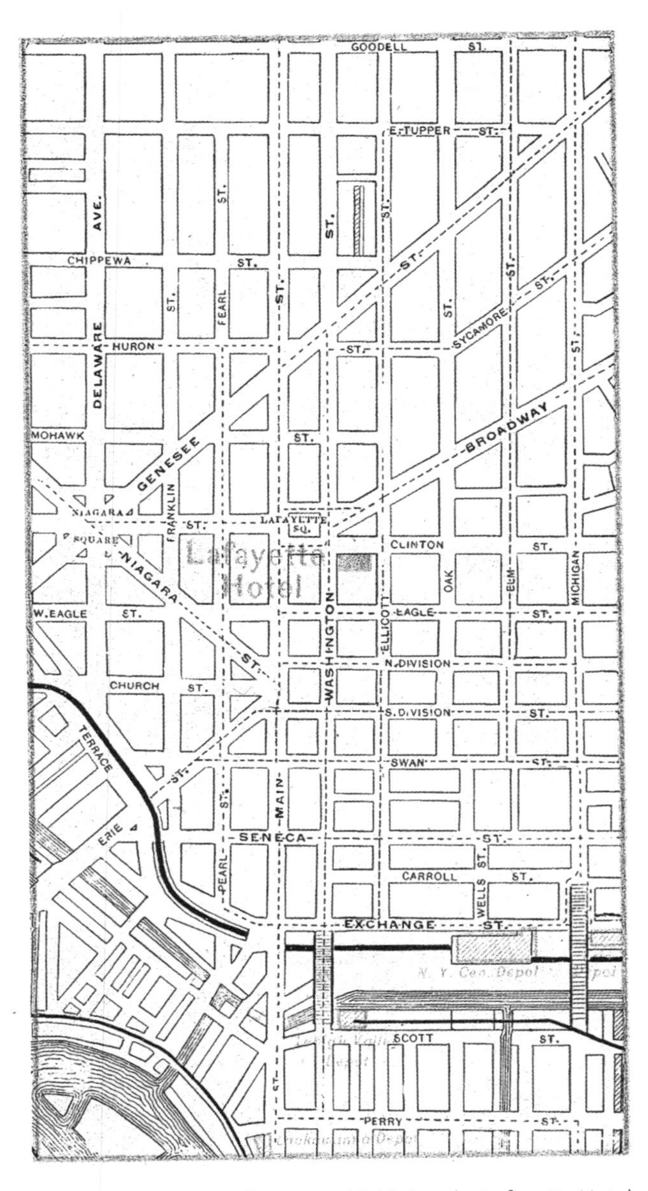

This map of Buffalo's downtown highlights the Lafayette Hotel in Lafayette Square, and its relationship to the neighboring Niagara Square and Lake Erie. From the circa 1904 pamphlet, "Lafayette Buffalo, Washington and Clinton Sts." (Buffalo History Museum, used by permission.)

storefronts. For public entertainment, choices included a variety of restaurants and bars and, by most cities' standards today, a booming theater district offering live vaudeville and variety acts, melodramas, traveling road shows from New York City, or movies.

Louise Bethune intended the hotel to fit harmoniously into its setting on Lafayette Square, orienting its original main entrance to directly align with one of the park's radial sidewalks. Her French Renaissance Revival design's compatibility is not so apparent today because many of the original buildings surrounding Lafayette Square have been demolished or altered in appearance. The style was not only suggested by the square's French honoree, but was already present on its northern boundary in the now-demolished German Insurance Building. Also on its northern boundary was the Olympic Theatre, a burlesque theater that was remodeled into a vaudeville and movie theater by 1914, and a restaurant, the Park Hof, which opened shortly after the Lafayette. These buildings were replaced in 1929 by an Art Deco-style skyscraper, the Rand Building (Franklin J. and William A. Kidd, architects), which possibly inspired New York City's Empire State Building. It was followed in 1959 by the Tishman Building, an international-style "curtain wall" skyscraper (Emery Roth & Son, architects) on the German Insurance Building's site. On the south side, the Renaissance-style Brisbane Building (1895, Milton E. Beebe and Son, architects, for James Brisbane and James Moody) featured a colored glass dome covering the lobby and second floor's "*bon marché*" of variety stores. It also housed banks, law offices, one of the first Woolworth stores, and the Kleinhans Company, a high-end men's clothing store. Today the Brisbane functions mainly as an office building, with a very humdrum "modernization" encasing its exterior at street level and the glass-domed arcade no longer evident. The Buffalo Central Public Library (1887-1961), a Richardson Romanesque building, sat on the western boundary. By 1964 it was replaced with the current Main Branch of the Buffalo and Erie County Public Library, designed by local architects James W. Kideney and Associates with Paul Harbach. The only conversation between this Postwar Modernist building and the Lafayette comes from the library's long entrance plaza fronting on Lafayette Square, which opens the hotel's entire Clinton Street façade to easy viewing.

"The Russians want to be French" says Nina L. Khruscheva. So do Americans!

The Niagara Frontier "boom" after the close of the Exposition made it possible for the Lafayette Hotel's construction to eventually move forward. The firm of Bethune, Bethune & Fuchs and the Lafayette Hotel's backers knew an invocation of French Second Empire charms would inherently advertise their luxury destination agenda. Beaux-Arts philosophy was all the rage following the great acclaim for its use at a series of U.S. expositions, starting with the 1876 Centennial in Philadelphia, and most famously at the 1893 World Exposition in Chicago's neo-classical White City. Additionally, it carried over into similar neo-revivalist designs for the 1895 Cotton States Centennial in Atlanta, the 1897 Tennessee Centennial in Nashville, the 1898 Trans-Mississippi and International Exposition in Omaha, and the colorful rainbow variations of Buffalo's Pan- American Exposition in 1901. The architects and owners were not alone in choosing this particular French Renaissance Revival model, described by Buffalo's architectural historians Martin Wachadlo and Christopher Brown as "characterized by red brick walls with white stone dressings around doors and windows and the adoption of Classical decorative details for ornament." Other examples, constructed during the Gilded Age at the behest of civic commissions and wealthy homeowners, can still be found scattered throughout North American cities from the Atlantic to the Pacific coasts. The Lafayette's French Renaissance Revival style, according to the Lafayette's National Register of Historic Places narrative, was inspired by:

> A number of residential squares surrounded by contiguous townhouses houses [built in Paris, when promoted by Henry IV in the early seventeenth century]. The most important of these addresses is the Place des Vosges (1605)... [which] was (and recently is again) an address of quality that helped to identify its style of architecture with comfortable urban living. Bethune's design for the Hotel Lafayette echoes the buildings of the place de Vosges, especially in the continuous ground floor arcade that forms the ground floor of the building... However the voussoirs of the Hotel Lafayette arcades, as well as the acroteria and moldings of the Classical cornice and other decorative elements on the exterior of the Buffalo building are made of glazed terra cotta rather than of cut stone. The decision to imitate the style of Henry IV or the French Renaissance... was most appropriate to the hotel's design, both because of its association with elegant Parisian domestic architecture and because its location on Lafayette Square also suggested the residential square—*places*—of Paris. The Marquis de Lafayette, despite his democratic views—would surely have been amused to

have his name attached to such a grand Francophile fabrication."

A President is Gunned Down

The Lafayette Hotel was first conceived in 1899, to accommodate the influx of visitors expected to attend Buffalo's Pan-American Exposition. Its site was then occupied by a small, stone, Greek Revival-style building, the Église Française St. Pierre (commonly known as the "French church," or St. Peter's Roman Catholic Church, 1844). Because Buffalo's churches reflected the separate heritages of its various immigrant communities, predominately from Germany, Ireland, Italy, and Poland, this congregation likely included French Canadians, many of whom chose Buffalo to obtain work in the area on waterworks and in the textile industry. The building was demolished in 1900, when hotel plans were given the go-ahead. The promoters initially planned to construct a first-class, 275-private-room, eight-storey, brick and terra cotta, fireproof hotel, "thoroughly modern… of the Romanesque style," according to a March 3, 1899 *Buffalo Commercial* article.

Its design was drafted by H. H. Little (c. 1848-1917), the first architect hired. Based in Buffalo, he was well known for many residential and commercial projects, including the still-standing Red Jacket Apartments (1894, southwest corner of Main and Allen Streets). Two houses, his personal favorites, chosen to illustrate his promotional materials were two residences, at 3 St. John's Place and 869 Delaware. His preliminary design evolved into a 225-room luxury hotel and a theater.

However, by late 1899, due to financing difficulties, H. H. Little was replaced by Bethune, Bethune & Fuchs as the architects, and the plan revised into a twelve-storey hotel with three hundred guest rooms, without a theater. When a change in investors caused further financial delays, it also occasioned a third change in architects because there was concern that Bethune, Bethune & Fuchs lacked experience to take on a project of this size and ambition. The next hire was Henry Ives Cobb, a nationally known architect whose extensive experience included residential, commercial, and educational projects mostly built in the Chicago area. Among his commissions were one hotel, six structures for the World's Columbian Exposition (most famously the Fisheries Building), and various University of Chicago campus buildings. Their ten-storey, 315-room hotel, to be named the Hotel Lafayette, appeared to be moving forward with the foundation dug and two foundation walls in place. Once again, there were further delays due to financial problems and Cobb withdrew or was fired.

To provide accommodations for out-of-towners attending the Exposition, the Iroquois Hotel, considered the best hotel in town at that time, added three storeys topped by a steel-framed Mansard roof to their existing building, and other existing Buffalo hotels remodeled their buildings. The Lafayette had been the only new hotel planned to meet the Exposition's opening deadline, and when it became evident that the hotel would not be ready, it increased the need for tourists to make do with any temporary housing they could find. *Buffalo's Pan-American Exposition* quotes one family who reported, "They had two beds at 573 Potomac for $2 per day. A *New York Times* reporter claimed some paid $4 for a cot and $5 for a 'bed on a billiard table.' Buffalo's $10 per week apartment dwellers were evicted to make way for visitors who paid $30 and $40 for their seven-day stay."

Even though the partners in the Hotel Lafayette project could no longer expect to benefit from a launch timed to the Pan-American Exposition, planning did go forward slowly. The promoters rehired Bethune, Bethune & Fuchs in 1901. In the summer of 1902, the project had to be rescued from yet another financial collapse after a Buffalo savings bank turned down a loan at the last minute to the now principal promoters, hotelman Charles J. Spaulding and restaurateur Joseph A. Oaks. Their friend, Walter B. Duffy, a Canadian-born Rochester distiller who had previously invested 140,000 dollars to purchase the site, raised an additional 525,000 dollars to finance construction of the project. Duffy saved the hole in the ground from remaining the local punch line it had become, even ensconced in a vaudeville ditty. Relabeled the Lafayette Hotel, its revised structural plan was realized as a seven-storeyed, 225-room hotel.

The initial building phase of the hotel was completed in 1904, three years after the close of what some called the ill-fated Pan-American Exposition, so called because President William McKinley was assassinated by anarchist Leon Czolgosz, or more accurately, McKinley was shot by Czolgosz on the Exposition grounds on September 6 while appearing at the Temple of Music to give an address. He died September 16, 1901, his doctors' malpractice as much to blame as the assassin's two unrecovered bullets. Some say this tragedy caused the fair's ending days to be melancholy, that the Expo did not meet its investors' financial goals, and contractors never received over one million dollars due for their work. Others, however, say Congress provided monies to prevent bankruptcy and in the big picture, Buffalo's economy actually benefitted. *A History of the City of Buffalo*, published in 1908 by the *Buffalo News* explained:

> One has but to examine the city chronicles of the past six years, which constitute the most progressive period in Buffalo's history—the transition of this community from a large, unwieldy, cumbersome town to the eighth city of the United States, foremost in many classes of industry… Immediately after the close of the exposition these benefits became manifest, first in inquiries from businessmen throughout the country, concerning the availability of factory sites, the price and supply of labor, the shipping facilities and the thousand and one things that contribute to the success of the modern industrial plant. The return was immediate. In the outlying sections factories sprang up almost in a day—great institutions, employing thousands of men. What benefited Buffalo also benefited Niagara Falls and there was such a boom in that community as had never before been witnessed. All this is contributory to Buffalo, and may be properly considered a part of the general advance made along the Niagara Frontier in the past six years.

Construction History: Putting the Pieces Together

The complicated business dealings surrounding the Lafayette's beginning almost seemed to set up the building for a destiny of changes whose ups and downs mirrored those of the city and its inhabitants. The National Register of Historic Places Chronology of the building's Construction and Alteration (Section 7, page 9) lists twenty-one significant dates in the hotel's history, previous to the restoration that the 2010 granting of Historic Preservation status made possible:

- 1899 Hotel for this site first mentioned (H. H. Little / Bethune, Bethune & Fuchs)
- 1900 Construction begins and stops at foundation (Henry Ives Cobb)
- 1902 Construction begins again, with new design (Bethune, Bethune & Fuchs)
- 1904 The original hotel is dedicated
- 1906 Expansion first proposed
- 1909 Construction begins on east addition (Bethune, Bethune & Fuchs)
- 1911 Addition is largely complete
- 1912 Addition is formally opened
- 1913 New marquee for main entrance (now gone); beginning of Esenwein & Johnson involvement
- 1914-1922 Bathroom alterations in original section (Esenwein & Johnson)
- 1916-1917 Ballroom addition (Esenwein & Johnson)
- 1924-1926 South addition, interior alterations (Esenwein & Johnson)
- 1928-1929 New elevators (Esenwein & Johnson)
- 1942 New main lobby installed (Roswell E Pfohl and Design, Inc)
- 1946 Dining room remodeled
- 1952 New windows installed in all guest rooms
- 1962 Sold by Yates family to Carter chain
- 1970 Dropped ceilings installed in main floor spaces
- 1978 Sold by Carter chain to Tran Dinh Truong

The Lafayette's glazed terra cotta roof detail. (Photo: Tania Martin.)

Tellingly, no modifications were noted during the thirty-two years of Tran Dinh Truong's ownership.

The original hotel was constructed on a stone foundation as a steel-frame building with concrete floors. The May 29, 1904 *Buffalo Times* named eighty-eight contractors hired to supply materials, construct, or furnish the Lafayette Hotel, with most structural materials obtained through Western New York or New York City sources. Buffalo Structural Steel Company provided the iron and steel; R. O. Riester of Buffalo supplied leaded glass; John H. Black of Buffalo supplied the dark-red vitreous bricks and terra cotta. Excelsior Terra Cotta Company of New York also brought in the ivory-white, semi-glazed terra cotta that would almost completely sheath the first and seventh floors and the corners of all floors. It would also provide the characteristic French Renaissance Revival decorative motifs of lions' heads, fiery torches, cartouches, and floral details, besides an egg-and-dart belt molding topped by a projecting cornice masking the flat roof with fleur-de-lis garlands and wreathed cartouches. The wrought iron Marquise-carriage porch and window balconies were the work of August Feine of Buffalo; a New York firm, Van Kannel Revolving

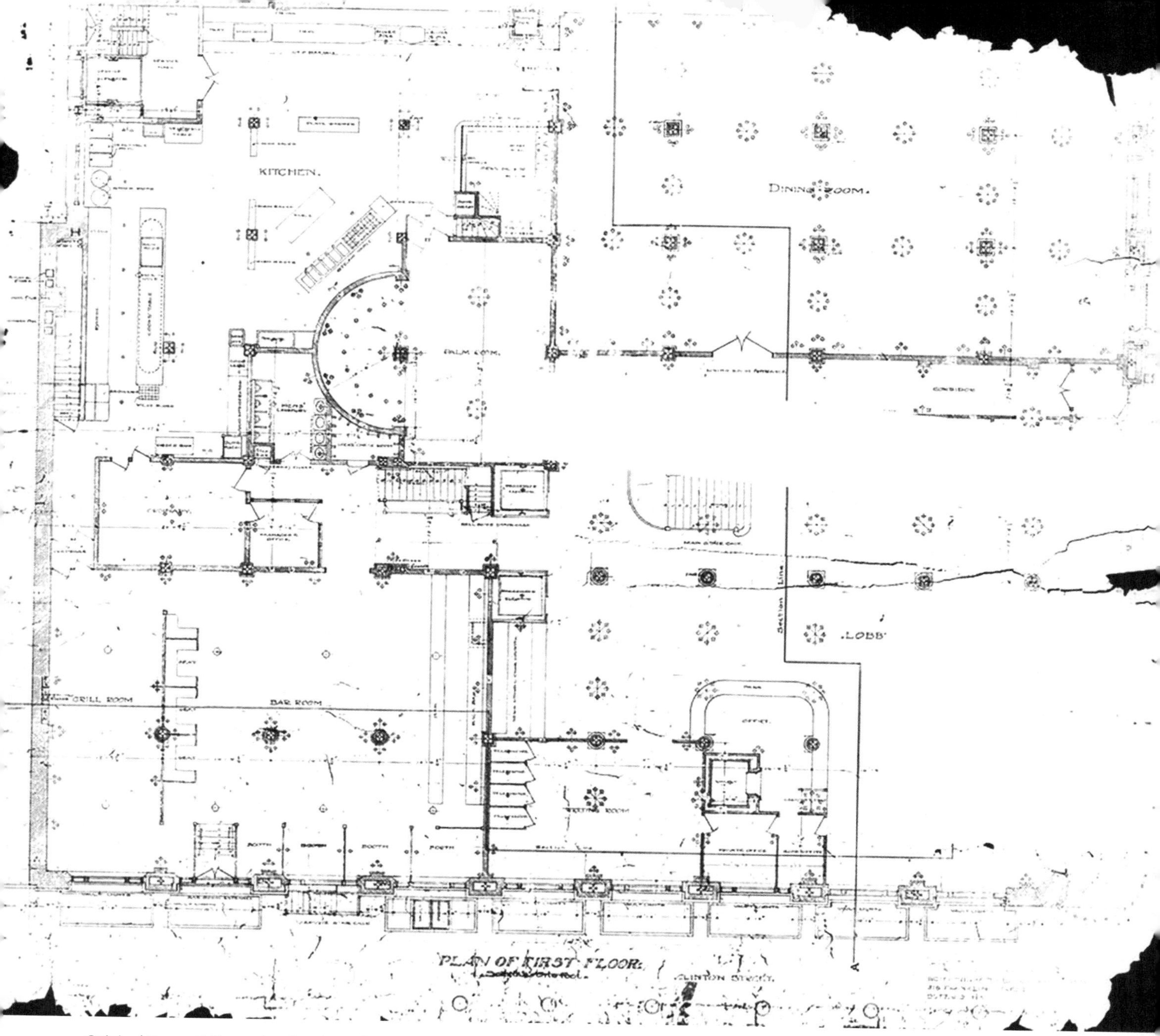

Original Ground Floor plan for the Lafayette Hotel by Bethune, Bethune & Fuchs.

Door Company, supplied the main entrance door at the corner of Washington and Clinton Streets; Buffalo's Byrne & Bannister executed the plain and ornamental plastering; A. K. Gibson, painting and finishing; and Niederpruem, Gibbs & Schaaf Company executed the largest contract, for masonry and carpentry. In an arrangement Robert Bethune described to the press as unusual at that time, the hotel was Buffalo's first large construction site not to employ a general contractor. Instead, the architects assumed responsibilities for arranging and supervising all aspects of each contract, including coordination on site.

On the 1902-1904 Ground Floor Plan, the entrance lobby was adjacent to the Washington Street side of the building, with its centrally placed grand staircase in front of two cage elevators. This center area flowed into a Palm Room, with a newsstand and cigar counter, men's check room, and men's lavatory immediately behind. The business offices, a public writing room with four telephone booths, a Bar Room with booths, and a Grill Room were aligned on the Clinton Street side of the building. On the opposite side of the building, adjacent to the Dining Room facing Washington Street, were a service elevator and the extensive kitchen and service areas. To properly manage a first-class, modern dining experience, the plan indicated placement for a dumbwaiter, work tables, ranges, broilers, a steam table, bain-marie, meat block, cake griddle, stock and vegetable pots, a salad refrigerator, and dish racks and sinks, including a designated salad sink, dish sink, and silver and china sinks.

The Basement Floor Plan included a barbershop, public bathroom, and billiard room for male guests, and for staff there was a baggage room, vegetable storeroom, four refrigerators of varying sizes, a beer cooler and wine room, laundry and dry rooms, slop sink, carpenter and repair shops, boiler room, bathrooms, and servants' kitchen, with separated dining rooms and locker rooms for men and women servants. Placement for lighting was indicated throughout both plans.

The Second and Third Floor Plans showed a few luxury suites offered full bathrooms, including both bath and shower facilities in some or bath alone, to be shared between two suites. All single rooms provided a sink, with one male and one female lavatory placed on every floor. At the time the Lafayette opened, this arrangement of bathroom facilities was considered a luxury for hotels. If the Lafayette's plumbing was Louise Bethune's idea, as would be consistent with her earlier assertion that she took responsibility for the firm's sanitation solutions, she came up with a unique solution that continues to function to this day. Hidden inside some of the free-standing columns in the grandly appointed Neo-Classical lobby, water flowed up and sewage flowed down from the public and individual guests' bathrooms inside pipes encased within vertical shafts that passed through those columns, on its way to and from the city's water and sewer system. This plumbing arrangement continues to function, even to this day. Jonathan Morris, the architect of the recent renovation, said it was the first time he had ever seen such a solution, and it works well. They were able to reuse the pipes inside the column shafts, obtaining permission from the building department to re-line the existing pipes and prolong their useful life.

The Lafayette Hotel featured energy-saving devices, innovative compared to what was present in most high-end hotels of that time: the electric lights in guests' rooms were wired to shut off when patrons closed and locked their doors; the elevators were operated on a unique system using electricity in summer months and steam during winter months; and a central air vacuum system extended to every room and corridor throughout the building, reducing housekeeping costs. Steam-heat radiators were provided in every room, and a gravity-fed ventilation system using airshafts and roof ventilators to draw cool air through the building in a kind of natural air-conditioning system, taking advantage of the basic law that hot air rises. In her 1939 Federal Writers' Project interview, Henrietta Dozier speaks of employing this same system, adding, "It is not as quick as some other much advertised systems, but it is reliable and satisfactory and there is no cost for upkeep—just the original outlay for the initial installation." (An air-conditioning system was installed during the Lafayette's 1940s Art Moderne remodel.) Air vents, still being used today, drew kitchen exhaust fumes out of the building through vaults underneath the sidewalks around the building. If you walk around the outside of the building, you will likely see clouds of steam releasing heat through the sidewalk's iron grates.

The Lafayette Hotel can lay claim to being the first hotel in the city of Buffalo to provide the then-modern amenities of electricity throughout the hotel and hot and cold running water, as well as telephones in every room. Other North American hotels had already claimed to be the very first to be wired with electricity. Thomas Edison must have been a very busy man; he first successfully used a three-wire electric lighting system on July 4, 1881. Amidst the hullabaloo of a brass-band performing marches and cheering residents, Edison personally switched on the current to a hundred-candle-power light mounted over the City Hotel (soon to be renamed the Hotel Edison), in Sunbury, a town in Northumberland County's Susquehanna Valley, Pennsylvania. That same year, Edison supervised arrangements for the first hotel in the world to have an electric light in every room, at Frederic Durant's Prospect House (1881-1915), a six-storey, three-hundred room Adirondack wilderness resort hotel frequented by many of the nation's most influential and wealthy citizens.

The Hotel's Gilded Grand Opening

Billed as the "Gateway to Niagara Falls," the Lafayette Hotel was ranked among the nation's fifteen finest. *The Buffalo Morning Express* (June 2, 1904) gave a detailed account of the grand opening event one night earlier, when "A great throng of well-wishers eagerly took advantage of the opportunity to inspect every department of the hotel." All guests were taken care of by experienced "negro bellboys… selected from New York hotels," as well as "imported" waiters; "30 from New York and six from Cleveland." (No explanation was given for this expense. Perhaps the hotel managers decided no one in Buffalo was sufficiently trained in the protocols of luxury hotel service.)

Investors Mr. and Mrs. Walter B. Duffy were the first guests to register, brought to the party from Rochester by Arthur G. Yates, president of the Buffalo, Rochester & Pittsburgh Railroad Company, via his private railroad car. They presided over the festivities, joined by the other Lafayette Hotel Company stockholders, each of whom had invested twenty-five thousand dollars:

New York hotel man George W. Sweeney, president; Arthur's son, Harry Yates, treasurer; Charles Tracey of Albany; manager Charles J. Spaulding; and Joseph A. Oakes, in charge of food service. The hotelmen were showered with great bouquets of flowers, telegrams, and congratulations from friends and reporters, some of whom arrived in the early evening from New York City.

The *Buffalo Express* reporter praised the interior's décor, designed by a well-respected New York firm, Duryea & Potter. They noted:

> [The main lobby's] walls are lined twelve feet up with exquisite slabs of Numidian marble. The entire ceiling is treated in harmonizing shades of gold. The decorative frieze above the wainscoting is carried out on gold-leaf tapestry. A bronze plaque effect is produced between each panel, giving the profile of General Lafayette and his associated officers. Harmonious drapings and real lace are at each window facing the main lobby and office. The furnishings of the lobby are in genuine rawhide coverings, with bronze-head nails.
>
> The outer restaurant or tapestry dining room is finished in English oak, the panels being in tobacco brown, figured material. The side walls above the oakwork are decorated in genuine Gobelin bordered tapestries. Marble forms the wainscoting, and the columns are in canyon green. The window drapings are in green, trimmed with antique gold galoon. Genuine Arabian laces also set off the windows, the curtains having embroidered on them the Lafayette coat-of-arms.
>
> The inner restaurant is known as the red and gold room, and has oak woodwork, the columns, pilasters and ceiling being also of oak. All the plain surfaces are inlaid with gold leaf. Coffee-brown ename's [*sic*] mark the woodwork in the palmroom, the ornamental work being in gold. The side-wall panels are in silk damask, and secreted electric lights beam forth from the elliptical ceiling, which is done in gold leaf.
>
> The woodwork in the grillroom and bar is Flemish oak. The decorations are on genuine leather, representing different studies of Falstaff, the execution of that work being hand tooled, diverse colors being inserted. The drapings are of leather, and the windows have obscure leaded glass.
>
> The ladies' parlor is decorated with old ivory enameled woodwork. The side walls and drapings are in helitrope [*sic*]-colored silk, the window laces being of the renaissance style. The banquet-room is treated the same as the ladies' parlor, but the color scheme is red.

Another small article in that day's *Express* noted the public particularly praised pianos, made by the Buffalo firm of C. Kurtzmann & Co., with custom wood finishes to match each of the several parlors in which they were placed.

Doubling the Footprint

The original footprint of the Lafayette was about eighteen thousand square feet. *The Buffalo Commercial* of June 20, 1906, reported it cost about one million dollars, including the land, building, and 250,000 dollars for interior furnishings. In 1906, owner Walter B. Duffy bought additional land to extend the hotel east on Clinton Street to Ellicott Street, adding continuous frontage of nearly five hundred feet on Washington, Clinton, and Ellicott Streets. This addition, also designed by Bethune, Bethune & Fuchs, enlarged the Lafayette to about twice its size at a cost of another one million dollars. Walter B. Duffy did not live to celebrate its opening on May, 20, 1912, when *The Buffalo*

Commercial's headline pronounced it "palatial," and even "down to the smallest detail... without a flaw." The ground floor was significantly rearranged, with the kitchen moved to the basement, underneath the main dining room. The carriage entrance, sheltered by a fifty-foot porch, was moved to Clinton Street, where male and female guests entered into the forty-by-fifty-foot Lafayette Room, the principal public parlor, which had been the former Grill Room. It had three large plate glass windows. The *Commercial* described the décor as:

> English domestic style of the Elizabethan period. The soft brown tint in English oak is aptly set off by furnishings and draperies of deep blue... There is a massive carved oak fireplace from Knole House, Sevenoaks, the ancient seat of the archbishops of Canterbury England. Its center panel bears a remarkable painting of the coat-of-arms of the Marquis de la Fayette. This blazon was obtained in Paris and is thought to be the only authentic copy in this country. The coats-of-arms of other heroes of Revolutionary days occupy other panels. A dozen of the prominent hotels in the country have authorized the use of their heraldic emblems on this unique frieze.

The 72 x 84 feet neo-classical lobby of the Lafayette Hotel, finished in Numidian marble and scagliola and mahogany with furniture covered in soft red leather, as it appeared shortly after the hotel opened. As published in the hotel's brochure, circa 1904. (Buffalo History Museum, used by permission.)

One broad doorway led into the lobby, with its elevators and main staircase. The enlarged connecting corridors appeared "materially changed" to this reporter. Another led into the new Orchard Restaurant, said to be favored by female guests for its Tiffany-like motif in pale green, white, and gold, with depictions of orchard scenes. The former carriage entrance was designated to be the men's entrance, and provided easy access to the now ground-floor barbershop, billiard room, and men's lavatories. One new dining room was created in the

The wrought iron canopy over the Clinton Street carriage entrance to the Lafayette Hotel was installed by 1912 during the first addition. (Buffalo History Museum, used by permission.)

basement. To adequately service three restaurants, extensive kitchen modernizations were installed. The Automobile Club, a major commercial rental that continued for decades, was accommodated with a large, ground-floor space. Two hundred rooms were added with the expansion, and each new guestroom was equipped with "a well-appointed bathroom with solid porcelain bath and basin." The heating and electrical plant was moved to an outside brick building on Darrow Alley (demolished in 1961), which supplied power to the hotel through a connecting tunnel.

Prelude of Changes to Come

This was a far cry from the Lafayette Hotel I first saw, during a visit to Buffalo in 2006. I was fortunate to be introduced to the hotel by three women architects, all of whom currently or recently had a practice in Western New York, and all of whom have been active in restoring the name and work of Louise Blanchard Bethune to the historical record. They are Beverly Foit-Albert, founder, CEO, and then-president of Foit-Albert Associates, an architecture, engineering, and surveying firm; Adriana Barbasch, recently retired Fellow of the American Institute of Architects; and Kelly Hayes McAlonie, then Education Chair of the Buffalo/Western New York Chapter of the AIA, who served as 2012 President AIANYS, and is currently Director of the Capital Planning Group, University of Buffalo.

We met in front of the Lafayette Hotel, during the time when the building's fate was uncertain at best. Although the exterior had remained largely intact, it was evident the hotel had seen better days. In fact it was hard to conceive that the Lafayette could once have been honestly described as "the best that science, art and experience can offer for the comfort of the traveling public." However, something about the building would keep bringing me back—something about the way it sits, angled just so into its site, looking "delicious," as my daughter Tennessee with her poet's eye says, "like a red-velvet layer cake."

Later I would learn the details of what was sensed at that first look—how the hotel's decline had paralleled the city's financial decline, as investments in the hotel's maintenance, sixty years and onward after its opening, could not have been intended to maintain the building as a "luxury hotel."

The Founding Families

For the first sixty years, the business of the hotel was primarily owned by three generations of the Duffy and Yates families, through their majority control of stocks in the Lafayette Hotel Corporation. When the hotel's corporation was organized in 1903, it issued six thousand shares of non-cumulative preferred stock and two thousand shares of one dollar par common stock, according to the April 9, 1957 *Buffalo Evening News*.

In the 1870s, Walter B. Duffy built his fortune upon his inheritance of his father's cider-refining business, and by the early 1880s was listed in the Rochester City Directory as a "Distiller & Rectifier of Alcohol, French Spirits, Malt, wheat, Rye and Bourbon whiskies." The company had two distilleries in Lexington, one in Baltimore, and another in Waterloo, New York. In pre-Prohibition times and even during the Prohibition era, when it was common to advertise liquor as a "medicine," the company created a popular product in their "Duffy's Pure Malt Whiskey," patented and advertised nationwide in newspapers by 1886 as "the greatest known heart tonic." One Duffy's ad showed a man looking like a medieval alchemist examining a vial. The ad copy asked, "If you have not tried it why not? DRUGGISTS AND GROCERS keep it." Among his other business interests, Duffy was president of the American Fruit Products Company, a stockholder in the National Hotel Company (which owned the Rochester Hotel), a director of the German Insurance Co., and owner of the Sam Shubert and Rochester theaters, all located in Rochester.

Arthur G. Yates (1843-1909) headed the Yates family, which owned bituminous coal mines in Pennsylvania and also the Buffalo, Rochester & Pittsburgh Railroad, the railroad on which much of this coal was shipped. They were regarded as one of the Northeast's leading coal traders. In 1891, the Duffy and Yates families had been united by the marriage of Harry Yates and Walter and Teresa Duffy's eldest daughter, Mary. When Duffy talked Harry into being the hotel's chief financial officer, he was already director of the Rochester-Pittsburgh Coal Co., the American Steamship Company, the Liberty Bank of Buffalo, and a chief stockholder in New York City's Commodore Hotel, now Donald Trump's Grand Hyatt. At the time of his death at age eighty-six in 1956, he was a former chairman of the board of the Buffalo and Fort Erie Public Bridge Authority, which supervises the Peace Bridge, and current chairman of the board of the Lafayette Hotel Corporation. His wife, Mary, died nine months later, in October 1956. At the time of their deaths the family still maintained controlling shares in the Lafayette Hotel Company.

After Walter B. Duffy died on January 14, 1911, Harry Yates became the principal director of the Lafayette Hotel Company. Between 1913 and 1937, they hired the Buffalo firm of Esenwein & Johnson to preside over various renovations and two significant additions, constructed between 1916-1917 and 1924-1926. Both of these additions maintained the basic design elements established by Bethune, Bethune & Fuchs, while expanding the hotel to its present size. By 1917, they had completed the Neo-Classical grand ballroom, the Lafayette's largest public space, inside a two and three-storey addition that lengthened the building on its southeastern corner. Ongoing major alterations in the original building's bathroom accommodations provided all guestrooms with self-contained baths and/or showers, and replaced each floor's communal bathrooms with new guest rooms. Esenwein & Johnson's interior changes also removed the skylight and its grand staircase from their dominant position in the center of the lobby. Between 1928 and 1929, the original hydraulic, open-cage Otis steel elevators and elevator shafts were filled in. New shafts were constructed on the lobby's southeast, aligned with the Washington Street entrance, where two electric Otis elevators were installed, their bronze frames and doors handsome in their Art Deco detailing; they have remained in this location since that change. In the 1930s, more hotel rooms were created in a seven-storey addition on the south, which also changed a billiard room on the ground floor into a bar. Known as Lafayette Tap Room, this was the first Buffalo hotel bar to open after the repeal of Prohibition in 1933. The Lafayette's 2010 National Register of Historic Places application describes the additions as "simpler" or "more restrained in

The Lafayette Hotel's 1940s Art Moderne-styled lobby renovation, as it appeared in 1980. (Buffalo History Museum, used by permission.)

design than that used on the earlier building, but nonetheless in sympathy to the original building."

The third major remodel, from 1942 to 1946, was designed by Buffalo-based architect Roswell E. Pfohl, with Earl Davenport, Vice President of the St. Louis firm Design, Inc., as general contractor. The lobby was transformed from its original Neo-Classical style into a streamlined Art Moderne style, similar to how it appears now, after undergoing the most recent preservation effort. New flooring was installed of terrazzo, a durable composite material with origins in Neolithic times that, because less expensive than marble, became popular in fifteenth-century Venice and Beaux-Arts architecture. Most dramatically, the scagliola columns and wainscoting were covered with plaster and painted, and a dropped ceiling eliminated the beams and plaster detailing.

Buffalo was enjoying its second heyday in the 1940s. Five billion dollars in war-supply contracts created plenty of jobs at fifteen shipyards, the country's largest aircraft industry, a major railroad hub, and steel mills, the main economic engine of Buffalo's World War II and postwar growth. The influx of migrant workers who came to Buffalo looking for defense industry jobs during World War II included many Southern blacks, such as my partner's mother and stepfather. Bethlehem-Lackawanna Steel alone, the world's biggest steel-making operation, was able to employ twenty thousand workers.

Buffalo's population peaked in 1950 at 580,000. Between 1950 and 1960, assisted by G.I. Bill educations, first-home subsidies, and roads built with 1956 Federal Highway Act funding, nearly eighty thousand white Buffalonians moved out to suburbs, in a pattern of "white flight" happening around the country. As Buffalo's population shrank, so did its economy. Key manufacturing plants began to leave, relocating to build new plants where they could pay lower taxes and wages, never to return. Bethune's prestigious former client, Spencer Kellogg, was among those who closed their businesses forever. His linseed oil processing plant had been the largest in the U.S. The slow beginning of the hotel's downward spiral paralleled these changes going on in Buffalo.

In 1952, the Lafayette's "modernization" program, costing about three hundred thousand dollars, was intended to update or renovate what now totaled 370 guest rooms, including metal replacements of wood window frames. However, to my eye, which admittedly has trouble appreciating 1950s decor, archival photographs of guest rooms during this era suggest the hotel's luxury category shifted toward a more practical, affordable, "business class" model.

By the 1960s, people stopped having reasons to come downtown, attracted by new suburban malls instead of the city's department stores. Downtown's live theaters and movie houses closed as televisions transformed home entertainment. These were patterns happening throughout North America. Another serious blow to the downtown core was the decision to expand and relocate the University of Buffalo's main campus to Amherst, a Buffalo suburb, in the late 1960s. In their November 27, 2013 article, "Renewing Economically Distressed American Communities," on the website *Issues in Science and Technology*, Michael Greenstone and Adam Looney describe:

> [T]hree harsh recessions between 1969 and 1982 pushed Buffalo and many other manufacturing-based cities off the path to prosperity. During each recession, manufacturing employment in the United States plummeted by between 9 and 15%. These were not temporary layoffs; jobs disappeared, shifts shrank, and plants closed. Buffalo's steel mill, which had employed 20,000 workers in 1965, was shuttered completely in 1982. That year, unemployment in the Buffalo area, which had been well below the national average for at least a decade, topped 12%. Local income, which was more than 6% above the national average in 1970, is today 9% below the average. When jobs disappeared, so did workers—in droves. By 2000, Buffalo's population had fallen by half. Property values dropped, and neighborhoods crumbled into disrepair, pocked with abandoned homes. More than a quarter of the city's residents lived in poverty.

From A Residence of Presidents to a Crack House

Under the Duffy and Yates families' watch, the Lafayette had managed to keep up with the times. Its downward spiral started to accelerate in 1962, when they sold the hotel to Hyman B. Cantor (1902-1980), owner of the Carter Hotels Corporation, which included hotels in New York City, Boston, Albany, and New Haven, in addition to Buffalo's Lafayette. Mr. Cantor wanted to make the Lafayette affordable for business travelers without a "large expense account." Unsuccessful in securing a twenty-million-dollar loan to achieve this goal, he nonetheless made significant changes during his tenure, which likely represented savings in terms of heating and cooling fees and general maintenance. However, in design terms, these measures worked against the Lafayette's charms. For instance, by installing dropped ceilings in the public rooms and passageways, it effectively covered over much of the original, elegant detailing that remained after the 1940s remodel, and reduced volume, a major ingredient when creating a luxurious atmosphere. Luckily for the hotel, just as the standard linoleum flooring Cantor had installed protected the original marble, tile, and wood parquet floorings, these changes also meant that the overall integrity of the building was still there, just covered over, and this was to prove very fortuitous in the long run.

In October 1977, the Carter chain sold New York's Carter Hotel to the Lavan Hotel Corporation, headed by the late Tran Dinh Truong (1932-2012), a Vietnamese-born businessman who had become a business partner of Cantor. In 1978, the Carter chain also sold the Lafayette to Mr. Truong. As someone who was born and grew up in Vietnam during its French colonial era, his attraction to the Lafayette made sense to me.

Tran Dinh Truong was the former CEO, chairman, and principal owner of the Vishipco Line, South Vietnam's largest shipping company. He frequently claimed his company's twenty-four commercial ships and hundreds of trucks rescued U.S. civilians and military stranded in remote parts of South Vietnam as the war was coming to an end, until the day before Saigon fell in 1975. This was when he and his family also found it necessary to leave everything behind except two suitcases, one filled with U.S. currency and the other with gold, variously claimed to be worth around one million or seven million dollars. Mr. Truong and his family eventually made their way to the United States in 1975.

Mr. Truong's humanitarian claims were refuted in two articles in *The New York Times*, posted July 5, 1994, and July 6, 1994, except for the detail about carrying gold on his U.S. arrival, which explains how he was able to purchase so much real estate. The former article quoted Kiem Do, former deputy chief of staff in the South Vietnamese Navy, who stated Mr. Truong "'operated there as he has in New York. He thinks with money and resourcefulness he can get away with anything… He was a war profiteer. But now the war is over.'"

Under the umbrella of his Lavan Hotel Corporation, Mr. Truong bought his first hotel, the Hotel Opera, in New York City's Upper West Side, after which he bought other New York City hotels, including the Hotel Carter, the Times Square Hotel, and the Kenmore, where back in the day, Dashiell Hammett lived and Nathanael West worked as a night manager. When Mr. Truong purchased the Lafayette, he stated he wanted to invest ten million dollars in a major renovation, but after convoluted twists and turns, this plan went nowhere.

As I suspected, the two *New York Times* articles, by Seth Faison with Jo Thomas also credited for the July 6 article, confirmed in copious detail that his *modus operandi*, not only in Buffalo but also in New York City, was to buy run-down hotels and deliberately keep them in that condition or worse, while harboring criminals, prostitutes, and addicts. Then the hotels were changed into housing for welfare and homeless tenants, for which cities paid high rentals, while LaVan Hotel Corporation would continue to cut operating costs by skimping on maintenance, repairs, and security so that crime still flourished. It went to such an extent that Truong was regularly fined in New York City and by 1983 was sued by the city for failures to correct health, safety, and building code violations. My suspicions were confirmed July 3, 2014, when a scandal involving the Kenmore Hotel was exposed by *The New York Times'* article, "Takeover of a Hotel: An Informer Recalls his Complicity." At the Kenmore, where there were 1899 narcotics arrests between January 1991 and mid-1994, and where crack dealers were known to rob and even kill older tenants for their cash, police and FBI informant Earl Robert Merritt revealed, "My main job was to hand out cash envelopes to the building and elevator inspectors… The only thing they inspected was their envelopes." Quoted in 1994 that he hadn't "taken a day off in 19 years," Mr. Truong had to be aware of all this as he lived out his days in three rooms at the Carter, which TripAdvisor's website voted for three consecutive years "the dirtiest hotel in America." This informant's revelations of setting up tenants for false arrests have led to speculations as to how many poor Hispanics and black were framed due to policies of the former Giuliani and Bloomberg administrations, and how many unscrupulous hotel owners cooperated with this corruption.

Somehow Mr. Truong made a lot of money even though the Lafayette Hotel and the other Cantor/Truong hotel properties were said to sometimes operate at a loss. Like Mr. Cantor, whose *New York Times* obituary (October 9, 1980) featured his philanthropic work through his H. B. Cantor Foundation's support of the United Jewish Appeal, the Grand Street Boys' Association, the New York Microscopical Society, and Lincoln Center for the Performing Arts, Mr. Truong represented himself as someone who was doing the right thing by "taking care of so many poor and homeless." Truong's most touted humanitarian gesture was a two-million-dollar donation to The American Red Cross Disaster Relief Fund after the September 11, 2001 terrorist attacks, their largest single donation ever received at that time. Mr. Truong also provided two hundred Hotel Carter rooms for five months, for use by rescue workers, firemen, and others involved in relief work, for which he was given a Vietnamese American's Golden Torch Award, as featured in his *Times*' death notice (May 14, 2012). Evidently his "covers" worked, at least until July 27, 2014, when in a lengthy *New York Times'* article entitled "Sifting a Messy Life and Legacy," the career of the man who nearly destroyed Louise Bethune's legacy was exposed before a world audience. This article was occasioned by legal battles being waged among the sixteen children and five wives or mistresses who all claim their rights to inherit Mr. Truong's one-hundred-million-dollar estate, left without a will.

However, even on that 2006 visit, I could see traces of the grand lady's glorious past in spite of the deteriorating façade's broken cast-iron balconies, chipped stonework, and the cobalt blue paint wrapping the base of the building and interrupting the integrity of the red and white motif so central to Bethune's original, elegant styling. I imagined the graceful, curved canopy that created an ornate passageway through the revolving door of the original main entrance at the intersection of Washington and Clinton Streets, anticipating guests' deluxe expectations. It had been removed in the 1940s, at the time of the Art Moderne remodel, when a side entrance on Washington Street became the new main entrance, signified by an incongruously hard-edged, flat, rectangular aluminum awning installed during a 1956 remodel. With white plastic letters spelling "Hotel Lafayette," it likely quashed anyone's excitement. As Jonathan Morris, the architect of the 2010-2012 renovation described to me later, the hotel "was in really rough shape."

When the three women architects and I entered the main lobby, we could see it had been stripped of most of its opulent past. Though painted white, it still maintained the Bethunes' eight original free-standing smooth columns with Numidian marble column bases. Instead of elaborately detailed plasterwork surrounding a high coffered ceiling, the smoothly surfaced ceiling was from the lobby's 1942 Art Moderne remodel by Roswell E. Pfohl, when it was lowered and its recessed center indirectly lit from a decorative ledge surrounding the room. The lobby's polished, polychromatic terrazzo floor also remained from the 1940s remodel, and its curving, geometric pattern in glittery green, gold, and white still functioned to lead guests from the Washington Street entranceway to the brass elevators with a bit of flair. The Fronterra mahogany-paneled walls and entrance desk were other remnants of the 1940s renovation, as were two handsome murals assembled using various types of inlaid woods in a technique known as intarsia, similar to marquetry. Hung on opposite sides of the lobby, their Art Deco style was a perfect fit for images of what were then the latest modes of transportation: on the south wall, with an Army propeller plane flying over Buffalo airport; on the north wall, with lake freighters dwarfed by a bank of grain elevators lining the Buffalo River.

Intarsia mural of grain elevators and a boat on the Buffalo River, displayed on the south wall of the Lafayette's lobby since circa 1940s. (Photo, Tennessee Reed.)

Even though we had telephoned ahead to request a tour of the building, when we asked the front desk clerk, Gideon, to view other parts of the interior, we were told we would have to check with the then-manager, Hung Thi Nguyen, one of five women with claims to being Mr. Truong's partner or wife. Ms. Nguyen lived with her family in the hotel's most commodious apartment, one floor above the original corner entrance that from the exterior exhibited the most elaborate wrought iron balcony. (This apartment has been designated as the bridal suite in the present renovation.) When I phoned later that day, the desk clerk on duty told me Ms. Nguyen had turned down our request, an evasion that aroused our suspicions—suspicions that would become facts-based.

Gideon had described his fascination with details glimpsed in its basement. Not being allowed past the lobby and main hallway, I was left to imagine what I had read in reports of the hotel's early days. The fabled crystal chandelier-hung grand ballroom, added to the original structure in 1917 by Esenwein & Johnson, was still being used in the 1970s, according to Bonnie Foit-Albert, when it was adapted by an architecture firm for their office space.

Also, in the 1970s, *Hot L Baltimore*, an award-winning play by Lanford Wilson that premiered in 1973 and later became a hit TV comedy series, is reported to have been inspired by Mr. Wilson's protracted stay at the Lafayette Hotel while working on a project with a local theater company. Probably reflecting his observations of the "outsiders'" world of the hotel's inhabitants, two of the play's characters are prostitutes (one of whom is an illegal immigrant), and it featured one of the first gay couples seen on an American television series.

I continued to hear one positive memory from various Buffalonians, black and white, of good times in the Lafayette Tap Room. That space is now called the Tap Room and serves beer made from scratch on-site. But from 1998 until 2010, it was a blues bar, established by local investors Dominic N. Puntoriero and Bill Barrons. With its own entrance on Washington Street, people enjoyed live jazz and blues bands, both local and national, in a high-ceilinged, long rectangular space featuring a vintage oak bar and mosaic tile flooring, whose separate street entrance kept them from witnessing happenings inside the rest of the Lafayette complex.

Once the stopover choice of Presidents Woodrow Wilson and Franklin D. Roosevelt, Governor Alfred E. Smith, movie stars, and longtime leader of the American Federation of Labor Samuel Gompers, the hotel, like the city itself, had fallen upon hard times; it had become a crack house. Buffalo's Mayor Byron W. Brown, whom I interviewed in 2006, confirmed the building had been cited by the city for committing a number of code violations, and some tenants had been evicted for engaging in criminal activities or having substance-abuse problems.

Rescuing the Fallen Lady and Other Buffalo Architectural Gems

Mayor Brown gave me an update on the hotel's story when I returned to Buffalo in the summer of 2007, as did architect Clinton E. Brown, who had recently filed an application with the United States Department of the Interior's National Park Service to gain historic preservation certification for the hotel. This time we were allowed to tour the hotel's long halls on upper floors, entering guestrooms undergoing basic maintenance upgrades necessary to be in compliance with current building codes. We observed repairs to correct deterioration of window frames, to replace faulty plumbing that had caused significant water damage to walls and ceilings, and stained and worn carpeting removed that was long past its prime. The hotel still had some tenants, but those who were causing disturbances had already been evicted, and Clinton Brown was proposing ways to generate income for the hotel, such as promoting its use by students and overseas travelers as a good bargain base when touring Niagara Falls and other sights in the region.

Clinton E. Brown's June, 2008 update on the Hotel Lafayette did not sound as upbeat. He stated that at present, "we are not involved in and do not know of any work underway," and his office's efforts to achieve historic preservation certification had only achieved Part I approval—certification that the Hotel Lafayette was historic for tax purposes. So the question remained as to whether it would be possible to continue to salvage and restore this historical hotel—historical not only because of its style and its period, but because of Mrs. Bethune.

In their discussion of Buffalo's architectural legacy, Beverly Foit-Albert, Adriana Barbasch, and Kelly Hayes McAlonie stated that buildings in Buffalo designed by famous male architects are considered prime examples of their work. Their assessment was confirmed by a *New York Times* quote in the city's official visitors' guide, describing Buffalo as "a textbook for a course in modern American buildings." In fact, Buffalo has come to embrace the amazing variety of its architectural heritage, and now features the city as an architectural museum in its tourist literature and well-researched websites.

As is true of many North American cities, until recently Buffalo had a history of not even preserving many of their internationally respected architectural gems. Buildings designed by out-of-towners, including H. H. Richardson and McKim, Mead & White, along with those by esteemed local architects, including Louise Bethune, were torn down. Most famously, Frank Lloyd Wright's Larkin Administration Building, built in 1904 to great acclaim for its innovative design (a central atrium surrounded by tiered floors of offices with coordinated interiors of built-in cabinets and futuristic metal office furniture), was demolished in 1950. Acquired in tax forfeiture by the City of Buffalo, it remains to this day an empty lot—except of course that it functions as a parking lot. As Elson Strahan explained to Tania and me in Vancouver, Washington—where the same land use pattern can be observed—it is hard to transform a parking lot into a built structure, as parking lots are low-maintenance "cash cows." Rocco Termini gave basically the same explanation for what we saw in Buffalo, with Tania adding that this maxim holds true in most every North American city. However, perhaps because of Buffalo's colossally embarrassing mistake, Wright's only example of a multi-residential Prairie house structure, the 1905 Darwin D. Martin House Complex, has been restored to its original glory through financing by a group of private Buffalo citizens who understood the importance of its preservation. Another citizens' preservation group long championed restoration of the Richardson Olmsted Complex (formerly Buffalo State Asylum for the Insane, built 1870-1896), the twin-towered red medina sandstone, Romanesque castle-like assemblage of buildings that was designed by Henry Hobson Richardson (1838-1886) with its surrounding two hundred acres landscaped by Frederick Law Olmsted and Calvert Vaux. Noted as the first example of Richardson's personalized revival of French Romanesque style and since 1986 a National Historic Landmark, its conversion into a hotel, conference, event, and architecture center is projected to be completed in 2016.

The turnaround has been so dramatic that in April 2013, the Society of Architectural Historians (SAH) held their sixty-sixth annual conference in Buffalo, focusing on how Buffalo uses preservation as "a tool for long-term urban, cultural and economic sustainability." Canadian-born Despina Stratigakos, University of Buffalo associate professor of architecture and one of the conference's local co-chairs, explained:

> After arriving in Buffalo, I kept telling people elsewhere what an incredible city it is in terms of the architecture and the planning idea—the creative past and continuing spirit—and at a certain point, I realized that it really has to be seen, in a way, to be absorbed… Buffalo has many architectural gems, but more than that, there's a very interesting, radical history here of innovation. SAH has never been to Buffalo in its 65 years of holding meetings, and the last time the conference was held in New York State was in the 1960s, so it's a big deal that this event is coming to town.

While many of these male architects have gained worldwide attention and are the subjects of copious books, papers, and articles, Louise Blanchard Bethune and her accomplishments have received little national notice until recently, other than the AIA's prominent acknowledgement of her "firsts" on its website. This is evidently not a recent problem, for when the Thursday, June 2, 1904 *New York Times* headline announced in bold, "BUFFALO HOTEL OPENED. The Lafayette, $1,000,000 Structure, One of the Handsomest in the Country," the article, with most admiring tone and here quoted in entirety, failed to mention the name of the primary architect or her firm.

> BUFFALO, June 1. The Hotel Lafayette, one of the most perfectly appointed and magnificent hotels in this country, was formally opened to the public today. It was built by Walter B. Duffy, a Rochester capitalist, at the cost of more than $1,000,000.
>
> George W. Sweeney, proprietor of the Victoria Hotel, of New York, and President of the Hotel Men's Association, is President of the company which has leased the hotel for twenty-one years. It will be conducted by Spalding & Oakes.
>
> The Lafayette is located at Washington and Clinton Streets, facing Lafayette Square. It is seven stories high, and is French Renaissance in style.
>
> The lobby is finished in red Numidian marble, scagliola, and fronterra mahogany. The Transportation Club of Buffalo has retained the entire seventh floor for club rooms.
>
> Many well-known men participated in the opening of the hotel.

The Nineteenth-Century Luxury Hotel as a Model for Modern Living

From today's vantage point, it is hard to imagine the excitement surrounding the development of luxury hotels in nineteenth and early-twentieth-century North America. The first real hotel in the U.S. was Boston's Tremont House. When it opened in 1829, it naturally established many of the "firsts" in the types of amenities travelers have come to expect from hotels, including bellboys (who were known as Rotunda Men at the Tremont), room keys to provide guests with privacy, inside water closets rather than outhouses, menu cards, and a room designated for the ladies (which in this case was a Reading Room, a nod to Victorian conventions demanding "proper" women never appear alone in public spaces). In 1846, Boston's Eastern

Exchange Hotel provided the first central heating system; in 1882, New York's Hotel Everett was the first in that city to be equipped with electric lighting; and when the Fifth Avenue Hotel opened in 1859, about which an 1892 *King's Handbook of New York* claimed, "No single hotel in the world has ever entertained so many distinguished people...," they installed a "perpendicular railway," said to be the first hotel passenger elevator in the world.

In the hospitality business, competition was fierce, and the stakes high. To create excitement that attracted visitors, "the standards of the rich man's townhouse have been transferred to a hotel, and have in some respects been transcended," according to Arthur C. David in his article, "The St. Regis: The Best Type of Metropolitan Hotel," which appeared in the *Architectural Record*, Vol. 15, June 1904. By the 1870s, many hotels became apartment hotels, as they offered the option of permanent residency to those seeking the conveniences of a hotel or to rise from the middle class though not yet able to afford a single-family dwelling with an upscale address.

All these new, utilitarian conveniences and comforts, however delightful, needed to be packaged in a total environment elaborately and elegantly appointed on a scale grand enough to knock your socks off. Unless you were among the Modernists in agreement with Frank Lloyd Wright, who said that, "For five hundred years, architecture has been phony," for most tastes, that agenda could best be fulfilled by long-tested manipulations of historic styles, the academic heritage of "Neo-Classical" or "Renaissance Revival" endorsed and preserved by the École des Beaux-Arts in Paris. Tellingly, Beaux-Arts philosophy defined architecture as "the public building," as architectural historian Ada Louise Huxtable explained in her essay "Beaux Arts—the Latest Avant-Garde":

> These ideals are based on prescribed and elaborate rules of formal classical design. In beaux arts practice, the work was judged by composition—the relationship between exterior volumes and interior spaces; by *parti*—the way in which the plan was resolved; and by *marche*—the quality of the progression of the spaces as one imagined walking through them. Plans were usually axial and symmetrical.

Paradoxically, though the École was a rigid bastion of conservative orthodoxy, the effect of a building created using Beaux-Arts principals, when well executed, was more likely to conjure up feelings of romanticism and joy. In any one hotel, to achieve the maximum degree of exuberance, it was common to mix historical influences. The style of a hotel's exterior could differ from décors of its interior's public rooms, where variations might employ their rendition of "Elizabethan British" or "Italian Renaissance," "Greek Revival" or "Medieval" like interiors, each difference a convenient way to help guests distinguish between the many public spaces such as reception halls, tea rooms and other dining rooms, reading or writing rooms, and banquet or ballrooms. Staged to perfection, like theater or movie sets, each room's unique glamour or fantasy was created through blending coordinated colors, shapes, and textures. This could involve the fabrics chosen for upholstery and layers of draperies; hand-painted or gilded ceilings and walls (sometimes including murals or frescoes); the patterned intricacies possible with wood and tile flooring or carpets; the qualities and colors of different woods for wainscoting and furniture; the ornamental details of ceramic or brass knickknacks or plantings; and very importantly the amount and quality of light filling the space either from natural daylight or perfectly chosen electric lighting fixtures. Public spaces designated for men included a barber shop, smoking room, club room, and billiard room; for ladies, a particular parlor and reception room, and sometimes even a separate entranceway because no matter how grand a hotel's design, separation by gender continued to be expected even a decade beyond the turn of the twentieth century.

Although Bethune never studied at the École des Beaux-Arts in Paris, she had at least spent many evenings studying their texts in Waite's library while she was his assistant, and she proved how profoundly she understood how to achieve all of their historical revival styles in the most elaborate design of her career, for the Lafayette. In her "Women and Architecture" address, Bethune waxed eloquent on the value of:

> [T]he antiquity of the model as a means of architectural representation or vehicle of design; its great value in the centuries before linear perspective was understood, and its final almost total disuse upon the adoption of the more intricate varieties of mechanical drawing. In fact the abandonment of the model may be said to mark the line of separation between the amateur and the professional architect. Its use today would spare the blushing novice much confusion, particularly in that shibboleth of all amateurs, the staircase.

In my 2006 conversation with architects Adriana Barbasch and Kelly Hayes McAlonie, Ms. Barbasch felt Bethune "was inspired by proportion." Kelly Hayes McAlonie added that "she was very client-conscious, so I have a feeling that a lot of it came from collaboration with clients. I'm sure the Lafayette Hotel's owners had very strong opinions." Certainly Buffalo School Superintendent James F. Crooker did, as he expressed in his annual reports, specifying what he wanted to achieve with new school designs from the Bethunes.

While working out her Lafayette design, Louise Bethune is thought to have made a survey of some of those fourteen other American luxury hotels of the day. Most were located in major cities of the Northeast, but they were scattered across the entire nation, to San Francisco's Palace (1875-1906, rebuilt after the earthquake and fires, 1909) and San Diego's Hotel del Coronado (1891). Canada's premier grand hotel of the day was Montreal's Second Empire-styled Windsor (opened 1878 and currently converted into an office building, Le Windsor). Robert Bethune undoubtedly visited Cleveland's most luxurious hotel, the Hollenden Hotel, when the AIA held its 1903 convention there, although Louise Bethune did not attend. Completed in 1885 and designed by Cleveland architect George F. Hammond, the Hollenden (closed in 1962, and demolished) was considered a technological marvel in its time because it was fireproof, with every one of its one thousand guestrooms equipped with electric lights, and one hundred guest rooms providing private baths. The interior public spaces included paneled walls, redwood and mahogany fittings, and crystal chandeliers, and offered bars and clubs, a theater, and a barbershop.

It is not known what other hotels either of the Bethunes actually visited, but it is likely they had at least seen photographs or drawings of the second

Palmer House, completed in 1875, or possibly had visited it when Mrs. Bethune attended a WAA meeting in Chicago in 1886. Designed by John Van Osdel, the Palmer House was seven storeys high and was set into its site with its main entrance visually aligned at the intersection of two streets, and with its two other entrances placed in the middle of the façades on those adjoining streets. Its markedly similar orientation to the original Lafayette can be found in other North American buildings from this period. To sustain excitement upon entering its luxuriously generous public spaces, the Palace employed a carpeted grand staircase, centered in the rear of the lobby, framed by two pairs of Corinthian columns of real or faux marble, and overhead, splendidly decorated plasterwork on the ceilings. Similarly, the placement of the Palmer House's staircase at the rear of the lobby, preceded by columns and elaborate plasterwork, were all central to the grand effects present in the original Lafayette Hotel's lobby. Like Van Osdel, Bethune mixed revival styles throughout the public rooms in her original hotel's design. Within her French Renaissance exterior, for instance, Bethune inserted dark oak vaulted ceilings and Welsh tiling to summon up the "man cave" effect of the Lafayette's English pub-style Grill Room, and the Elizabethan period was referenced for the main parlor for men and women, the Lafayette Room.

Corinthian capital topping a column in Bethune's ballroom/banquet room. (Photo, Tennessee Reed.)

The renovated Lafayette has restored much of the glory of its grand hallway linking the lobby to most of the ground-floor restaurants, restrooms, public event spaces, formal banquet halls, and ballrooms. Called Peacock Alley, this name often identified passageways adjacent to the main lobbies of opulent hotels, and was so named because they were popularly used as a promenade space where people, displayed in all their finery, could see and be seen. There is a Peacock Alley in Washington, D.C.'s Willard Intercontinental (Henry Janeway Hardenbergh, 1902) and another in Hardenbergh's German or Dutch Renaissance revival design for the Astoria Hotel (1897, between 33rd and 34th Streets on Fifth Avenue's west side, later adjoined as the Waldorf-Astoria, and demolished in 1929 to build the Empire State Building). Black-and-white photos of the Waldorf-Astoria's Peacock Alley display architectural details that are distinctly similar to the Hotel Lafayette's, as both create their sumptuous warmth and elegance with mosaic tile flooring, recessed and ornately decorated ceilings from which hang brass and glass ball chandeliers, and especially walls of marbled wainscoting lined with Romanesque Corinthian pilasters and columns. The Waldorf-Astoria's varying shades of ivory-colored wainscoting, pilasters, and columns were said to be carved from actual northern Russian marble, rather than the faux technique applied at the Lafayette, called scagliola, which was made from a paste of burnt red-to-rust-hued pigment mixed with plaster and sizing or glue. The Lafayette's first interior designers, Duryea and Potter, who collaborated with Bethune, Bethune & Fuchs, may have suggested these darker colors to effectively hide the ubiquitous oily soot emanating from gasoline-powered motorcycles and automobiles, an increasingly popular means of private transportation. Early photographs of the Lafayette's exterior, however, show horse-and-carriage liveries on the square, which could be hired, for example, to bring guests from a train station to the carriage entrance of the hotel, and continued to be a common sight on Buffalo streets for some time. Of course, the designers were correct; automobiles were about to become the vehicle of choice, likely to be coveted by those who had the wherewithal to arrive at the doorstep of a luxury hotel. In 1901, Oldsmobile's Olds Motor Vehicle Co. sold six hundred cars. By 1904, the year the Lafayette opened, sales had increased tenfold, and Cadillacs, Wintons, and Fords had started up production, as well as the pricey "Great Arrow" by the Buffalo-based Pierce Arrow Motor Car Company, manufacturer of some of the world's finest cars. By the 1910s, the number of automobiles on the road would exceed the number of buggies.

The Lafayette Hotel lobby's original elevator and grand staircase, as designed by Bethune, Bethune and Fuchs, led to the women's parlor and grand banquet hall. As published in the hotel's brochure, circa 1904. (Buffalo History Museum, used by permission.)

In spite of its many charms and confections, the Lafayette's design manages what to my modern eye is a welcome restraint from the over-ornamentation of some Gilded Age Renaissance Revival buildings. A sensibility of utilitarian simplicity and directness appears to be inherent to all the works of this architect. Besides, as Bethune was known to complete projects within or even under their budget projections, her designs likely reflected the given constraints of the projects' financial realities: a city the size of Buffalo would probably not be able to sustain support for as extravagantly over-the-top a spectacle as could be possible in a New York or Chicago hotel. Tellingly, buried in an old file box of the Lafayette's financial records now at the Buffalo Historical Society are typed orders for kitchen equipment to be delivered and installed during construction of the first addition. A comparison of the initial quote and a second quote requested by Bethune, Bethune & Fuchs shows that the revised budget came back with a considerably reduced price tag, with one-third of the equipment initially itemized by the vendor stripped away. The second quote got approved.

In fact, luxury hotels such as the Lafayette pushed the envelope for what comforts of modernization people began to desire and even expect in terms of indoor plumbing, electricity, air conditioning, and telephones—not only in hotels, but in their homes as well. This was why, between 1914 and 1922, the Lafayette felt the necessity of undertaking renovations, in response to the latest amenities in hotel living offered by Buffalo's Hotel Statler, the first hotel in town to offer a self-contained bathroom in every guestroom. Built at the corner of Swan and Washington Streets by Buffalo hotelman Ellsworth M. Statler from 1905 to 1908, it was designed in Art Nouveau style by Esenwein & Johnson, the same local team of architects engaged to work on various Lafayette additions and renovations between 1913 and 1937. Although Statler's ambition was to offer a more practical experience for travelers, with less emphasis on luxuriousness, its new amenities and close downtown location made the Lafayette feel the heat of its competition. (Incidentally, the first Statler was renamed Hotel Buffalo after Statler built the second Hotel Statler in 1923 at 107 Delaware Avenue in Niagara Square, now under renovation. The first Hotel Statler was demolished in 1968, and is now an open plaza in front of the present baseball stadium.) Designed by George W. Post & Sons, the second Hotel Statler's nineteen-storey, 1,100-room towers combined Italian and English Renaissance styles, meant to attract luxury hotel clientele. The Lafayette's second series of upgrades, by Esenwein & Johnson, made certain they, too, could boast that every guestroom was appointed with its own, self-contained bathroom.

The seven-storey building that comprised the 1904 Lafayette cost one million dollars and opened the same year as Jack Astor's St. Regis (Trowbridge & Livingston, architects) in New York City. The latter was a nineteen-floor French Beaux-Arts tower called a wonder of modernism, presumably because it qualified as a skyscraper. It cost six million dollars. Similarly, if we fast forward to 2012, in time for the Lafayette's forty-three million dollar restoration, we see that it cost about one-quarter of the 170-million dollars spent on the recently completed renovation of Chicago's Palmer House.

The Lafayette Hotel's 43-Million-Dollar Restoration

> *Carla Blank*: Is there anything you would have done differently in terms of restoration of the architecture?
> *Rocco Termini*: No, because we brought it back to its original look... we took no shortcuts here. There is not a thing I would have done differently.
>
> From an August 8, 2013 interview
> with Buffalo developer, Rocco Termini,
> who made it possible to restore the Lafayette Hotel

Sometimes, good work does get rewarded, for as I watched and took notes over a period of seven years, this former fleabag slowly but surely transformed into as near to what it once was as present building codes and forty-three million dollars would allow, with its functions now expanded to include two boutique hotel floors, four floors of rental apartments, and ground floor restaurants and retail spaces that make it possible to serve as a one-stop wedding and event facility.

The hotel officially reopened in May 2012. In August 2013, with a Baraka Books' contract secured, my co-author Tania Martin and I left the cloistered Seattle archives of the Sisters of Providence to experience living at the Lafayette Hotel for a few days and to interview people essential to the restoration of the Lafayette and resurrection of Bethune's legacy. When we arrived, 1980s pop tunes and variously-colored fluorescent lighting effects throbbed from a skylight outside, one floor below our third-floor suite's wall of windows. It was Saturday night, August 10, 2013, and three weddings and an anniversary party were in full swing. Just the volume of noise announced we had entered a different world. Magically, around midnight, all went silent and dark.

The following morning, we explored the Lafayette inside and out, to experience for ourselves what had been steadily reported in local newspapers and Internet blog sites, of this renovation that employed thirty companies and more than two hundred workers, many skilled in the historic techniques that had created the original building. We had heard how Termini searched both worldwide and locally to find these master craftsmen and women, and how his finds included two Russian master plasterers, identified without surnames in newspaper and Internet reports during the renovation, as Oleg and Umar. Their centuries-old "Old World" training made it possible to replicate the original ceiling moldings, among other decorative details, using the same techniques that were used in producing the original plaster work. We heard how among the local companies, Buffalo Plastering and Architecture, under co-owner Gary Bolles and his team, solved other replications with newer techniques by creating liquid-rubber molds in order to recast various plaster ornamental details for areas including the ballrooms and foyer. We also heard how the scagliola was restored by Michael Mammana and his Faux F/X team, including artist Joe Teresi; and how another local company of conservation specialists, Kevin Gleason's ConservArt team, took on the responsibilities of cleaning and restoring the lobby's wood marquetry and oil paintings in the Lafayette Tap Room.

We saw the results of how various crews had meticulously stripped years of paint from the ground floor's wood panels, ceilings, walls, and doors; again employed scagliola, a seventeenth-century Tuscan *trompe l'oeil* painting technique that imitates the appearance of the real marble at the bases of columns and wainscoting in the first floor's lobby and hallways; patched or matched patterns in the original mosaic tile and wood parquet floors uncovered under layers of linoleum; discovered etched-glass doors tucked inside walls and matched them with more, to create room dividers; and where cutaways of dropped ceilings revealed ornate ornamental plastering patterns on the original ceilings and support columns, their poured molds exactly replicated damaged sections. Years of dirt and grime that I remembered seeing were now removed from paintings and the two inlaid wood marquetry murals that were centerpieces of the lobby's 1941 Art Moderne remodel. All that had been reported was there, and more.

I felt the echoes of "WPA Art Moderne," one of America's reigning architectural styles, evoked in the architects' and developers' decision to retain elements of both the 1940s Art Deco and the 1900s Beaux-Arts traditions in the lobby and other public areas of the ground floor. This coexistence of Art Deco and various Revival styles had already been initiated during the Lafayette's 1940s redo, when WPA Art Moderne was at the height of its popularity. The style evolved out of President Franklin Roosevelt's New Deal programs, such

A mold created from an existing capital of a column demonstrates how replacements were created to replicate damaged or missing sections of the original ceilings and columns. (Photo, Tennessee Reed.)

as the Public Works of Art Project (PWAP, December 1933-June 1934) and Works Progress Administration (WPA, August 1935-June 1943), when schools, post offices, courthouses, and other government and municipal structures were built from scratch, added to, or modified. Western New York benefitted from forty-five million New Deal dollars, giving forty thousand people jobs on three hundred projects. Among Buffalo's large-scale WPA projects were the Municipal Auditorium (opened 1940, demolished 2009); an entry court and gateways to the Buffalo Zoo designed by John Edmonston Brent (1889-1962, the first African-American architect to practice in Buffalo), which were placed on the National Register of Historic Places in 2013; the Scajaquada Bridge built over Delaware Avenue; and a new stadium, now called War Memorial Stadium.

In particular, those two privately funded lobby murals and the Lafayette Tap Room's two murals—oil paintings by Aldo Lazzarini (b. Bergamo, Italy 1898, d. 1989) featuring George Washington and General Lafayette—could be easily mistaken as federally-funded WPA projects. Created during that era, they provide glowing proof that WPA arts projects did, by example, help to bring about a new kind of renaissance in American Art, including a willingness to support "cultural democracy" so that artworks would not only be seen by rich collectors, as Franklin Roosevelt said, in a "guarded room on Sundays and holidays." In this case, the art was available to all who entered the hotel.

Leaving the lobby, Tania and I wandered into the restored Peacock Alley amidst its fully-burnished scagliola-clad glory, passing underneath the restored lead-and-golden, Tiffany-like tinted glass skylight, noting how the newly-refreshed Impressionist-style painting by Avery Graves evoked what was once a palm-lined art gallery. At the end of this long corridor we found the stairway to the basement and what had been described as the biggest surprise of all, as a section of the first floor had covered over a former speakeasy in the Clinton/Ellicott corner of the 1912 addition. From the street, the original, opaquely-frosted glass windows had continued to effectively hide its existence from passing pedestrians. I wondered if there were any connection between the placement of a speakeasy in the Lafayette's basement and the fact that descendants of the Lafayette's major investor, Walter B. Duffy, owner of Duffy's Malt Whiskey Company, were then directors in the Lafayette Hotel Company. This most recent renovation has transformed the speakeasy's space into one supply-

Peacock Alley showing scagliola, the faux marble painting technique used for the walls, tinted glass skylight, and tile flooring.. (Photo, Tania Martin.)

ing different kinds of sinful pleasures. Now called Butterwood Sweet and Savory, it is a restaurant that includes a bakery outlet, which supplies weddings, banquets, and East Coast restaurants with their sculptural delights. Of course, Tania and I treated ourselves to a sample.

Once we went outside and circled the building, we could more easily understand the story of the Lafayette's E-shaped footprint: the vertical seams that revealed where the first and second additions had been added to the original hotel's structure; where and how the latest renovation had met present-day fire-code requirements to provide occupants with access to two exits on all floors, besides the newly-inserted glassed-in entranceway and stairwell designated for apartment dwellers' units on the upper floors. The stairwell also functions to separate the comings and goings of apartment dwellers from those using the boutique hotel floors and commercial and public spaces. From Ellicott Street, the hotel's long history was evoked by two still-clearly-readable painted signs on the brick façade of the first addition, one's letters simply advertising "Lafayette Hotel" and underneath, the other's oval logo, "Headquarters AAA Buffalo." From the open space of the adjacent parking lot, you can view the "backsides" of the now-conjoined seven buildings, including five seven-storey units and two two-storey units, one built as the Grand Ballroom addition and the other containing the former Lafayette Tap Room and hotel service rooms. Their lower height allows maximum daylight into the four light courts. There is only a suggestion of the rest of the exterior's terra cotta decorative motifs wrapping the top corners of the east and west elevations. For me, this assemblage of vertical and horizontal rectangles, stripped to their red brick skins, exposes how a surprisingly modern core informs the entire structure.

Early the next morning, on Monday, our first interview was scheduled with Rocco Termini, the developer who cobbled together the means to

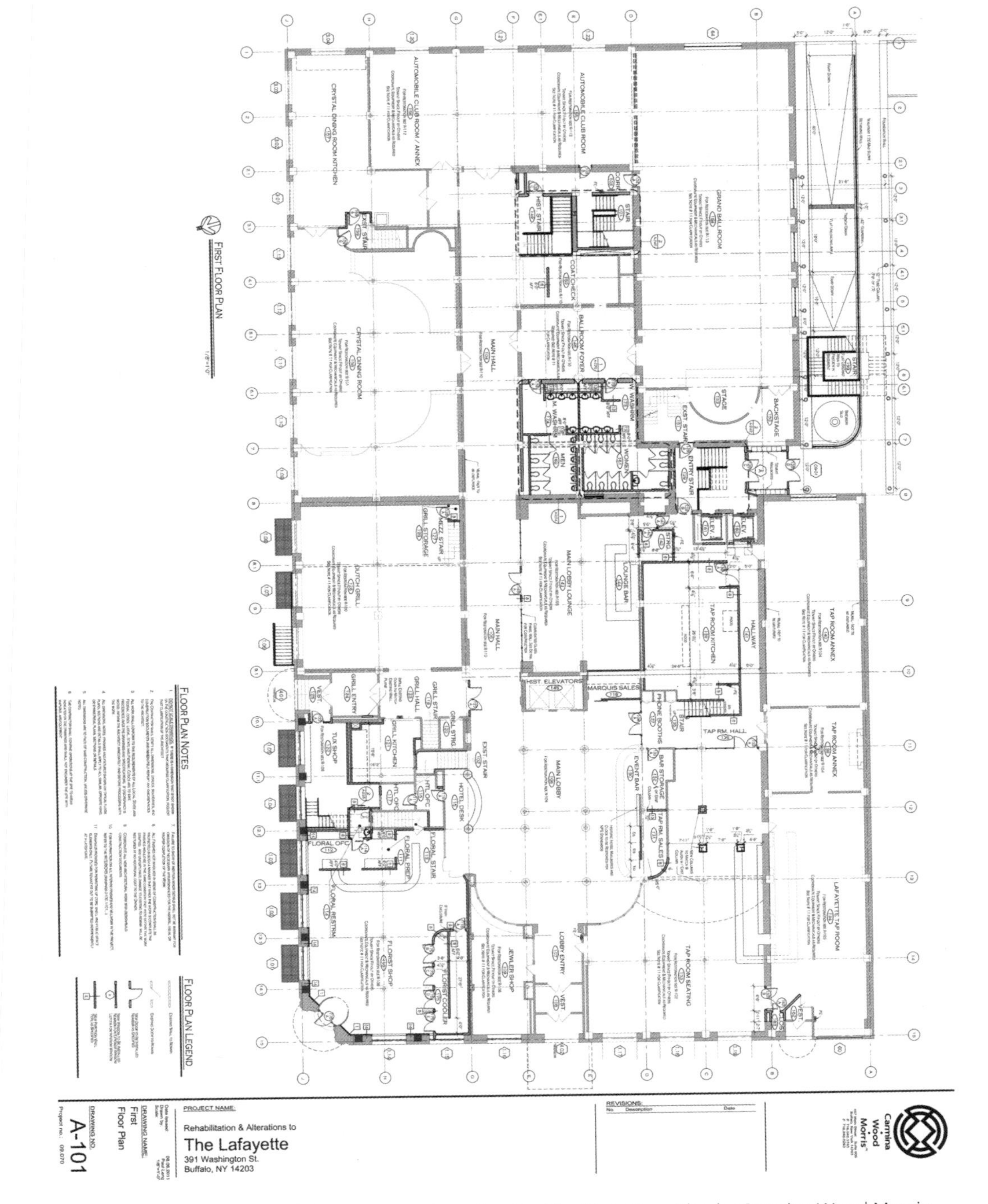

Projected Rehabilitation and Alterations to the Lafayette: The First Floor Plan by Carmina Wood Morris. As realized in 2012, except for the stair and balcony structure located towards the rear of the building, which was never built due to budget concerns during construction. (Courtesy, Jonathan Morris, AIA.)

restore and renovate the building's entire interior and exterior with funding from Buffalo's Urban Renewal Agency, New York State, and sales of historic tax credits. When we asked Mr. Termini how he decided to take on this project, he responded:

> Well, this is one of the only French Renaissance buildings left in downtown Buffalo. This is the Central Business district and I knew it was in danger of becoming a parking lot, so I knew it had to be saved. That's really why I decided to tackle it.
>
> *Carla Blank*: So you have a strong interest in the preservation of historic buildings in the city?
>
> *Rocco Termini*: Yes, this is the seventh historic building that I have rehabilitated in the city of Buffalo... I concentrate my efforts in downtown, because we need to develop critical mass downtown. We need to do as much as we can just to rebuild downtown.
>
> *Tania Martin*: Why was this slated to be demolished?
>
> *Rocco Termini*: It wasn't scheduled to be demolished, but it was ready to be demolished because it was in such poor condition. The ballroom was collapsing, the roof leaked for over thirty years, so everything inside of it had started crumbling... So the city was ready to close the building up anyway.
>
> *Carla Blank*: How did you decide the uses that you wanted to put the building to?
>
> *Rocco Termini:* What I wanted to do is make a one-stop shop for weddings. That was our main focus. We have a gift store, we have a florist, we have a bridal store; we have a bakery that makes wedding cakes. We have the banquet facilities and we have the hotel so you can come here and have your wedding and get everything right here in the building.
>
> *Carla Blank*: We saw that this weekend.
>
> *Rocco Termini*: It was mobbed, full of people... It's like that every single weekend. It's probably two other days during the week when we have different events here. It went from a place where you had pedophiles, to a place that has become an attraction for the city.
>
> *Carla Blank*: So it is working.
>
> *Rocco Termini*: It's absolutely working.

Before Termini could begin the hotel's restoration, it was necessary to go through a three-year preliminary process. The first step required filing an application for the building's designation on the National Register of Historic Places. It then became possible to apply for federal, state, and local funding. Termini has been credited with getting revisions in New York State's historic preservation tax credit program (known as HTC) passed by the New York State Legislature. The changes, approved by Gov. David A. Patterson on August 30, 2010, expanded the acceptable finance sources to banks and insurance companies, giving developers a wider net from which to secure financing for their projects through sales of tax credits for historic buildings, which in addition to saving the Lafayette, according to developer Paul F. Ciminelli (member of Empire State Development Corporation's board of directors), also "helps Western New York leverage its historic architecture to promote redevelopment." This revised program ended a six-month hiatus after the closing of the hotel, when it sat empty while awaiting the state's decision. Termini moved very fast once he got the result he needed. He summoned a news conference at the Lafayette on August 31, where he announced crews would begin working on the hotel within thirty days. As

George Washington and his servants greet Lafayette on a visit to Mount Vernon in Aldo Lazzarinni's oil painting, located in the Pan-American Grill & Brewery's dining area. (Photo, Tennessee Reed.)

our conversation continued, Mr. Termini detailed the hoops he jumped through to accomplish his mission.

Rocco Termini: We went to the State of New York and convinced them that the project was worthy of a grant… they gave us a two-million-dollar grant.

Carla Blank: For what purpose?

Rocco Termini: For the preservation of the building. We got a bill passed that allowed the state to give historic tax credits for historic buildings. We worked on that for three years. That was part of the money that we used. We used federal historic tax credits, we used Erie County Industrial Development Agency, and the city of Buffalo gave a grant. National Grid, which is the electric company in Buffalo, gave a grant; National Fuel gave a grant. So there were a lot of different layers of money that came in to do this project.

Carla Blank: Were there individual donations also?

Rocco Termini: No. Just corporations.

Carla Blank: Would you please explain to us how tax credits work? They seem to be very important to your project.

Rocco Termini: Here's how they work. Say you have forty million in qualified expenses. Twenty percent of that would be eight million. You then sell the federals for ninety-five cents and they get sold to large corporations that have a need for tax credits, so somebody like Chevron or Sherman Williams or Bank of America, they buy those tax credits and they will pay you 7.7 million dollars of the eight million dollars in tax credits.

Carla Blank: Does that mean they then have a share in the building?

Rocco Termini: That means they are partners in the building for five years. They have to be a partner. That is the way the tax laws are written. But we still get that equity from them. Not only do you get the federal equity… you get the state equity, too. It's not only money from the federals but you sell the state credits also. That raises a lot of equity that you need to do these buildings. [Termini also got an eight-hundred-thousand-dollar loan from the city of Buffalo.] Because the big thing in Buffalo is the rents are so cheap that you'd never be able to advertise costs to redo this building. Of course… you could never get that financing without putting in your own money first [on] all of these projects.

Termini explained that he is an accountant.

Rocco Termini: It's all about bean-counting. You're not going to be successful unless you are the bean counter. That's why a lot of these projects go under because there is nobody watching. It's all part of it.

Tania Martin: Do you consider yourself a developer then, too?

Rocco Termini: Yes. Jack of all trades. Master of none. [laughter]

Later that day, again starting our meeting in the Lafayette's lobby, we interviewed Jonathan Morris and Pamela Timby-Straitiff, the architect and interior designer for this renovation, who are both partners in the local firm, Carmina Wood Morris.

Jonathan Morris: I had lived here for a long time and never had gone inside the building. I had always just stayed clear of it because… it was kind of this spooky place. When Rocco approached us about working on it I came in for the first time and was just blown away by what was here… so much of it was still here, fortunately.

Tim Jones [who was the building's engineer for eighteen years] was such a pack rat fortunately. When anything broke or fell off he'd squirrel it away, and keep it. It was like walking into a treasure chest full of stuff, which was great. The previous owner and Tim had at least maintained the building and kept it going, kept it intact. It could have been a building where the owners stripped everything, gotten rid of it all. Fortunately they didn't do that so we had a lot [of fabric] to work with when we got here. That was really fun to walk in for the first time and start exploring.

Carla Blank: You reminded me of an intriguing comment Tim Jones made when I met him in the winter of 2012, while visiting the site in the midst of its renovation. He said whenever you tried to do something to the building, the building would push back. What did he mean by that?

Jonathan Morris: We researched and began to understand the building, from the way it was designed and what it was used for historically. Then we had to take what we had, and… take all this new programming and try to fit it into what we were doing.

Carla Blank: By new programming do you mean bringing it up to code?

Jonathan Morris: Well, yes, and then the new uses, like the restaurants and the ballrooms, the hotel, the commercial space, the apartments, and how to fit all that in the best way back into the building with the most efficient use. We tried to match up the right spaces with the right tenants. So often the uses ended up back where the original uses were designed. An example of this was when the original building opened in 1904… the Pan-American Restaurant here was the outer dining room and behind it was the inner dining room. That was the formal dining space for the restaurant.

Carla Blank: These were not privately owned spaces?

Jonathan Morris: No. This was all hotel restaurant. The other restaurant space was the Lafayette Grill, the Dutch Grill. It was sort of the man cave… Englishmen's club. It had its own separate entrance from the street. The formal, fancy dining rooms were [to the left of the Washington Street entrance]… The lobby was configured differently. The entrance was over at the corner through what is now the florist. The back corner of the building, which would be the southeast corner of the building, was the service end of the building. That was where the freight elevator was and the back stair. That was where the kitchen was. So when we started to redesign this for the tenant who was taking over, creating the Pan-American Bar and Grill, we really struggled with all their kitchen requirements. We ended up splitting their kitchen into three different components, but the place that had ended up making most sense for their largest kitchen was in the back, in the southeast corner of the building where the original kitchen was. Similarly, when Butterwood Desserts came on line and moved their entire operation from West Falls to downtown, and we did this large space where thirty-five employees operate a commercial bakery, they ended up occupying the entire basement of this 1912 addition that originally was all food service. That was where the bakery and butcher, all the steam tables, and all of the major food service prep were. And when the building expanded, things changed and everything got moved downstairs. The entire basement became food services, and lo and behold that space has become a major commercial bakery. They are utilizing the same space that was intended for that originally. That kind of thing happened over and over again. The building just seemed to work as originally laid out and continued to function that way for the uses [needed now].

Morris and Timby-Straitiff described how they figured out the "character" of the hotel—what was its original look:

Jonathan Morris: We had an original set of drawings from Bethune's office. It wasn't all the floors, but it was the basement, the foundation plan, a first floor plan, and a second floor plan, I think, and parts of drawings of a typical upper floor. So we had a pretty good idea of how it was laid out and those were large original drawings. So that was part of it. Most of it was just climbing around the building with Tim, through trap doors and up above ceilings. We went up above this [lobby] ceiling. The first time I climbed through this trap door… I shined my flashlight and saw all of the original plaster ceilings.

Pamela Timby-Straitiff: They are still all up above here. You can see that ceiling in Anatomy [one of the hotel's stores, which offers clothing design services, especially for wedding parties].

Jonathan Morris: A lot of that kind of stuff. There were other places where we were trying to decide, what was the original look of this thing? Like the end of that corridor over there, the end of Peacock Alley. When we walked in everything was white-washed, everything was painted white. We had an idea of the character of what it was from what we saw above the ceiling, when we were poking around. We found one example when they were doing this demolition…, a piece of the plaster [frieze that] looked like it was relatively untouched. We were able to take down a two-foot section, and clean it and that sort of became the pattern for all of the colors and the color schemes that we and the interior designers came up with for the restoration. The faux painters and the retouchable painters took that and we worked with them to come up with a series of layers of glazes, paints.

Pamela Timby-Straitiff: We did lots of research on what kind of colors would have been used at that era, what was appropriate. There was a lot of work with the Buffalo Historical Society. Just knowing what would have been used, or appropriate, kind of geared us in one direction. And then coming on site and peeking behind walls and peeling off [layers of paint] and seeing a glimpse of what was there originally, [we] fine-tuned it, to really get it back to what we hope is what was there when she designed it, for the renovations going forward.

Jonathan Morris: We found a lot of black-and-white photographs and old [watercolor-washed] polychrome postcards. We had some idea of what it looked like realistically, in the photographs, and the postcards filled in the details of what colors might have been used. Then just poking around and finding bits and pieces of things that were covered up and left untouched. A combination of stuff.

With Morris and Timby we revisited some questions we asked Termini, to better understand the process to get designation as a National Historic Site, and how the funding was patched together, both ingredients which made it possible to realize this restoration.

Jonathan Morris: The first year and a half of that process—we worked on this for about three years—was writing the historic preservation application, which is the document that has to get approved through New York State and then gets passed on to Washington and gets approved by the National Parks Service. And that approved document is the basis for the Historic Tax Credit itself.

Tania Martin: And that's through the Secretary of the Interior?

Jonathan: Right.

Tania Martin: And they're applying their standards?

Jonathan Morris: Yes, the Secretary of the Interior's standard for rehabilitation. Typically when you implement those you must identify the period of significance for the structure that says this is the most important time period and this is what we are going to take it back to. In this case there were so many periods: there was 1904, 1912, 1917, and then the 1920s and 1940s, all of which had a significant story to tell.

Tania Martin: Talk about the tax credits.

Jonathan Morris: The syndication of tax credits, it's a whole structuring of all the financing, the packaging, and selling of the tax credits. There are lawyers and accountants that do that; it's a specialized field. What we do is the Historic Preservation Application. It's a three-part document. Part One establishes the significance of the building. Part Two is the description of what you are going to do—what is here and what you are going to do to restore it. And once they approve that then you are eligible for tax credits, if you do what you say you are going to do. When you are all done you file the Part Three, where you take photographs and prove what you have done. When Part Three is approved the tax credits are available.

Pamela Timby-Straitiff: Which is after the building is constructed and finished.

Jonathan Morris: Once the Part Two is approved, then the project is eligible for a developer like Rocco to go sell those tax credits to large corporations who are looking for tax breaks. Typically banks and insurance companies, that sort of business. They will purchase the tax credits from someone like Rocco, and so when they go file their tax reports, instead of paying ten million dollars, they can file for their purchase of three-million-worth of tax credits, which [because] they bought for something less than a dollar on the dollar, they can get relief from their tax burden at a savings. By selling those it generates income to do the project.

Tania Martin: It provides the liquidity? Basically it gives you the money, the working capital you use to pay the contractors? I guess on the individual level the analogy would be comparable to the amount of charitable receipts you have to get deductions that reduce your income taxes?

Jonathan Morris: Right. It generates working capital to do the project... There is a big market out there. There are different tax credit programs. There are energy efficiency tax credits, there are housing tax credits for subsidized housing, there's new energy tax credits, there's historic preservation tax credits, there are new

The Lafayette Hotel's lobby, as renovated in 2012, mainly evokes the Art Moderne 1940s renovation. (Photo, Tania Martin.)

market tax credits… along with the New York State and Empire State Development Fund. And the New York State Blueprint Program gives some funding, and the city gives some funding. That's what Rocco as developer does: to package all that. He has the cost to buy the building and he has the cost to restore it. And to offset those costs with historic tax credits, he raises capital that then becomes equity against which he borrows the difference. So there is a mortgage on the building, as well as to the bank. But the bank will loan only up to the assessed value of the building. In a market like Buffalo, the assessed value isn't as high as it would be in a place like Manhattan. So the tax credit income is what bridges the gap between what is needed to pay contractors and what is needed to actually do the project. The lawyers and accountants figure that all out. Our part is to get the preservation document approved and then to see to it that is followed and the work gets done.

Jonathan Morris: What we negotiated through the process with Albany and the Park Service was that the period of significance was not one period but five different dates, and what we were trying to do was tell the story of the evolution of the hotel... [For example,] we wanted to restore the outside of the building to what it looked like in 1912, but we had to keep the Art Moderne fabric from the 1940s... [Now] you don't see the arched top windows from the inside... But we were able to restore those windows from the outside and get a lot more light in here. That was one of those compromises between the 1940s and 1904, to get the look from the outside, but then keep this [Art Moderne look inside].

Pamela Timby-Straitiff: Part of the story of this building was the progression through history... You can see that where the one ballroom, the Crystal Ballroom, is almost like a meld. You have some Art Deco flavor and some French Renaissance. And part of it was bringing those two together and having them work... harmoniously without it feeling totally disjointed. You'll... have the French Renaissance... clear and distinct by itself and then you'll have this weird mix and then the Art Moderne. That is part of the beauty of the building.

When Ishmael, Tennessee, and I returned to Buffalo one weekend in March 2014, we were booked into the Lafayette again, amidst many wedding parties again. In the lobby, the long counter surrounded by high stools that did not appear to have any designated function during our August visit was now active as a coffee bar, completing an idea Jon Morris and Pam Timby had mentioned was under consideration during our August 2013 interview. Although the hotel is to remain basically as planned for at least five years, it appears the staff will continue to fine-tune aspects of the decor, to better enhance visitors' experiences.

Creating a Place in the Historical Record

On the evening of the second day of the AIA's annual convention in Buffalo, New, York, in 1888, "the Buffalo architects hosted the attendees at a dinner in the Niagara Hotel. After the speeches, the following exchange closed the evening's proceedings:

Mr. Stone: Before we separate let us drink a toast to the lady member of the Buffalo Chapter, Mrs. Bethune.

Mr. Moser: Long may she live and may there be many more."

From the proceedings of the Twenty-Second Annual Convention of the American Institute of Architects, held in Buffalo, October 17, 18, 19, 1888, p. 120.

Carla Blank: I assume Louise Bethune was totally aware of what the competition was. Did you feel she was trying to make her expression in the context of all this architectural grandness around the city that happened during the ten or so years she was working on the Lafayette?

Rocco Termini: There is a lot, but... she wanted to go one better than everybody else. And I think [the Lafayette] is more decorative than... the Richardson, the Sullivan, the Burnham, the Frank Lloyd Wright. I think this is probably more over the top than those buildings. She probably was competing with them. She wanted to do better than the guys.

Carla Blank: I get that feeling. [laughter]

Rocco Termini: She was one that was ahead of her time and she wanted to make a statement that "I can do it too," and that "I can do better than you." And I think she did.

From interview with Rocco Termini, August 2013

In the 1910 through 1919 decade, the average life span for a woman was 55.0 years and for a man it was 50.3 years. Louise Bethune exceeded the average by two years, when she died from complications of kidney disease in 1913 at age fifty-seven, eleven years after the death of Mother Joseph at age seventy-nine. Bethune was survived by her mother, Emma Blanchard, her husband, Robert, and their son, Charles. After the death of his wife, Robert Bethune and William Fuchs continued to practice as partners for two more years. Following an unknown illness of five weeks, on July 17, 1915, Robert Bethune died at the age of sixty. Fuchs continued to practice on his own until the Great Depression, when he dissolved his practice. Only a few papers and photographs in the possession of his family, from the years Bethune, Bethune & Fuchs were in business, are known to have survived that closing. Dr. Charles Bethune died at the age of sixty-nine in Buffalo on October 2, 1952. His distinguished medical career included service as consultant to the County Health Department, as examining physician for child labor. His granddaughter, Zina Bethune, a respected dancer, choreographer, actress, and teacher who was the last-known living descendent of Louise and Robert Bethune, was killed at the age of sixty-six on February 17, 2012, in a tragic Los Angeles freeway accident.

Louise and Robert Bethune are buried together in Buffalo's famous Forest Lawn Cemetery, along with President Millard Fillmore, funk star Rick James, and Seneca orator Red Jacket, whose monumental statue stands watch over all. Founded in 1849 and listed in the National Register of Historic places, Forest Lawn remains an excellent example of the park-like landscape style known as the "rural" cemetery movement. Fittingly, its eclectic examples of crypts, walls, and walkways were designed by the full spectrum of architects who practiced in Buffalo during the Gilded Age.

For reasons unknown, the original stone marker at the Bethunes' burial site was engraved only with the name and birth and death dates of Robert Bethune. In 2002, the Buffalo/Western New York chapter of the AIA placed a bronze plaque in Forest Lawn Cemetery on the road close to the gravesite, to help visitors seeking its location. It provides Louise Blanchard Bethune's likeness, some biographical information, and explains that her ashes were interred with her husband's. The Buffalo/Western New York chapter of the AIA also succeeded in having Louise Blanchard Bethune inducted into the Western New York Women's Hall of Fame in 2007.

On the hundredth anniversary of her death, in an event sponsored by the American Institute of Architects New York State chapter and the Buffalo Architecture Foundation, and attended by eighteen men and women, including Rocco Termini and Kelly Hayes McAlonie, they celebrated Louise Bethune's life and the installation of a new memorial marker which they arranged to have placed in the ground next to Robert Bethune's. Its engraving simply states: "JENNIE LOUISE BLANCHARD BETHUNE / July 21, 1856 / December 18, 1913."

Things are looking up for Buffalo this summer of 2014 as I complete this chapter. Although property values are still down, slowly but surely new businesses are arriving, employment rates are improving, and incomes and the unemployment rate, while still below national averages, have stabilized rather than continuing to drop. In 2010, *Forbes Magazine* named Buffalo one of "America's Best Places to Raise a Family." An August 17, 2014 *Buffalo News* article about the downtown's development declared: "Good news about Buffalo's present begets more good news… It is stunning to think about the progress made in just the past few years. Better still, that progress is generating new hope for what we will see in the next few years."

Bethune's landmark achievement, now sporting its new name, Hotel @ The Lafayette, received the Preservation League of New York State's award for Excellence in Historic Preservation in 2013. As I wrote in my August 11, 2013 *Wall Street Journal* article, "How Buffalo's Lafayette Hotel Went from Fleabag to Fabulous," even though the National Women's Hall of Fame has rejected three applications to include Louise Blanchard Bethune in their ranks, if the imagination, creativity, and sheer drive that it took to revive this grand lady, the Lafayette Hotel, is an example of Buffalo's grit, will, and determination, then the town can say with former resident Mark Twain that "the reports of my death have been greatly exaggerated."

The look of the 1904 lobby's decorative ceiling plasterwork and columns painted in Numidian scagliola to match the Numidian marble wainscoating, as originally created by Bethune, can be viewed in Anatomy, a shop for bridal and other kinds of dressmaking. (Courtesy, Ali Eagen, owner + designer of Anatomy. Photo, Tania Martin.)

CONCLUSION

"....ARCHITECTURAL PRESERVATION is real estate driven—but so is everything else. Old buildings must earn their way."

Ada Louise Huxtable in "Manhattan's Landmark Buildings Today," *New York Times,* February 25, 1964

"Storytelling is part of the game."
—Tania Martin

Some buildings we just cannot let go of. Others are still around because of dumb luck. The Lafayette Hotel in Buffalo, New York, and the House of Providence in Vancouver, Washington, are two cases in point. Both survived in part because they were located in economically depressed downtown areas where, because they nonetheless served a purpose, their respective owners continued to maintain them, at least minimally, and in part because a core group of people had developed such strong emotional attachments to the buildings that they lobbied long and hard in favor of their rehabilitation.

People who engage in historic preservation expect a return on their investment. Rarely is a building saved, or built in the first place, for its own sake. The building, existing or new, has to have a vocation, a function, housing people or machines. It can also fulfill one or multiple needs. A religious structure may be erected to the Glory of God and given symbolic importance; it will also function as a place of assembly, and perhaps in a second or third life as a concert venue or community library. However, even an architectural gem appreciated for its exemplary construction system, its impeccable workmanship, or its designer's creative mastery will fall to the wrecking ball if no contemporary use for it can be found.

To preserve a building simply for its association to a historical event or person is tantamount to commemoration and very costly given the resources it takes to restore and maintain it without pouring money into it year after year to ensure its sustainability. Civic pride alone could not justify the preservation of either the Lafayette Hotel or the

House of Providence. Their importance had to be demonstrated and political will had to be mustered before public or private investors became interested. Be they governments, corporations, or individuals, stakeholders need to be reassured that the rehabilitation, the adaptive reuse of the building will generate a tangible economic or social benefit.

The Hidden Brothers, the board members of the Fort Vancouver National Trust, Rocco Termini, and their collaborators all exerted tremendous efforts in order to convince stakeholders of the worthiness of their projects. They devoted considerable time and energy to amass the financial resources and obtain the permissions and permits necessary to finally realize their plans. In hindsight, their stories are enough to give anyone pause before trying similar endeavors. However, their drive and success should also give hope to those like them, who believe that historic preservation can leverage urban revitalization and sustainable development.

In both Buffalo and Vancouver, we can detect a feminist agenda among the early defenders of the two women architects' signature buildings—Adriana Barbasch and Kelly Hayes McAlonie, whom Carla interviewed in Buffalo, and Ann King and even Sister Susanne Hartung in Vancouver. For them, there was a larger project behind the restoration of the Lafayette Hotel and of the House of Providence: first, acknowledgement of the designers Louise Blanchard Bethune and Mother Joseph and of their places in history; second, having their last remaining major architectural works stand as memorials to their careers.

The Hiddens, King, and Hartung all had very personal reasons to boost historic preservation of the House of Providence. For two generations of the Hidden family, the fact that their ancestor, Lowell Mason Hidden, provided the bricks for its construction was not negligible in forging a visceral connection to the building, in spite of its potential real estate value. For Ann King, the fact that one of her great aunts knew Mother Joseph in her lifetime sparked curiosity and pride. For Susanne Hartung, the fact that Mother Joseph, foundress of her order in the Pacific Northwest, had had the building at the heart of her life's mission erected provides the *raison d'être* of the training program she developed to inculcate Providence values among Providence Health and Services lay employees. So architectural preservation cannot be all about real estate; storytelling is also part of the game.

Since 1953, Mother Joseph has been, until recently, unfailingly portrayed as "an architect and builder of recognized ability, unerring judgment in choice of material, and in testing brick, lime, lumber, nails, and measurements." Such statements must have been of service when it came to having this French Canadian, Roman Catholic sister inducted to the U.S. National Statuary Hall and the House of Providence, listed in 1978 on the National Register of Historic Places. While they prove that she and the building with which she is associated go beyond local interest, we must also consider them for their rhetorical uses. For why else would Catherine McCrosson relate in Mother Joseph's biography, *The Bell and the River*:

> Every evening after the workers went home, Mother Joseph made a meticulous inspection of the day's work, climbing the ladders to test the beams or prying under flooring to check the foundations. She was always known as a taskmaster when building was

the job on hand. It had to be well done; there was no such thing as tawdry or mediocre construction. She had been known to disassemble brick chimneys not built according to specifications, and to reconstruct them herself from the foundation, to the amazement of the workers who returned the next day.

Her story, in fact, serves a dual purpose. It provides glimpses of historical events as gleaned from the documentary record and oral history and, cast in a particular literary style, makes for fun reading. It also elevates the reader. Mother Joseph's story is meant to inspire; she is to be a role model for those who follow her spiritual path, much like hagiography or the lives of saints are meant to do.

However, we also like to have heroes, and sometimes take liberties in embroidering the facts. Local newspaper reporter Dave Jewett, writing in *The Columbian* in 1956 (the centennial year of the Sisters of Providence's arrival), boasted how Mother Joseph personally drew the plans of Providence Academy; she inspected every brick that was used in construction. This is hyperbole. I seriously doubt the sister had this kind of time to spend and I am sure she had other things to do than inspect every brick. Sacred Heart School, Colville, Washington, and St. Patrick Hospital, Missoula, Montana, also demanded her attention in 1873.

Jewett additionally claimed Mother Joseph was said to be the daughter of a noted architect in Montreal, having learned the art of building by frequently helping him with his work. Journalist James Stevens had mentioned in 1953 Mother Joseph's father was an "architectural designer and artist in wood," as well as a carriage maker, a statement reporter Frances Blakely exaggerated twenty years later, telling her readers that Mother Joseph's father

was "an eminent architect in Montreal" and that she herself was an "architect… [a] free mason and carpenter, many times taking her own trowel to the three-foot rock foundation to see that her plans were being followed." Even if there had been some basis in fact that Mother Joseph was undeniably involved in the practice of architecture in a variety of ways—as builder, contractor, client, and architect—much like the children's game of pass-the-word, the original version got distorted each time her story was repeated.

Nonetheless, that does not answer Carla's burning question: was Mother Joseph an architect? I guess it depends on who you are asking. I suspect that were I to put that question to colleagues in the world of architecture, some would dismiss her out of hand; others would be in firm agreement that she was an architect. What is important, however, is that by considering a person's true place in history, in putting her life in context, as modest as that may be, we begin to understand how she can stand in for and be an example of the thousands of people who shaped the North American landscape, the physical milieu in which we live, and who, unlike the two women we singled out, will remain uncelebrated and probably unacknowledged.

Ultimately, I have strived to debunk a few myths circulating about Mother Joseph, clarify the history of the evolution of Providence Faubourg and offer new understanding of the construction and historic preservation of the House of Providence. This I hope will help Fort Vancouver National Trust interpret the importance of the sisters in founding Vancouver, even though their material culture at the Fort has disappeared. What can be said after sifting through the hearsay, rumors, and mythology—Mother Joseph's energy and her ambition made the hostile environment she and her associates inhabited tolerable and livable. Providence Academy is a testament to her story.

Anthropologist Serge Bouchard has since 2005 been uncovering the forgotten persons who have shaped French America. In broadcasting the underdog's side of history to Radio-Canada listeners, he sheds light on such characters as François-Xavier Aubry, fastest horseman of his day who made his fortune leading caravans to Santa Fe, New Mexico and helped open roads to California in the early 1840s and the Métis Jean-Baptiste Charbonneau, born of Sacajawea of the Shoshone Nation and French-Canadian Toussaint Charbonneau who were guides to Lewis and Clark. To this day the couple and their son remain obscured by the glorification of the famous expedition and the conquest of the West. Many of these unsung heros, like Mother Joseph, are virtually unknown to English Canadians and Americans and not much better known in Québec. Yet, as the story of the "Sister with the Hammer" reveals, there are strong links between French Canada's four-hundred-year history and the development of the Pacific Northwest. Perhaps she can join the illustrious cast of Bouchard's *remarquables oubliés* [the remarkably forgotten].

"Women architects are not confined to modest projects." —Carla Blank

Although I have been a practicing artist since the early 1960s and taught a twentieth-century history of arts course at the University of California, Berkeley, in the 1990s, it never crossed my mind that women architects were hard at work in the late 1800s and early 1900s. The exception was Julia Morgan, who is famous in the San Francisco Bay area. When I lived in the Cambridge, Massachusetts, area for about six months while Ishmael taught the spring 1987 semester at Harvard and I was a consultant to Harvard's Office for the Arts, I passed by and probably admired houses renovated or designed by Lois Lilley Howe from the mid-1890s into the early twentieth century, without noting their architect's name. One does not expect a woman architect, even when you might pass one of her buildings daily.

Working on this book, I began to recognize how women's contributions to history disappear or are appropriated. When I would share a photograph of the Lafayette Hotel with people curious to learn more about the subject, the most common reaction was a surprised exclamation, "It's really big!" as though women architects were confined to modest projects, like designing cottages.

While no one can legitimately question including Louise Bethune in the history of North American architecture, it is likely people will need to continue to fight the pattern of neglect. In defense of their request to place the Hotel Lafayette on The National Register of Historic Places, Martin Wachadlo and Frank Kowsky explained:

> Louise Bethune occupies a foremost place in the select pantheon of early women architects in America. Ironically, many other women architects have achieved more recognition for their careers and greater scholarly study has been dedicated to their body of work. Women including Theodate Pope Riddle (1867-1946), Julia Morgan (1872-1957), Mary Jane Colter (1869-1958), and to a lesser degree, Lutah Marie Riggs (1896-1984). Like Bethune, these architects cast their designs in established styles of their times, however most worked for more nationally visible clients, unlike Bethune who's practical and often utilitarian designs were overlooked by the architectural press.

Authors Tania Martin and Carla Blank at the Lafayette, August 2013. (Photo, Tennessee Reed.)

However, the scale of the Lafayette Hotel, with its accessories which modernists would find gratuitous, is anything but "utilitarian." Is French Renaissance or any other revival of a historic style "practical"?

Before becoming so fixated on Bethune's Lafayette Hotel, I had not realized how popular its particular red-brick and glazed, white-terra-cotta-clad French Renaissance Revival style had become throughout North America. Nor had I recognized how the rules of what qualifies as original architectural work are somewhat different than those applied to the processes that create new literature and performing and visual arts forms. It was when I found photographs of four other early-twentieth-century, French Renaissance, red-brick and white-terra-cotta-clad hotels and one commercial building that I finally grasped that in architecture, plagiarism is not only acceptable, but even encouraged. Although these buildings were not identical carbon copies, their exteriors and interiors were obviously influenced by the Lafayette Hotel's model. Their differences were minimal, mostly related to requirements posed by the particulars and orientations of each site.

I feel justified in assuming this because of a few major facts. All five of the other French Renaissance red-brick and white-terra-cotta-clad buildings were constructed within two to nine years of the Lafayette Hotel's opening. Rochester's two downtown luxury hotels and one commercial building were all financed by the first owner of the Lafayette, Walter B. Duffy, and his associates, and were completed during the same years that Duffy hired Bethune, Bethune & Fuchs to design and supervise construction of the Lafayette's first addition. The designers of one of the Rochester hotels, the eight-storey, three-hundred-room Seneca Hotel (opened 1908, razed in 1969) were the Buffalo-based team Esenwein & Johnson. While I do not know the name of other Rochester buildings' designers or who financed Utica's Hotel Utica (1910) and Worcester's Bancroft Hotel (1912-1913), these two hotels were also both designed by Esenwein & Johnson.

The Bancroft was completed the same year Esenwein & Johnson landed the first of their twenty-four years of commissions to design renovations and additions to the Lafayette itself, widely lauded for maintaining consistency with the original Bethune design. Of course, Bethune, Bethune & Fuchs held no trademark on Second Empire or French Renaissance Revival style. I saw no evidence that anyone questioned the integrity of the Esenwein & Johnson designs for these three French Renaissance-revival hotels; by the 1920s they had become architects for the United Hotels Company, the biggest hotel chain in North America. On the contrary, Buffalo-based architectural historians have given far more deferential attention to the works of Esenwein & Johnson than they customarily have given to those of Louise Bethune and her firm, whose models they appropriated. This is a complaint made by black Americans, Native Americans, and others who have been denied credit for their work. Thankfully for Louise Bethune, this is no longer so evident, due to those Buffalo architects and historians who revived her reputation in the twenty-first century and the warm reception accorded the recent renovation of the Lafayette Hotel.

Like other buildings that have survived one hundred years or more, the Lafayette went through many changes, large and small, some to its benefit, and some not. Rescuing Bethune's Lafayette Hotel from further ignominy makes the efforts of those who restored the building that I found in 2006 even more ennobling; it was akin to taking what in the nineteenth century was called a "fallen woman" and restoring her dignity.

Cities such as Buffalo, Detroit, Cleveland, Pittsburgh, Oakland, and other once industrial boomtowns were abandoned by their manufacturing bases and populations, especially as globalization wooed the capitalists, who provided employment for millions, to seek cheaper labor abroad. However, these cities do not necessarily have to remain ghost towns littered with abandoned buildings. The examples from Buffalo and Vancouver show that spaces like the Lafayette Hotel and the Academy are not dead, but only dormant, and can be put to new uses with multiple positive benefits, through creative civic and private leadership.

Pan-American Grill & Brewery, as it appeared in spring 2014, maintains much of Bethune's original design, with carved oak bar, mosaic tile floor and the ceiling's elliptical groins. (Photo, Tennessee Reed.)

At the Lafayette, the thoughtful stewardship of the building reveals itself in choices that were made to honor its history and to most efficiently recycle its treasures. Some are inferred, like ancient tracings: the sweeping arc of each entrance and exit through the original entrance's revolving door remains etched into the floor of Woyshner's Lafayette Flower Market, the present occupant of this section of the lobby; a century of finely-clad footsteps add random patterns to wood and tile mosaic floors, now carefully interspersed with modern patchwork. New mechanicals run through many of the original ventilation system's airshafts. Where round light fixtures hung in the 1940s lobby, new round diffusers of the same diameter were found to most efficiently position the new air conditioning and heating systems. Other renovation solutions can be easily observed. Generally, two original hotel rooms now equal one hotel room; three original hotel rooms equal one apartment. All the original doors along the hallways of each floor remain, some functional as apartment entry doors, some hiding mechanicals, and some walled-over on the inside. Marble slabs that once divided restroom facilities into stalls are now recycled into sink and table-tops throughout the building. Polished wood banisters supported by wrought iron work have been repositioned in the stairwells of the new apartment entranceway, where they continue to provide a smooth, hand-sized grip hold.

"The Greenest Building: Quantifying the Environmental Value of Building Reuse," the 2011 Report from the Preservation Green Lab of the National Trust for Historic Preservation, details both economic and environmental justifications to demonstrate how preservation of existing buildings can go beyond those "strictly cultural and sentimental." The study's Introduction states:

Until now, little has been known about the climate change reductions that might be offered by reusing and retrofitting existing buildings rather than demolishing and replacing them with new construction. This groundbreaking study concludes that building reuse almost always offers environmental savings over demolition and new construction. Moreover, it can take between 10 and 80 years for a new, energy-efficient building to overcome, through more efficient operations, the negative climate change impacts that were created during the construction process. However, care must be taken in the selection of construction materials in order to minimize environmental impacts; the benefits of reuse can be reduced or negated based on the type and quantity of materials selected for a reuse project.

The study documents how the cumulative savings and environmental benefits can be substantial when factored over an entire city, especially, as the study concludes:

> Every year, approximately one billion square feet of buildings are demolished and replaced with new construction in the United States. The Brookings Institution projects that some 82 billion square feet of existing space will be demolished and replaced between 2005 and 2030—roughly one-quarter of today's existing building stock.

Ben Austen reports on Detroit's multiple approaches to regenerating its city in his July 13, 2014 article in *The New York Times Magazine*, "Buy Low," where investments by "black and white, young and old, billionaires and shop owners… find the raw material for new enterprise in the wreckage of the Rust Belt." Following his maxim to "do well by doing good," the buying spree of hometown boy Dan Gilbert, the billionaire owner of Quicken, scored dirt cheap purchases of architectural gems, including "a Daniel Burnham, a few Albert Kahns, and a Minoru Yamasaki masterwork with a soaring glass atrium. 'They're like old-school sports cars,' said Dan Mullen, one of the executives who took over Quicken's newly formed real estate arm. 'These were buildings with so much character, so much history. They don't exist anywhere else.'" Rufus Bartell, an African-American entrepreneur and investor in local small business properties, believes, "To grow Detroit, you have to shrink it." In this city that in its heyday sprawled to encompass 139 square miles, this can involve more pain to those still hanging onto properties in outlying areas. The city's 2012 Master Plan says this will require tearing down buildings and clearing junk from the land, "with half the overabundant land reclaimed as parks and mixed-green communities, a flowering of carbon-reducing forests and industrial buffers, of greenways and retention ponds, of camp-grounds and community gardens." Whether the combined efforts of all of Detroit's large and small redevelopers will work is still very much in question.

In San Francisco, one of the United States' hottest real estate markets, real estate issues stem more from problems of over-regulation by city planning authorities. When combined with the growing trend of tech workers to prefer to live in cities rather than near suburban office park-projects, this has led to tech companies practicing adaptive re-use. According to *The New York Times*' architectural critic Michael Kimmelman in his June 1, 2014 article, "Urban Renewal, No Bulldozer":

> Flush with cash and encouraged by a payroll tax incentive from the city, [these tech firms rush] like hermit crabs living off whatever's around,... [taking] over more than three million square feet of existing office and industrial space... the equivalent of New York's new 1 World Trade Center.

San Francisco is likely to run out of old buildings to adapt long before the tech companies' demands are satisfied. Kimmelman believes that in San Francisco, the choice for adaptive reuse is "driven as well by a taste for 'authenticity,' 'character,' and other buzzwords today's tech firms love."

Perhaps the aesthetics of these choices were given the green light in 1975, when, after years of dismissing nineteenth-century's Beaux-Arts aesthetics as dead weight best ignored, the New York Museum of Modern Art mounted a show of drawings from l'École nationale supérieure des Beaux-Arts' storehouse in Paris, rediscovered to be timeless keys synthesizing our past with our present.

Investing in making a future for women architects

As Tania said above, notwithstanding the recent tremendous efforts on its behalf, there is more than a little serendipity in the fact that Bethune's Lafayette Hotel did survive while other famous Buffalo buildings met the wrecking ball. It fortunately remains a living testimony, instructive in its turnaround into what is now enthusiastic recognition and agreement that some buildings are irreplaceable; it creates the particular sense of place that each city gives to its inhabitants and the future generations who will come to know it.

Adriana Barbasch and Kelly Hayes McAlonie have invested much time into spotlighting women's contributions like Bethune's to architecture, in large part to encourage more young girls to consider the profession. Kelly, with Despina Stratigakos, created a successful campaign to get Mattel to produce an "Architect Barbie," which we understand was a commercial success. The fact that over one hundred years ago, Mother Joseph and Louise Bethune were able to storm the old boys' citadel, with little support and few allies, should also be an inspiration to young women of today.

The focus and dedication exemplified by these two women proved that avenues once closed to women can be available now. Historic preservation of places in which women had significant roles in their making is another, more traditional way of sharing that history with the general public. Tania and I wish all those fundraising to restore Mother Joseph's Academy an equal success to the one being enjoyed by the Hotel @ the Lafayette and its community, in large part because historic preservation of places such as the Academy and the Lafayette ultimately showcases how women, although lost in the shadows of history, have had significant roles in making our communities.

BIBLIOGRAPHY
Related to Individual Architects

Mother Joseph of the Sacred Heart
Providence Archives, Seattle, Washington
(13) Mother Joseph S. H.
Box 8. Correspondence, French, 1856-1901.
Folder: Correspondence-O, collection of five letters, 1856-1857
Letter to Mother Caron, dated December 21, 1856.
Letter to Mgr Bourget, dated December 29, 1856.
Letter to Mgr Bourget, dated January 27, 1857.
Letter to Très Revérend A. F. Truteau, V.G. [Vicar General], dated April 19, 1857.
Folder: Correspondence-O, set of five letters, 1856-1864.
Letter to Mother [Caron], dated May 1857.
Letter to Mgr Laroque [supérieur des SP à Montréal] dated August 15, 1857.
Letter to Mother [Caron], dated November 18, 1857.
Letter to Mother [Caron], dated August 20, 1858.
Letter to Reverend L. Rossi, dated February 5, 1859.
Letter to Mgr Bourget, dated February 1859.
Letter to Mgr Laroque, dated March 6, 1859.
Letter to Sr Martin, dated June 6, 1859.
Letter to Mgr Bourget, dated January 1860.
Letter to Très Revérend A F Truteau, V. G, dated March 21, 1860.
Letter to Rvd mère Philomène, dated August 19, 1860.
Letter to Très Revérend A. F. Truteau, V. G., dated October 21, 1860.
Lettre à Revd H. Moreau, chanoine en date du January 15, 1861.
Letter to Rvd mère Philomène, dated 28 April 1861.
Letter to J. B. A Brouillet, V. G., dated 27 juillet 1861.
Letter to J. B. A Brouillet, V. G., dated 23 March 1862.
"Preliminary Inventory of the Correspondence of Mother Joseph of the Sacred Heart 1856-1875," Volume 1 and Volume 2.
«Nécrologies des Filles de la Charité Servantes des Pauvres, 1891-1903,» Sœur Joseph-du-Sacré-Cœur, pp. 169-175.

(22) Providence Academy
Series 1: History.
Box 1, Folder 1, Chronicles, 1856-1875 (set 1).
Box 1, Folder 2, Chronicles, 1875-1892 (set 1).
Box 1, Folder 3, Chronicles, 1892-1908 (set 1).
Box 2, Folder 1, Chronicles, 1908-1952 (set 1).
Box 2, Folder 2, Chronicles, 1952-1966 (set 1).
Box 3, Folder 1, Chronicles, 1856-1886 (set 2).
Box 4, Folder 2, Chronicles, 1866-1881 (set 3, "draft").
Box 5, Folder 2, St. James Mission.
James, Sister Mary, "Claims of the Missionary Station of St. James," handwritten on a pad of lined paper, undated.
Plate XXVI, Diagram of Survey of St. James' Mission Claim, Surveyed July 10, 1872, Len Farnsworth, U.S. Deputy Surveyor.
Box 5, Folder 6, "Providence Academy, Vancouver, Washington, 1874-1950," by Sister Mary Claver Morrow, pp. 3-5.
Box 5, Folder 7, "Providence Academy: Its Construction and Contribution" by Sister Merilu Vachon, 1974.
"Portrait of Mother Joseph of the Sacred Heart."
"Notes on Mother Joseph of the Sacred Heart."
Box 5, Folder 10, Closure of Providence Academy, 1966.
"Act of Council," January 25, 1966.
Letter to Most Reverend Thomas A. Connolly Archbishop of Seattle from Mother Mary Loretta, Provincial Superior, dated January 5, 1966.
Letter to Mother Mary Loretta from Archbishop Thomas A. Connolly, dated January 25, 1966.

Letter to Mother [Loretta] from Sister Cecilia Mary, dated February 4, 1966, about dismantling Providence Academy and salvaging building materials.

Letter to Mother Mary Loretta from Sister Jeanne Marie, dated March 9, 1966.

McDonald, Lucile, "Changing education patterns to bring End to State's Oldest School Building," *The Seattle Times*, July 10, 1966.

Pratt, Gerry, "Making the Dollar, Historic Academy Forced to Close," *Sunday Oregonian*, March 20, 1966.

Modie, Judi, "Age Catches Up With Providence," *Columbian*, January 28, 1966.

"Age Overtakes Providence Academy," *The Progress*, February 4, 1966.

Van Arsdol, Ted, "Closing Sparks Memories: Student of Earlier Era Recalls Days at Providence Academy," *The Columbian*, June 1, 1966.

Series 2: Administration, Local Community, *Procès Verbal* Acts of Council, Box 6.

Folder, Administration, Local Community, *Procès Verbal* (Official Visits), 1881-1956.

Folder, Administration, Local Community, *Procès Verbal* (Official Visits), 1938-1966.

Folder, Administration, Local Community, Acts of Council, 1892-1916, ledger book.

Folder, Administration, Local Community, Acts of Council, 1916-1939, ledger: Deliberations of the local council, House of Providence, Vancouver, WA.

Series 3: Personnel.

OS Folder 1, Orphans' Letters to Bishop A. M. A. Blanchet, 1885, 1886.

Series 6: Property Records.

OS Folder 4, Building Plans, Plan of water tower by J. B. Blanchet, one linen drawing, undated.

OS Folder 5, Building Plans, Floor Plans, six linen drawings, undated.

OS Folder 6, Building Plans, Convent and Music School, 1951, four blueprints,

John W. Maloney, Architect, Seattle and Yakima, WA.

OS Roll 1, Building Plans, Basement, First Floor, Second Floor, three linen drawings.

OS Roll 2, Building Plans, Incinerator Addition, two blueprints, 1947.

OS Folder 7, Plat Maps, Sisters of Providence property near river (aka Farm on River Road), three blueprints, one paper.

Plat Map, Martin Rapp, Civil Engineer, Vancouver, WA, December 5, 1894, two typewritten pages.

OS Folder 8 Plat Maps, Vancouver maps.

Homan, W. P., *Map of the City of Vancouver, Washington*, December 1912.

Map of the City of Vancouver, Washington, Edson M. Rowley, Real Estate Dealer.

OS Folder 9 Plat Maps, J. B. Blanchet's Land, Township 2, N. R. 1 E (aka Minnehaha Farm, two linen drawings, one paper.

OS Roll 2 Plat Maps, Property at River Road, one blueprint, Map of Beard [Fruit Company], Sisters [of Charity], and Port Tract in Short-Mellick and Prulx [*sic*] D. L. C. in Clark County, WA, scale 1:200.

OS Folder 10 Plan of St. James Mission Buildings in 1866 by J. B. Blanchet, three blueprints.

Series 10: Post-closure.

Box 31, Folder 1, Action to save Providence Academy building, 1966-1968.

"Providence Academy" petition and "Preservation of Historic Providence Academy" document prepared by Robert Hidden, Donald J. Stewart, and Merv Simpson, January 1968.

Krohn, Barbara, "The Preservation of Providence" May 1966.

Rohrer, Kathy, "Group Moves to Preserve Old Academy," *The Columbian*, January 8, 1968.

— "Group tries to breathe new life into old Providence Academy," *The Columbian*, January 17, 1968.

"Providence group led by Hidden." *The Columbian*, January 17, 1968.

"Invitation for tonight," *The Columbian*, January 25, 1968.

"Academy's fate hangs on a deadline," *The Columbian*, January 26, 1968.

"Academy alum has plea on Provident," *The Columbian*, January 31, 1968.

"Academy studied as agency office," *The Columbian*, September 13, 1968.

Hopkins, Jack, "Providence Academy's future," *The Columbian*, May 13, 1973.

Box 31, Folder 3, Academy Plaza, 1972.

Bacon, Leonard, "Plans revealed for $14.5 million Providence Academy development," *The Oregonian*, June 8, 1972.

Hopkins, Jack, "Vancouver condominium project's future uncertain," *The Columbian*, December 1972.

Pierce, Steve, "Lack of communication scored," *The Columbian*, undated.

Box 31, Folder 4, The Academy.

"Academy drew praise, complaints," *The Columbian*, November 8, 1981.

Letter to Hidden Brothers from Sister Barbara Ellen Lundgerg, S.P., dated June 4, 1973, about loaning the structural item [chapel] and pews.
Hamilton, Don, "Owners write 'For Sale' on historic Academy – for right price," *The Oregonian,* copy dated June 6, 1984.
Box 31, Folder 7, The Academy, Chapel.
Johnson, Janis, "Old Academy to celebrate chapel opening," *The Oregonian,* Septemberıo, 1982.
Box 31, Folder 9, Moving of the bell, 1975.
Excerpt, Chronicles: Providence Heights, Issaquah, WA, February and March 1975.
"Two men killed in copter crash near Chehalis," *The Oregonian,* February 20, 1975.
"Trip for bell ends in tragic copter crash," *The Columbian,* February 20, 1975.
Bacon, Leonard, "19-century bell rehung in academy by Vancouver firemen," *The Sunday Oregonian,* March 2, 1975.
Box 31, Folder 11, Sale to Fort Vancouver Historic Trust, 2011-2012.
Email from Hartung, Susanne SP to Sister Karin Dufault, dated December 13, 2011, "Providence Academy Update."
Series 11: Subject.
Box 32, Folder 2, Benefactors.
"Benefactors of the Sisters of Charity of Providence, Providence Academy, Vancouver, Wn."
Box 32, Folder 6, Cornerstone.
"Order to Be Observed At the Blessing of the Corner-stone of the Orphans' New Building in Vancouver, on Sunday, Sept. 21st, 1873, at 2:30 P.M."
Box 32, Folder, Hidden family.
"Hidden Brick Company Close To Century Mark After Pioneer Found Suitable Clay on His Farm," *The Columbian,* January 5, 1965.
"Vancouver Family Buys St. Joseph Hospital," [??], March 20, 1969.
Craft Rozen, Sydney, "The Hidden Family," *Old Portland Today,* April 1976.
Dietrich, Bill, "The Hiddens: A foot in the past, a hand in the future," *The Columbian*, November 8, 1981.
Finken, Dee Anne, "Hidden Family—Cornerstones of Clark County," *Vancouver Business Journal*, January 19, 1998.
Series 12: Newspaper Clippings.
Box 32, Folder 15. 1865-1965.
"Providence School For Young Ladies," newspaper ad, 1865.
"Providence Sisters Centennial," *The Progress*, May 4, 1956.
Stevens, James, "Mother Joseph, Builder of Hospitals, Is Called This Region's First Architect," *The Seattle Times*, June 14, 1953.
Stevens, James, "Mother Joseph: Pioneer Architect," *The Sunday Oregonian Magazine*, October 4, 1953.
"Banquet and Drama Note Providence Centennial," *The Columbian*, May 9, 1956.
Van Arsdol, Ted, "Providence and Past – 1: Sisters of Providence and Northwest History Are Interwoven Skeins in Pattern Out or Past," *The Columbian,* November 5, 1963.
Van Arsdol, Ted, "Providence and Past – 2: Colorful Formal Ceremonies Marked the Start of Construction Job for House of Providence," *The Columbian,* November 6, 1963.
Van Arsdol, Ted, "Providence and Past – 3: Vancouver Institution Draws Noted Figures But Money. Problems Plague Building Pace," *The Columbian,* November 8, 1963.
Van Arsdol, Ted, "Providence and Past – 4: Chapel Still Highlight of Building Today, as it Was When Dedicated," *The Columbian*, undated.
Van Arsdol, Ted, "Providence and Past – 5: Tradition, History Have Carved Markings On Providence. Structure Over Its 90 Years," *The Columbian,* November 13, 1963.
Van Arsdol, Ted, "Providence and Past – 6: Apartments or Shopping Center May Take Over Historical Tract," *The Columbian,* November 14, 1963.
Box 32, Folder 16, 1966-2009.
[see also OS Folder 12]
OS Folder 11.
"When Mass Was First Said At Vancouver," *The Sunday Oregonian,* January 1, 1911.
"Vancouver 'Dig' Yields Old Stockade Remains," *Sunday Oregonian,* October 19, 1947.
Jewett, Dave, "Early Morning Bell Tolls the Start of Busy Day For Sisters At Academy," *The Columbian*, April 2, 1956.
Jewett, Dave, "Providence Academy, Pioneer Northwest School, Founded 100 Years Ago," *The Columbian,* April 2, 1956.
"Vancouver's Providence Academy prepares to Celebrate 100th Anniversary," *Oregon Journal,* April 4, 1956.
Blakely, Frances, "Providence Academy Observes 100 Years," *Oregon Journal*, April 6, 1956.
"Celebration Honors Heroic Achievements."
Pratt, Gerry, "Thanks Be to Providence," *The Sunday Oregonian,* May 6, 1956.

"Schools Ripped, Twisted by Clutching Fingers of Storm," *The Columbian*, October 15, 1962.

OS Folder 12.

Van Nostrand, Elisabet, "Old Academy envisioned as "period" arcade site," *The Columbian*, March 19, 1969.

Arenson, Kathy, "Providence Academy Prepares for Last Graduation," *The Columbian*, May 20, 1966.

"Vancouver Academy Safe From Wrecker," January 1, 1974.

Mosey, Ed, "Searching for Tenants, The Academy: making the old relevant," *The Columbian*, April 28, 1974.

Van Arsdol, Ted, "Providence Academy stirs with new life," *The Columbian*, September 9, 1974.

Bacon, Leonard, "Historic Vancouver school enters new career," *Sunday Oregonian*, April 6 1975.

Burnett, Bob, "The Academy," *The Columbian*, January 28, 1977.

Gianelli, Diane, "The church in Vancouver Sitting on the state's culturally richest soil," *The Progress*, November 16, 1979.

Beck, Bob, "History lessons: Academy still teaches about a nun's courage," *The Columbian*, July 8, 1979.

Beck, Bob, "The Academy: Standing guard over Vancouver's heritage," *The Columbian*, Sunday edition, undated, 1989.

Jones, Tricia, "Best Architecture"; "In Its Own Classic Class"; "Readers' Top 10"; "Building a List Vexed Architects"; "Architects" Top 10"; *The Columbian*, August 19, 2007.

Sisters of Providence Washington Corporation/Property/ Property Records (Vancouver), c. 1871-c. 1951, incomplete.

Fletcher-Daniels Abstract Co., Abstract of Title.

"An Act to Incorporate An Institution of Learning and Charitable Purposes In the County of Clarke, Washington… passed January 28, 1856," typescript, File No. C49101, filed July 25, 1927.

"Proposed Agreement between Providence Academy and St. Joseph's Hospital, Vancouver, Washington."

Sisters of Providence, Washington, Property Deeds, Agreements, 1858–1878.

Folder: Deeds, 1858-1898.

Deeds of Sisters of Charity of the House of Providence in the Territory of Washington, from February 23, 1858, ledger book containing Quit-Claim Deed, Act of Incorporation, Deeds, Ordinances, etc.

Folder: Deeds (Missions), 1863-1892.

Missions, Deeds of Sisters of Charity of the House of Providence in the Territory of Washington, from September 15, 1863, ledger book.

Folder: Property Agreements/Deeds, various.

Folder: Property, Deed of A. M. A. Blanchet, 1858.

Vente du terrain où se trouve actuellement l'orphelinat des garçons aux Srs Joseph, Praxedes et Blandine (1858) Quit-Claimed *de l'Évêque de Nesqually aux Srs de Charité*, February 3, 1858.

Deed, A. M. A. Blanchet to the Sisters of Charity of the House of Providence, July 19, 1864.

Deed, A. M. A. Blanchet, Bishop of Nisqually, to the Sisters of Charity of the House of Providence, dated November 15, 1877.

Folder: Property, Petition to City Council to close street, 1867-1873, Vancouver Petition.

Letter to Common Council of the City of Vancouver from Sisters of Charity, dated June 5, 1873.

Ordinance No. 76.

Letter dated June 3, 1873, signed Sr. Praxède.

Folder: Property. Deeds and Sale, Sections 21 and 28, Township 2, Clark Co. WA, Vancouver Farm, 1873-1944.

Folder: Property, Deed, Petrain Property, Amos Short Land Claim, 1874-1929.

Folder: Property, Deed, and Sale, section 11 and 12, Township 2, 1875-1927.

Description of Minnehaha Farm, The Dodd Claim.

Sisters of Providence Washington Corporation, Property/ Vancouver property sale to Robert Hidden, 1967-1974.

Letter to Sister Ernestine Marie from F. H. Andrews, real estate consultant, dated February 8, 1967.

Letter to Sister Ernestine Marie from F. H. Andrews, real estate consultant, dated February 22, 1967.

Letter to F. H. Andrews from Robert L. Harris, dated April 25, 1967.

Letter to Mr. Fran Andrews from Sister Cecilia Abhold, FCSP, dated January 2. 1968.

Letter to Sister Cecilia from Mr. and Mrs. John Repman, dated January 25, 1968.

Letter to Sister Rita from Virginia Hidden, dated January 26, 1968.

Letter to Sister Rita from Mrs. Alice L. Wright, dated January 27, 1968.

Letter to Sister Rita from Harley Mays, dated January 27, 1968.

Letter to Sister Rita from Virginia Hidden, dated January 28, 1968.

Letter to Sisters of Charity from Lesla E. Scott, dated February 2, 1968.

Letter to Mr. Robert A. Comfort from F. H. Andrews, dated October 11, 1968.

Letter to Sister Ernestine Marie from F. H. Andrews, real estate consultant, dated November 1, 1968, in which is included a handwritten sheet entitled "Principles of

Purchase" signed by William Foster Hidden and Robert A. Hidden.

Handwritten note/memo to Sister Cecilia, dated November 27, 1968.

Letter to Sisters of Charity of Providence from Robert and Virginia Hidden, dated January 3, 1969.

Letter to Irwin C. Landerholm, Esq. from Donald L. Johnson of Law Offices of Bogle, Gates, Dobrin, Wakefield & Long, dated January 23, 1969.

"Sale of Providence Academy Property," March 5, 1969, document included with a letter to Sister Ernestine Marie from Donald L. Johnson of Law Offices of Bogle, Gates, Dobrin, Wakefield & Long, dated March 7, 1969.

"Certified Copy of Corporate Resolution," signed by Sister Rita Bergamini, dated March 5, 1969.

Letter to Mr. Donald L. Johnson from John L. Warme of Rahn and Company Inc., dated March 7, 1969.

Letter to Sister Marie Paule Levaque from Sister Susan Hunsaker, dated April 14, 1970.

Letter to Mr. Bill Hidden from Tina Youngquist, dated February 13, 1973.

Letter to Rev. James H. Gandrau, Editor of *The Catholic Northwest Progress* from Sister Rita, dated March 22, 1974.

Letter to Robert Hidden from Sister Lucelle Dean, SP, dated August 20, 1984.

Handwritten note by Sister Rita Bergamini, stamped September 20, 1988, "Sister Barbara Schiller relates the following… Si Sheeley, County Officer worker…"

"Drive to Save Academy Set," *The Oregon Journal*, January 10, 1968.

Regional Book Collection, Vancouver.

A Brief History of the Hudson's Bay Company, Incorporated 2 May 1670, Winnipeg, s.n., 1988, pamphlet.

A Report to the Citizens of Vancouver WA by the City Planning Commission, 1945, pp. 10-12 and plate no. 8.

Berger, Brian, "The Economy," *Beautiful Vancouver U.S.A.*, 1979.

Burnham, Howard, *Early Land Titles In Vancouver, Washington*, Vancouver, WA, Clark County Abstract & Title Co., 1947.

Clancy, Kathleen, "The Pacific Northwest's White-Headed Eagle," *St. Joseph Magazine*, September 1957.

Providence Archives, Seattle, digital database, http://providencearchives.contentdm.oclc.org/cdm/.

Cadastral map of Saint Joseph Hospital, Vancouver, WA, 1919, http://providencearchives.contentdm.oclc.org/cdm/singleitem/collection/p15352coll1/id/183/rec/5.

Cadastral map of Providence Academy, Vancouver, WA, 1919, http://providencearchives.contentdm.oclc.org/cdm/ref/collection/p15352coll3/id/400.

Cadastral map of Providence Academy, Vancouver, WA, 1919, http://providencearchives.contentdm.oclc.org/cdm/ref/collection/p15352coll3/id/399.

Cadastral map of Providence Academy, Vancouver, WA, July 1919, http://providencearchives.contentdm.oclc.org/cdm/ref/collection/p15352coll3/id/401.

Title History of Saint Joseph Hospital, Vancouver, WA, 1919, http://providencearchives.contentdm.oclc.org/cdm/singleitem/collection/p15352coll1/id/180/rec/3.

1948 photograph of the interior of the chapel at Providence Academy, http://providencearchives.contentdm.oclc.org/cdm/singleitem/collection/p15352coll3/id/514.

Chapel of the former Providence Academy, Vancouver, WA, 1977, http://providencearchives.contentdm.oclc.org/cdm/singleitem/collection/p15352coll3/id/518/rec/103.

The five foundresses of the Sisters of Providence Northwest mission in Oregon Territory, http://providencearchives.contentdm.oclc.org/cdm/singleitem/collection/p15352coll3/id/853/rec/48.

Statue of Mother Joseph of the Sacred Heart by Felix de Wel don, 1980, http://providencearchives.contentdm.oclc.org/cdm/singleitem/collection/p15352coll15/id/174/rec/34.

Sisters Mary of Nazareth (left) and Mary Conrad on horseback, preparing to leave on a begging tour at St. Eugene Mission, Kootenay, British Columbia, c. 1896 http://providencearchives.contentdm.oclc.org/cdm/singleitem/collection/p15352coll5/id/316/rec/85.

Mother Joseph of the Sacred Heart, 1823-1902, c. 1882, http://providencearchives.contentdm.oclc.org/cdm/singleitem/collection/p15352coll15/id/198/rec/51.

Mother Joseph of the Sacred Heart, 1850s, http://providencearchives.contentdm.oclc.org/cdm/singleitem/collection/p15352coll15/id/204/rec/142.

Mother Joseph of the Sacred Heart, 1823-1902, c. 1900, http://providencearchives.contentdm.oclc.org/cdm/singleitem/collection/p15352coll15/id/199/rec/127.

Architect J. B. Blanchet, 1883, http://providencearchives.contentdm.oclc.org/cdm/singleitem/collection/p15352coll1/id/264/rec/177.

Visitors filing into Providence Academy for the centennial celebration of the arrival of the sisters in the northwest, Vancouver, WA, 1956, http://providencearchives.

contentdm.oclc.org/cdm/singleitem/collection/p15352coll3/id/802/rec/218.
Newspaper article announcing a fundraising fair to benefit the orphans at Providence Academy, Vancouver, WA, c. 1873, http://providencearchives.contentdm.oclc.org/cdm/singleitem/collection/p15352coll3/id/1057/rec/6.
The first convent of the sisters in the Northwest (water tower in background), http://providencearchives.contentdm.oclc.org/cdm/singleitem/collection/p15352coll3/id/870/rec/91.
The first convent of the sisters in the Northwest (Providence Academy in background), http://providencearchives.contentdm.oclc.org/cdm/singleitem/collection/p15352coll3/id/419/rec/124.
First convent of the Sisters of Providence in the Northwest, Vancouver, Oregon Territory (water tower in background), http://providencearchives.contentdm.oclc.org/cdm/singleitem/collection/p15352coll3/id/429/rec/137.
Providence Academy, Vancouver, WA, 1901, http://providencearchives.contentdm.oclc.org/cdm/singleitem/collection/p15352coll3/id/1063/rec/17.
Interior of a classroom circa 1900, http://providencearchives.contentdm.oclc.org/cdm/singleitem/collection/p15352coll3/id/1067/rec/2.

Books, Monographs, Dissertations

96th Congress, 2nd Session, Senate Document No. 96-70, *Acceptance of the Statue of Mother Joseph (Esther Pariseau) Presented by the State of Washington, Proceedings in the Rotunda of the United States Capitol, Washington, D.C., May 1, 1980,* Washington, United States Government Printing Office, 1980.
Corriveau, Claude, *Les voitures à chevaux à Québec*, Sillery, Septentrion, 1991.
Danylewycz, Marta, *Taking the Veil: An Alternative to Marriage, Motherhood, and Spinsterhood in Quebec, 1840-1920*, Toronto, McClelland and Stewart, 1987.
Erigero, Patricia C., *Fort Vancouver Cultural Landscape Report, Volume II*, National Park Service, U.S. Department of the Interior, 1992, http://www.nps.gov/history/history/online_books/fova/clr.htm.
Hussey, John A., *Fort Vancouver Historic Structures Report: Historical Data, Volumes I and II*, National Park Service, U.S. Department of the Interior, June 1972 (Vol. I), April 1976 (Vol. II), http://www.nps.gov/history/history/online_books/fova/hsr/hsr.htm.
Kinney, Thomas A., *The Carriage Trade: Making Horse-Drawn Vehicles in America*, Baltimore, Johns Hopkins University Press, 2004.
Lacoursière, Jacques and Robin Philpot, *A People's History of Quebec*, Montreal, Baraka Books, 2009.
Lamb, W. Kaye, "McLOUGHLIN, JOHN," *Dictionary of Canadian Biography,* Vol. 8, University of Toronto/Université Laval, 2003, http://www.biographi.ca/en/bio/mcloughlin_john_8E.html.
Lapointe-Roy, Huguette, "PARISEAU, ESTHER, Joseph du Sacré-Cœur," *Dictionary of Canadian Biography,* Vol. 13, University of Toronto/Université Laval, 2003, http://www.biographi.ca/en/bio/pariseau_esther_13E.html.
Laurin, Nicole, Danielle Juteau, and Lorraine Duschesne, À la recherche d'un monde oublié: Les communautés religieuses de femme au Québec de 1900-1970, Montreal, Le Jour, Éditeur, 1991.
Lentz, Sister Dorothy, s.p. *The Way It Was in Providence Schools: Stories of Seven Providence Schools in the West Founded between 1856-1920*, Montreal, Sisters of Providence, Providence Mother House, 1978.
Lessard, Michel, *Antiquités du Québec : Objets anciens*, Montréal, Éditions de l'Homme, 1994.
Luxton, Donald, editor, *Building the West: Early Architects of British Columbia,* Vancouver, British Columbia, Talonbooks, 2003.
Martin, Tania, "The Architecture of Charity: Power, Gender, and Religion in North America, 1840-1960," Ph.D. Dissertation, University of California, Berkeley, 2002.
McCrosson, Sister Mary of the Blessed Sacrament, with Sister Mary Leopoldine and Sister Maria Theresa, s.p. *The Bell and the River*, Palo Alto, Pacific Books, 1956, 2006.
Ochsner, Jeffrey Karl, editor/co-author, *Shaping Seattle Architecture: A Historical Guide to the Architects*, Seattle and London: AIA Seattle and University of Washington Press, 1994.
Rousseau, Louis and Frank W. Remiggi, *Atlas historique des pratiques religieuses: Le Sud-Ouest du Québec au XIXe siècle*, Ottawa, Les Presses de l'Université d'Ottawa, 1998.
Taylor, Terri A., *Fort Vancouver Cultural Landscape Report, Vol. I*, National Park Service, U.S. Department of the Interior, 1992, http://www.nps.gov/history/history/online_books/fova/clr.htm.
United States Department of the Interior, National Park Service, *National Register of Historic Places, Inventory – Nomination Form, House of Providence*, received April 12, 1978.
The Institute of Providence, History of the Daughters of Charity Servants of the Poor, Known As The Sisters of Providence, Vol. V, Montreal, Providence Mother House, 1949.
Venerable Development, LCC, "Providence Academy: Due Diligence and Development Recommendations Report," Portland, Oregon, October 26, 2012.

"Women in Architecture Exhibits Committee," Vancouver, B.C., Women in Architecture Exhibits Committee, 1996.

Internet

Andrews, Mildred, "Sisters of Providence arrive at Fort Vancouver on December 8, 1856," February 15, 2003, HistoryLink File #5207, http://www.historylink.org/_content/printer_friendly/pf_output.cfm?file_id=5207.

Andrews, Mildred, "Sisters of Providence open their first Seattle hospital on August 2, 1878,"

December 8, 1998, revised February 5, 2001, corrected August 3, 2008, HistoryLink File #461.

Andrews, Mildred, "Seattle's Providence Hospital moves to a new building on September 24, 1911," December 9, 1998, updated May 12, 2002, HistoryLink File #471, http://www.historylink.org/_content/printer_friendly/pf_output.cfm?file_id=471.

"Bishop Augustin Blanchet dedicates Washington's original St. James Cathedral at Fort Vancouver on January 23, 1851," HistoryLink File #9126, http://www.historylink.org/_content/printer_friendly/pf_output.cfm?file_id=9126.

Caldbick, John J., "Lowell Mason Hidden opens the Hidden Brick Company in Vancouver, Clark County, in 1871," September 1, 2009, HistoryLink File #9132, http://historylink.org/index.cfm?DisplayPage=output.cfm&file_id=9132.

Glowen, Ronald P., compiler, "Timeline: Native Americans in the Inland Northwest: Wars and Treaties," http://www.narhist.ewu.edu/native_americans/timelines/timeline_wars_treaties.html.

Metz, William, "Seattle," *The Catholic Encyclopedia*, Vol. 13, New York, Robert Appleton Company, 1912, http://www.newadvent.org/cathen/13665a.htm.

"Mother Joseph of the Sisters of Providence (Esther Pariseau), 1823-1902," HistoryLink File #5483, http://www.historylink.org/_content/printer_friendly/pf_output.cfm?file_id=5483.

Paulus Jr., Michael J., "The Sisters of Providence establish St. Vincent's Academy in Walla Walla on February 18, 1864," August 18, 2010, HistoryLink File #9517.

Paulus Jr., Michael J., "Cornerstone is laid for St. Mary's Hospital in Walla Walla on August 3, 1879," August 17, 2010, HistoryLink File #9518, http://historylink.org/index.cfm?DisplayPage=output.cfm&file_id=9518.

Parmenter, Jon R., David Edmunds, and Gregory Moore, "Wars With Indian Nations," *Dictionary of American History*, Stanley I. Kutler, editor, 3rd edition. Vol. 8, New York, Charles Scribner's Sons, 2003, pp. 395-405, *U.S. History in Context*, September 17, 2014, http://ic.galegroup.com/ic/uhic/ReferenceDetailsPage/ReferenceDetails Window?displayGroupName=Reference&disable Highlighting=true&prodId=UHIC&action=e&windowstate=normal&catId=&documentId=GALE%7CCX3401804479&source=Bookmark&u=lnoca_hawken&jsid=eb550ceb5d50c37372e4dbd87626b41b.

Hidden Family, http://history.columbian.com/hidden-brick-company/.

"History of Willamette University," *Wikipedia*, https://www.willamette.edu/about/history/index.html.

"Yakima War, " http://en.wikipedia.org/wiki/Yakima_War.

"Hudson's Bay Company, 19th Century," *Wikipedia*, http://en.wikipedia.org/wiki/Hudson's_Bay_Company#19th_century.

Metsker, Thos C., Historic Map, Township 2N, range 1W, Vancouver, Tomahawk Island, *Clark County 1961 Atlas, Historic Map Works,* http://www.historicmapworks.com/Map/US/1253495/.

Metsker, Thos C., Historic Map, Township 2N, range 1W, Vancouver, Hazel Dell, Lakeshore, Hidden, Smith Lake, *Clark County 1961 Atlas, Historic Map Works,* http://www.historicmapworks.com/Map/US/1253494/Township+2+N+++Range+1+W+++Vancouver++Hazel+Dell++Lakeshore++Hidden++Smith+Lake/Clark+County+1961/Washington/.

Clark County Historical Museum, http://www.cchmuseum.org/.

Aerial View of Vancouver, 1972, Photographs Collection, P02.1.4, cchm00024.tif.

School for the Deaf, Photographs Collection, P03.3.4, cchm00175.tif.

School for the Deaf, Photographs Collection, P75, cchm09660.tif; cchm09654.tif.

School for the Deaf, Photographs Collection, PN56, cmpn00072.tif.

Broadway Street in Vancouver, P79.1.7, cchm06505.tif.

Business People, Photographs Collection, P48.7.171, cchm07073.tif.

Clark County Historical Museum, Photographs Collection, P10.51, cchm01867.tif.

Court House Building, Photographs Collection, P10.19.15, cchm01029.tif.

L. M. Hidden at the Washington State School for the Blind Dedication Ceremony, Photographs Collection, P74, cchm09635.tif.

L. M. Hidden, Photographs Collection, P48.8.117, cchm07191.tif.

Main Street in Vancouver, Photographs Collection, P79.1.2.2, cchm06496.tif.

Vancouver, Clarke County, USA in the Great State of Washington, c. 1910, cchm00000p01_cchm00000p023 (includes a photograph of House of Providence; Hotel Columbia; State School for the Deaf; Vancouver Hospital).
Downtown Vancouver, Photographs Collection, P.15.34.3, cchm03185.tif.
Foster Hidden Home, Photographs Collection, P32.3.20, cchm04850.tif.
Hidden Brickyard, Photographs Collection, P10.13.2, cchm00946.tif.
Hidden Brickyard Crew, Photographs Collection, P10.13, cchm00947.tif.
Hidden House, Photographs Collection, P10.36.3, cchm01296.tif.
Hidden House, Photographs Collection, PN90, cmpn00136.tif.
Pacific Coast Architecture Database (PCAD).
"Sisters of Providence, Providence Hospital #1, Seattle, WA," https://digital.lib.washington.edu/architect/structures/4790/.
"MacKay, Donald," https://digital.lib.washington.edu/architect/architects/2693/.
"Roman Catholic Diocese of Nesqually, Saint James Cathedral #2, Vancouver, WA." https://digital.lib.washington.edu/architect/structures/8101/.
Pioneer Courthouse Historical Society, "The Pioneer Courthouse Architecture," http://pioneercourthouse.org/architecture.html.
U.S. General Services Administration, "Pioneer Courthouse, Portland, OR," http://www.gsa.gov/portal/ext/html/site/hb/category/25431/actionParameter/exploreByBuilding/buildingId/31, includes a copy of the National Register of Historic Places Inventory Nomination Form.
Providence Health & Services "Pioneer, Leader, Woman of Faith," sketch first published January 2002, http://www2.providence.org/phs/archives/history-online/MJSH/Pages/Pioneer.aspx.
The Academy Campaign, http://www.academycampaign.org/.

Newspapers

Vogt, Tom, "Sole Sister moves on," *The Columbian*, April 11, 2012, http://www.columbian.com/news/2012/apr/11/sole-sister-moves-on-jumppresence-of-sisters-of-pr/.
Vogt, Tom, "Vancouver National Trust to purchase The Academy," *The Columbian*, May 1, 2012, http://www.columbian.com/news/2012/may/01/historic-academy-moment-fort-vancouver-na/.
Joner, Cami, "Williamsburg of the West? The Academy could anchor historic area," *The Columbian*, May 1, 2012, http://www.columbian.com/news/2012/may/01/williamsburg-of-the-west-academy-could-anchor-hist/.
Kulmac, Nicholas Shannon, "Fort Vancouver National Trust announces plan to purchase the Academy for $10.6 million," *Vancouver Business Journal*, May 1, 2012, http://www.vbjusa.com/news/261-breaking-news/5084-breaking-fort-vancouver-national-trust-announces-plan-to-purchase-the-academy-for-106-million.
"In Our View: Multiple Winners," *The Columbian*, May 2, 2012, http://www.columbian.com/news/2012/may/02/multiple-winners/.
Kulmac, Nicholas Shannon, "A historic business deal," *Vancouver Business Journal*, May 4, 2012, http://www.vbjusa.com/news/top-stories/7115-a-historic-business-deal.
Vogt, Tom, "Off Beat: Old-school construction boosts Academy restoration," *The Columbian*, May 7, 2012, http://www.columbian.com/news/2012/may/07/old-school-construction-boosts-academy-restoration/.
Joner, Cami, "Trust sees Academy restoration as financially viable project," *The Columbian*, August 18, 2012, http://www.columbian.com/news/2012/aug/18/fort-vancouver-national-trust-academy-project-viab/.
"In Our View: Preserving Our History," *The Columbian*, August 27, 2012, http://www.columbian.com/news/2012/aug/27/preserving-our-history/.
Oliver, Gordon, "Portland developer DeMuro dies," *The Columbian*, September 10, 2012, http://www.columbian.com/news/2012/sep/10/portland-developer-demuro-dies/.
Joner, Cami, "Academy focus of fundraising efforts," *The Columbian*, December 10, 2012, http://www.columbian.com/news/2012/dec/10/preserving-the-academy-trust-has-raised-about-3m-0/.
Hewitt, Scott, "Alumnae return to The Academy for fun, future," *The Columbian*, February 13, 2013, http://www.columbian.com/news/2013/feb/09/alumnae-return-to-academy-for-fun-future/.
Vogt, Tom, "Trust launches campaign for Academy," *The Columbian*, March 18, 2013, http://www.columbian.com/news/2013/mar/18/trust-launches-campaign-academy/.
Kulmac, Nicholas Shannon, "Trust's 'P2' campaign targets business community," *Vancouver Business Journal*, March 22, 2013, http://www.vbjusa.com/news/top-stories/9014-trust-s-p2-campaign-targets-business-community.
Joner, Cami, "Academy fundraising efforts intensify," *The Columbian*, March 26, 2013, http://www.columbian.com/news/2013/mar/26/academy-fundraising-effort-intensifies/.

Mathieu, Stevie, "Senators support state funding for Children's Center, Academy project" *The Columbian,* April 9, 2013, http://www.columbian.com/news/2013/apr/09/senators-support-state-funding-for-childrens-cente/#.

Kulmac, Nicholas Shannon, "Academy campaign receives $100,000 matching gift," *Vancouver Business Journal*, August 21, 2013, http://www.vbjusa.com/news/news-briefs/9402-academy-campaign-receives-100-000-matching-gift.

Kulmac, Nicholas Shannon, "Fort Vancouver National Trust gets Academy purchase agreement extension," *Vancouver Business Journal*, November 22, 2013, http://www.vbjusa.com/news/top-stories/9674-academy-purchas.

Hewitt, Scott, "Vancouver residents issue Academy fund-raising challenge," *The Columbian,* August 22, 2013, http://www.columbian.com/news/2013/aug/22/vancouver-residents-academy-fundraising-challenge/.

"Fundraiser to Buy Academy Extended," *The Columbian,* November 22, 2013, http://www.columbian.com/news/2013/nov/22/fundraiser-to-buy-academy-extended/.

Nicholas Shannon Kulmac, "Fort Vancouver National Trust gets Academy purchase agreement extension," *Vancouver Business Journal*, November 22, 2013, http://www.vbjusa.com/news/top-stories/9674-academy-purchas.

Vogt, Tom, "Trust wins $650K grant for purchase of Academy," *The Columbian*, April 23, 2014, http://www.columbian.com/news/2014/apr/23/academy-grant-fort-vancouver-national-trust/.

Suffia, David, "Clark College exploring new restaurant and fermentation science program," *Vancouver Business Journal*, June 27, 2014, http://www.vbjusa.com/news/top-stories/10269-clark-college-exploring-new-restaurant-and-fermentation-science-program.

Louise Blanchard Bethune

Barbasch, Adriana, "Louise Blanchard Bethune: The AIA Accepts Its First Woman Member," *Architecture: A Place for Women*, Ellen Perry Berkeley and M. McQuaid, editors, Washington, Smithsonian Institution Press, 1989.

Barbasch, Adriana, "A Tribute to the First Professional Woman Architect Admitted to the American Institute of Architecture: Louise Bethune, FAIA," researched and compiled for the March 6, 2005 Induction of Louise Bethune to the Western New York Women's Hall of Fame, Buffalo/Western New York Chapter of the American Institute of Architects.

Bernstein, Peter L., *Wedding of the Waters: The Erie Canal and the Making of a Great Nation*, New York, W. W. Norton & Company, 2005.

Bethune, Louise, "Women and Architecture," address quoted in article, "Woman's Work," *The Inland Architect and News Record*, Vol. XVII, No. 2, March 1891, pp. 20-21.

Bethune, Louise, "Women as Architects," address reprinted in *Buffalo Daily Courier,* July 13, 1884, Buffalo History Museum archives.

Brown, Clinton, Historic Preservation Certification Application, undated.

Buffalo Architectural Guidebook Corporation, sponsor, *Buffalo Architecture: A Guide*, Cambridge, MIT Press, 1981.

Buffalo Projects: H. H. Richardson, Buffalo, New York, Burchfield Center, Western New York Forum for American Art, State University College at Buffalo.

By-Laws and Rules of the Women's Wheel and Athletic Club," Buffalo, July 3, 1888, Buffalo Historical Museum.

"The Convention," Official Report of the Second Annual Convention of the Western Association of Architects, held at St. Louis, November 18, 19 and 20, 1885, *The Inland Architect and Builder*, Vol. VI, No. 5, November 1885, p. 66.

Cromley, Elizabeth, "Lafayette Square Study: Buffalo Place Competition," Buffalo, SUNY School of Architecture, 1986, Buffalo History Museum archives.

Crooker, James F., *Department of Education Report: Superintendent of Education, City of Buffalo: 1882-1883*, Buffalo, Laughlin, 1884, Buffalo History Museum archives.

Crooker, James F., *Department of Education Report: Superintendent of Education, City of Buffalo: 1883-1884*, Buffalo, Laughlin, 1885, Buffalo History Museum archives.

Crooker, James F., *Department of Education Report: Superintendent of Education, City of Buffalo: 1884-1885*, Buffalo, Laughlin, 1887, Buffalo History Museum archives.

Crooker, James F., *Department of Education Report: Superintendent of Education, City of Buffalo: 1885-1886*, Buffalo, Laughlin, 1887, Buffalo History Museum archives.

Crooker, James F., *Department of Education Report: Superintendent of Education, City of Buffalo: 1886-1887*, Buffalo, Laughlin, 1888, Buffalo History Museum archives.

"Zina Bethune (1945-2012)," Obituary, *Dance Magazine,* February 2012.

Dillon, Michael, *The Life and Times of Edward H. Butler, Founder of the Buffalo* News *(1850-1914): A Crusading Journalist Navigates the Gilded Age*, Lewiston, The Edwin Mellen Press, 2003.

Atherton Fernald, Frederick, "Lafayette Hotel," *Index Guide to Buffalo and Niagara Falls,* pp. 95-96, Buffalo, Frederick A. Fernard, 1910, Buffalo Collection, Buffalo and Erie County Public Library.

Fox, Austin M., "Louise Blanchard Bethune (1856-1913)," *Buffalo Spree*, Summer, 1986, pp. 50-51, Special Collections, Vertical files, Buffalo and Erie County Public Library.

Goldman, Mark, *High Hopes: The Rise and Decline of Buffalo, New York*, Albany, State University of New York Press, 1983.

Grant, Kerry L., *The Rainbow City: Celebrating Light, Color, and Architecture at the Pan-American Exposition, Buffalo, 1901*, Buffalo, Canisus College Press, 2001.

Hays, Johanna, *Louise Blanchard Bethune, America's First Female Professional Architect*, Jefferson, North Carolina, McFarland & Company, Inc., 2014, includes list of works.

James, Edward T., editor, "Bethune, Louise Blanchard," *Notable American Women, 1607-1950: A Biographical Dictionary*, Vol. 1, pp. 140-141, Cambridge, The Belknap Press of Harvard University Press, 1971.

Jonnes, Jill, *Empires of Light: Edison, Tesla, Westinghouse, and the Race to Electrify the World*, New York, Random House Trade Paperbacks, 2004.

"*Lafayette, Buffalo*," brochure published by the Lafayette Hotel, c. 1904, TX 941, L34, Buffalo History Museum archives.

Leary, Thomas and Elizabeth Sholes with the Buffalo and Erie County Historical Society, *Images of America: Buffalo's Pan-American Exposition*, Charleston, South Carolina, Arcadia Publishing, 1998.

Leonard, Jon, editor-in-chief, *Woman's Who's Who of America, 1914-1915*, p. 98, New York, The American Commonwealth Company, 1914.

Logan, Mrs. John A., "Louise Bethune," *The Part Taken by Women in American History*, pp. 787-788, Wilmington, Delaware, The Perry-Nalle Publishing Co., 1912.

Longbottom, Tom, "New Hotel Statler Opens Tonight in a Blaze of Glory," *Buffalo Saturday Night*, May 19, 1923.

Hayes McAlonie, Kelly, "Louise Bethune: America's first woman architect," in a special architecture issue of *Buffalo Spree*, pp. 78-81, July/August 2006.

Men and Women of America, p. 147, New York, L. R. Hamersly & Co., 1910.

Miller, Page P., editor, *Reclaiming the Past: Landmarks of Women's History*, Bloomington, IN, Indiana University Press, 1992, Buffalo and Erie County Public Library, Vertical files.

The National Cyclopædia of American Biography: Being the History of the United States. Vol. XII, New York, James T. White & Company, 1904, Buffalo History Museum archives.

Nye, David E., *Electrifying America, Social Meanings of a New Technology, 1880-1940*, Cambridge, The MIT Press, 1997.

Olenick, Andy, Photography, and Richard O. Reisem, Text, *Classic Buffalo: A Heritage of Distinguished Architecture*, Buffalo, Canisius College Press, 1999.

Hubbell, Mark S., *Our Police and Our City*, pp. 705-707, 711, Buffalo, Bensler and Wesley, 1893, Buffalo History Museum Research Library.

Pettengill, George E., Hon. AIA, "How AIA Acquired Its First Woman Member, Mrs. Louise Bethune," *AIA Journal*, March, 1975, Special Collections, Vertical File, Buffalo and Erie County Public Library.

Quinan, Jack, *Frank Lloyd Wright's Buffalo Venture: From the Larkin Building to Broadacre City, A Catalogue of Buildings and Projects*, San Francisco, Pomegranate Communications, Inc., 2012.

"Richard A. Waite," *The Men of New York*, Vol. I, pp. 87-88, Buffalo, Geo. E. Matthews & Co., 1898.

Reitzes, Lisa, "Bethune, Louise Blanchard," *American National Biography*, Vol. 2, p. 703, New York, Oxford University Press, 1999.

Sanborn and Ferris Map Company, "City of Buffalo, New York," New York, Sanborn Map Company, 1889, Buffalo History Museum archives.

Sanborn and Ferris Map Company, "City of Buffalo, New York," New York, Sanborn Map Company, 1893, Buffalo History Museum archives.

Sanborn and Ferris Map Company, "City of Buffalo, New York," New York, Sanborn Map Company, 1916, Buffalo History Museum archives.

Saylor, Henry H., FAIA, "Institute Structure," *A.I.A.'s First Hundred Years*, pp. 10-23, Washington, D.C., The Octagon, 1957.

"Some Distinguished Women of Buffalo," *American Woman's Illustrated World,* October 7, 1893, p. 325, Buffalo and Erie County Public Library.

Stern, Madeleine B., "Louise Bethune, 1881," *We the Women: Career Firsts of 19th-Century America*, pp. 61-67, New York, Schulte Publishing Co., 1963.

Tesla, Nikola, *My Inventions and Other Writings*, New York, Penguin Classics, 2011.

"Third Annual Convention of the Western Association of Architects, Held at Chicago, November 17, 18 and 19, 1886," *The Inland Architect and Builder*, Vol. VIII, No. 8, December, 1886, pp. 76-79.

Wachadlo, Martin, *Louise Blanchard Bethune and her Office: Partial List of Known Works, 1883-1897* (as of March 1996), Blasdell, Martin Wachadlo, 1996, Buffalo History Museum archives.

Wachadlo, Martin, "RICHARD A. WAITE (1848-1911), Architect, Buffalo, NY, Preliminary List of work, 1875-1881," compiled February 1996.

Wachadlo, Martin, F. Kowsky, and D. McEneny, "Hotel Lafayette," National Register of Historic Places, Registration Form, July 6, 2010.
Wachadlo, Martin, & C. Brown, "Richard Waite: A Forgotten Master," *Western New York Heritage Magazine*, Winter 2004.
Wilner, M. M., "The City of Buffalo," *Truth*, Vol. XVII, No. 11, November 1899.
Willard, Frances E. and M. A. Livermore, editors, *A Woman of the Century: Fourteen Hundred-Seventy Biographical Sketches Accompanied by Portraits of Leading American Women in all Walks of Life*, pp. 80-81, New York, Charles Wells Moulton, 1893.
Willard, Frances, editor, *American Women: Fifteen Hundred Biographies*, revised edition, pp. 81-82, New York, Mast, Crowell & Kirkpatrick, 1897.
The Women's Wheel and Athlete Club, organized July 4, 1888, incorporated March 18, 1893, Buffalo, 1894, Buffalo History Museum Archives.

Internet Sources

"About the AIA," http://www.aia.org/about/index.htm.
"The AIA Historical Directory of American Architects," http://public.aia.org/sites/hdoaa/wiki.
"AIA Directory of Public Policies and Position Statements," amended 2013, http://www.aia.org/aiaucmp/groups/aia/documents/pdf/aias078764.pdf.
Association for the Advancement of Women, "Annual report of the Association of the Advancement of Women for 1881," Boston, Press of Cochrane & Sampson, 1882, Widener Library the Harvard University, http://nrs.hardvard.edu/urn-3:FHCL:506946.
"Arthur G. Yates." www.librarweb.ora/~digitized/books/Biographical_record_or_the_city_of_Rochester%20_and_Monroe _County.pdf.
"Buffalo Population 2014," *World Population Review*, June 22, 2014, worldpopulationreview.com.
Eck, Susan, "Lafayette Hotel: Part 1, The place to be Downtown," http://wnyheritagepress.org/photos_week_2012/hotel_lafayette/lafayette_part1.html.
Eck, Susan, "Lafayette Hotel: Part 2, The place to be Downtown," http://wnyheritagepress.org/photos_week_2012/hotel_lafayette/lafayette_part2.html.
Eck, Susan, "10 Lafayette Square-Roos Block, Buffalo German Insurance Building, Tishman Building," http://wnyheritagepress.org/photos_week_2012/german_insurance_tishman/german_insurance_tishman.html.
Fernandez, Manny, "What Do You Expect for $99.23 a Night?" http://www.nytimes.com/2005/11/20/nyregion/20carter.html.
Fincham, Jack E., "Did a Medicine Bottle Change History? Duffy's Malt Whiskey," *Bottles and Extras*, May-June 2013, http://www.peachridgeglass.com/2013/05/is-it-just-a-duffys-pure-malt-whiskey-bottle/.
Gee, Derek, "Progress at the Lafayette," *Buffalo News*, January 12, 2012, http://www.buffalonews.com/apps/pbcs.dll/gallery?Site=BN&Date=20120112&Category=PHOTOGALLERIES&ArtNo=301129999&Ref=PH&Profile=1413.
Hevesi, Dennis, "Zina Bethune Dies at 66; Actress, Dancer and Choreographer," *The New York Times*, February 18, 2012, http://www.nytimes.com/2012/02/19/arts/zina-bethune-actress-and-dancer-dies-at-66.html.
Kaplan, Thomas, "In Buffalo, Vision, Perhaps Illusions of a University-Fueled Revitalization," *The New York Times*, May 8, 2011, http://www.nytimes.com/2011/05/09/nyregion/buffalo-pins-hope-for-revival-on-university-expansion.html.
LaChiusa, Chuck, *Buffalo as an Architectural Museum*, http://www.buffaloah.com/a/DCTNRY/b/beaux.html.
LaChiusa, Chuck, *The History of Buffalo: A Chronology*, buffaloah.com/h/histindex.html.
LaChiusa, Chuck, "Lafayette Hotel-Table of Contents," *Buffalo as an Architectural Museum*, http://www.buffaloah.com/a/washngtn/391/index.html.
Meyer, Brian, "City approves $800,000 loan for Hotel Lafayette project," *Buffalo News*, May 12, 2011, http://www.buffalonews.com/city/communities/downtown/article421246.ece.
Meyer, Brian, "Work to start this month on Hotel Lafayette Makeover," *Buffalo News*, August 31, 2010, http://www.buffalonews.com/city/communities/article177226.ece.
McKelvey, Blake, "From Stagecoach Taverns to Airline Motels," *Rochester History*, Vol. XXXI, No. 4, October 1969, www.libraryweb.org/~rochhist/v31_1969/v3li4.pdf.
McKelvey, Blake, "Historic Predecessors of the Central Business District," *Rochester History*, Vol. XXXIV, No. 2, April 1972, www.libraryweb.org/~rochhist/v34_1972/v.34:2.pdf.
Ouroussoff, Nicolai, "Saving Buffalo's Untold Beauty," *The New York Times*, November 16, 2008.
Puma, Mike, "The Craftsmanship of Restoring the Hotel Lafayette," *Buffalo Rising*, November 7, 2011, buffalorising.com/2011/11/the-craftsmanship-of-restoring-the-hotel-lafayette/.
Reilly, Ed, "Hotel Lafayette Scheduled to Open in 4 Weeks," Eye Witness News, March 29, 2012, http://www.wkbw.com/video/Hotel-Lafayette-Scheduled-to-Open-in-4-Weeks-144987745.html.
"Richard Alfred Waite," http://familytreemaker.genealogy.com/users/s/t/u/Elizabeth-Stuerke-IL/WEBSITE-0001/UHP-0037.html.

Richert, George, "Congress for New Urbanism comes to Buffalo," News 4, June 4, 2014, http://wivb.com/2014/06/04/congress-for-new-urbanism-comes-to-buffalo/.
Sullivan, Mary Ann, photographer, http://www.bluffton.edu/%5C~sullivanm/newyork/buffalo/lafayette/bethune.html
"Tax breaks keep Hotel Lafayette alive," News 4, November 8, 2010, http://www.wivb.com/dpp/news/buffalo/Tax-breaks-keep-Hotel-Lafayette-alive.
Treehorn, Jackie, "Construction Watch: Hotel Lafayette," *Buffalo Rising*, May 10, 2012, http://www.buffalorising.com/2012/05/construction-watch-hotel-lafayette.html.
Walkowski, Jennifer, "Richard A. Waite, Architect," http://buffal.oah.com/a/archs/waite/walkow.html.
"Walter B. Duffy," *RocWiki*, Rocwiki.org/Walter_B._Duffy.

Newspapers

"Buffalo Hotel Opened," *The New York Times*, June 2, 1904.
"Contractors and Contracts for Building and Furnishing the Lafayette Hotel," *Buffalo Times*, May 29, 1904.
"Dr. Charles Bethune, Examiner for Child Labor, Dies at 69," *Buffalo Evening News*, date unknown, 1952, Buffalo History Museum archives.
Faison, Seth, "Clashing Stories of 4 Ships And a Disputed Heroism," *The New York Times*, July 5, 1994.
Faison, Seth with Jo Thomas, "Empire of Hotels Riddled With Crime and Drugs," *The New York Times*, July 6, 1994.
Ferro, Shaunacy, "A Century After Her Death, America's First Female Architect Gets Her Due," December 18, 2013, http://www.fastcompany.com/.
"Funeral of R. A. Bethune, architect, this afternoon," *Courier*, July 20, 1915.
Hevesi, Dennis, "Zina Bethune Dies at 66; Actress, Dancer and Choreographer," *The New York Times*, February 18, 2012.
"Hotel Corporation, Names of the Men Who Are Behind the New Lafayette Hotel Enterprise," *Name*, July 24, 1903.
"Hotel Lafayette, Founded On Loyalty, Is 50 Years Old," *Name*, May 26, 1954.
Charlotte Hsu, "Paying Tribute to first female architect," *UB Reporter*, January 3, 2014.
"Hyman B. Cantor, 78, An Owner of Hotels; Started a Foundation," *The New York Times*, October 9, 1980.
Jarvis, H. P., "Men You Ought to Know," *Buffalo Courier-Express*, p. 95, July 18, 1926, Buffalo History Museum archives.
"Ladies of the Wheel," *Buffalo Morning Express*, August 14, 1892, Buffalo History Museum archives.
"The Lafayette, a Fireproof Hotel," *Buffalo Times*, May 29, 1904.
"Lafayette Hotel to be Enlarged," *The Buffalo Commercial*, June 20, 1906.
"The Lafayette is a Palatial Hotel," *The Buffalo Commercial*, May 20, 1912.
"Lafayette to Remodel Lobby, Move Entrance," *Buffalo Evening News*, February 2, 1942.
Longbotham, Tom, "New Hotel Statler Opens Tonight in a Blaze of Glory," *Buffalo Saturday Night*, Vol. 3, No. 114, pp. 8-9 and 16-17, May 19, 1923.
"Mrs. Harry Yates, Widow of Prominent Businessman, Dies," *Buffalo Evening News*, October 8, 1956.
"Mrs. Yates, Financier's Widow, Dies," *The Buffalo Courier-Express*, October 8, 1956.
"A New Hotel," *Buffalo Commercial*, March 3, 1899.
"New Hotel Opened," *Buffalo Express*, June 2, 1904.
"Prominent Woman Architect is Dead," *Buffalo Evening News*, December 19, 1913, Buffalo History Museum archives.
Sommer, Mark, "Masters of recasting the past," *Buffalo News*, December 18, 2011.
"Who Built The Lafayette," *Buffalo Express*, June 16, 1912.
"A Woman Architect," *Buffalo Express*, January 11, 1914.
"Work to start this month on Hotel Lafayette makeover," *The Buffalo News*, August 31, 2010.
"Yates Estate Fights Ruling Asking More in Gift Taxes," *Buffalo Evening News*, April 9, 1957.

Other Women Architects

Adams, Annmarie and Peta Tancred, *'Designing Women': Gender and the Architectural Profession*, Toronto, University of Toronto Press, 2000.
Adams, Annmarie, "Marjorie's Web: Canada's First Woman Architect and Her Clients," *Rethinking Professionalism*, Janice Anderson and Kristina Huneault, editors, Montreal, MQUP, 2012, pp. 380-399.
Adams, Annmarie, *Architecture in the Family Way: Doctors, Houses and Women, 1870-1900*, Montreal, McGill-Queen's University Press, 1996.
Adams, Annmarie, "Gender Issues," *Architecture School: Three Centuries of Educating Architects in North America*, pp. 322-329, Joan Ockman, editor, Cambridge: MIT Press; Washington D.C., Association of Collegiate Schools of Architecture, 2012.
Anthony, Kathryn H., *Designing for Diversity: Gender, Race, and Ethnicity in the Architectural Profession*, Chicago, University of Illinois Press, 2001.
Allaback, Sarah, *The First American Women Architects*, Chicago, University of Illinois Press, 2008.

Beecher, Catherine Esther, *A Treatise on Domestic Economy: For the Use of Young Ladies at Home and at School*, BiblioBazaar Edition, 2008, original copyright 1845.
Beecher, Catherine Esther and Harriet Beecher Stowe, *The American Woman's Home*, New York, J. B. Ford and Company, 1869. Reprinted and with an Introduction by Nicole Tonkovich, London, Rutgers University Press with the Harriet Beecher Stowe Center, 2002.
Berke, Arnold, *Mary Colter: Architect of the Southwest*, New York, Princeton Architectural Press, 2002.
Berkeley, Ellen Perry and Mathilda McQuaid, editors, *Architecture: A Place for Women*, Washington: Smithsonian Institution Press, 1989.
Boutelle, Sara Holmes, *Julia Morgan, Architect*, New York, Abbeville Press, 1988, revised and updated edition.
Brooks, H. Allen, *The Prairie School: Frank Lloyd Wright and His Midwest Contemporaries*, New York: W. W. Norton & Company, 1972.
Cole, Doris, *From Tipi to Skyscraper: A History of Women in Architecture,* New York, G. Braziller, 1973.
Fried, Stephen, *Appetite for America: How Visionary Businessman Fred Harvey Build a Railroad Hospitality Empire that Civilized the Wild West*, New York, Bantam Books, 2010.
Friedman, Alice T., *Women and the Making of the Modern House: A Social and Architectural History*, New Haven: Yale University Press, 2006.
Fowler, Orson S., *The Octagon House: A Home for All*, New York, Dover Publications, Inc., 1973, originally published 1853.
Grattan, Virginia L., *Mary Colter: Builder Upon the Red Earth*, Grand Canyon: Grand Canyon Natural History Association, 1992.
Harrelson, Barbara J., *For La Fonda on the Plaza: From Every Window A Glimpse of the Past*, Santa Fe, 2011.
Hayden, Dolores, *Grand Domestic Revolution: A History of Feminist Designs for American Homes, Neighbourhoods and Cities*, Cambridge, MIT Press, 1981.
Hayden, Dolores, *Redesigning the American Dream: Gender, Housing and Family Life*, New York, W. W. Norton & Company, 2002 revised and expanded edition.
Horton, Inge Schaefer, *Early Women Architects of the San Francisco Bay Area: The Lives and Work of Fifty Professionals, 1890-1951*, Jefferson, McFarland & Company, Inc., Publishers, 2010.
Kullack, Tanja, editor, *Architecture, A Woman's Profession*, Berlin: Jovis Verlag GmbH, 2011.
Mahony, Marion, *The Magic of America*, two versions of unpublished manuscript viewed at The Art Institute of Chicago and The New York Historical Society.
Martin, Brenda and Penny Sparke, editors, *Women's Places: Architecture and Design 1860-1960*, New York, Routledge, 2003.
Martin, Tania, "Housing the Grey Nuns: Power, Women, and Religion in fin-de-siècle Montréal," *Perspectives in Vernacular Architecture*, Vol. VII, editors Annmarie Adams and Sally McMurry, Knoxville, University of Tennessee Press, 1997, pp. 212-229.
O'Gorman, James F., editor, *Hill-Stead: The Country Place of Theodate Pope Riddle*, New York, Princeton Architectural Press, 2010.
Rink, Deborah, *Spirited Women: A History of Catholic Sisters in British Columbia*, Catholic Church, Archdiocese of Vancouver, Sisters Association of Vancouver Archdiocese, 2000.
Rubbo, Anna, "Marion Mahony: A Larger Than Life Presence," *Beyond Architecture: Marion Mahony and Walter Burley Griffin: America, Australia, India*, Anne Watson, editor, Australia, Powerhouse Publishing, 1998.
Sklar, Kathryn Kish, *Catherine Beecher: A Study in American Domesticity*, New York, W.W. Norton, 1976.
Spain, Daphne, *How Women Saved the City*, Minneapolis, University of Minnesota Press, 2001.
Torre, Susana, editor, *Women in Architecture: A Historic and Contemporary Perspective*, New York, Whitney Library of Design, 1977.
van Slyck, Abigail, *Free to All: Carnegie Libraries and American Culture, 1890-1920*, Chicago, University of Chicago Press, 1995.
Wilson, Mark Anthony, *Julia Morgan, Architect of Beauty*, Layton: Gibbs Smith, Publisher, 2007, 2012 revised edition.
Wood, Debora, editor, *Marion Mahony Griffin: Drawing the Form of Nature*, Evanston, Northwestern University Press, 2005.
Wright, Gwendolyn, *Moralism and the Modern Home: Domestic Architecture and Cultural Conflict in Chicago, 1873-1913*, Chicago: University of Chicago Press, 1980.
Van Zanten, David, editor, *Marion Mahony Reconsidered*, Chicago, University of Chicago Press, 2011.

Internet

Adams, Annmarie, "Building Barriers: Images of women in Canada's architectural Press, 1924-1973, *Journal of the Royal Architectural Institute of Canada*, Resources for Feminist Research Fall 1994, Vol. 23, Issue 3, www.thecanadianencyclopedia.com.
"2014 AIA Gold Medal Awarded to Julia Morgan, FAIA," *American Institute of Architects*, press release, December 12, 2013, http://www.aia.org/press/releases/AIAB100853.

Ahrentzen, Sherry, "The Space Between the Studs: Feminism and Architecture," *Signs*, Vol. 29, No. 1, Autumn 2003, pp. 179-206, http://www.jstor.org.acces.bibl.ulaval.ca/stable/10.1086/375675.

"America's First Woman Architect?" *Journal of the Society of Architectural Historians*, Vol. 18, No. 2, May 1959, p. 66, http://www.jstor.org.acces.bibl.ulaval.ca/stable/987980

Beverly Willis Architecture Foundation, includes "Dynamic National Archive," bwaf.org.

Birmingham, Elizabeth, "The Case of Marion Mahony Griffin and The Gendered Nature of Discourse in Architectural History," *Women's Studies: An Inter-Disciplinary Journal* Vol. 35, No. 2, 2006, pp. 87-123, http://dx.doi.org/10.1080/00497870500488065.

Craven, Jackie, "Forgotten Women Designers: Women Have Always Played a Role in Home Design," http://architecture.about.com/od/greatarchitects/a/forgotten.htm.

Donoho, Julia, Petition to the American Institute of Architects, "Award the AIA Gold Medal to Women Architects." http://www.change.org/petitions/american-institute-of-architects-award-the-aia-gold-medal-to-women-architects.

Dunlap, David W. "An Architect Whose Work Stood Out, Even if She Did Not. The New York Times, July 31, 2013. http://www.nytimes.com/2013/08/01/nyregion/an-architect-whose-work-stood-out-even-if-she-didnt.html?ref=obituaries&_r=3&

The International Archive of Women in Architecture, maintained by College of Architecture and Urban Studies and the University Libraries at Virginia Tech, http://spec.lib.vt.edu/iawa/.

McMillan, Gail, "Women T-Squares: Developing a Regional Perspective by Tracing Forgotten Architects and Design Professionals," Virginia Polytechnic Institute and State University, International Archive of Women in Architecture, http://spec.lib.vt.edu/iawa.

Sharp, Leslie N., "Henrietta Dozier (1872-1947)," *New Georgia Encyclopedia*, http://www.georgiaencyclopedia.org/articles/arts-culture/henrietta-dozier-1872-1947.

Shepherd, Rose, interviewer, "Miss Henrietta C. Dozier, Architect," Jacksonville, Florida, 1939, *American Memory: American Life Histories Collection: Manuscripts from the Federal Writers' Project, 1936-1940*, Library of Congress, http://www.loc.gov/item/wpalh000450

Tucker, Lisa M., Ph.D. "The Architects' Small House Service Bureau and the American Institute Architects," *Enquiry: The ARCC Journal*, April 2009, http://www.arcc-journal.org/index.php/arccjournal/article/view/38/37.

Tuskegee University, Architecture Program Report, September 1, 2010, Table 1, "Chronology of Significant Dates for the Department of Architecture," p. 10, http://www.tuskegee.edu/sites/www/Uploads/Files/Academics/School%20of%20Architecture/APR-2010-Final,Addendum1.pdf.

Moonan, Wendy, "AIA Award 2014 Gold Medal to Julia Morgan," *Architectural Record*, December 16, 2013, http://archrecord.construction.com/news/2013/12/131216-AIA-Awards-2014-Gold-Medal-to-Julia-Morgan.asp.

R. H. Morrison Papers, 1820-1888, Collection Number 01131, The Southern Historical Collection at the Louis Round Wilson Special Collections Library, http://www.lib.unc.edu/mss/inv/m/Morrison,R.H.html.

Willis, Julie, "Invisible Contributions: The Problem of History and Women Architects" *Architectural Theory Review*, Vol. 3, No. 2, 1998, pp. 57-68, http://dx.doi.org/10.1080/13264829809478345.

General References on Architecture, Historic Preservation

Austin, Ben, "Buy Low," *The New York Times Magazine*, July 13, 2014.

Banham, Reyner, *A Concrete Atlantis: U.S. Industrial Building and European Modern Architecture, 1900-1925*, Cambridge, The MIT Press, 1989.

Berg, Scott W., *Grand Avenues: The Story of the French Visionary Who Designed Washington, D.C.*, New York, Pantheon Books, 2007.

Bledstein, Burton, *The Culture of Professionalism, The Middle Class and the Development of Higher Education in America*, New York: W. W. Norton, 1976.

Condit, Carl W., *American Building Art, the Nineteenth Century*, New York: Oxford University Press, 1960.

Collins Cromley, Elizabeth, *Alone Together: A History of New York's Early Apartments*, Ithaca, Cornell University Press, 1990.

Crossman, Kelly, *Architecture in Transition: From Art to Practice, 1885-1906*, Kingston: McGill-Queen's University Press, 1987.

Cuff, Dana, *Architecture: The Story of Practice.* Cambridge, MIT Press, 5th printing, 1996.

Dorsey, Leslie and Janice Devine, *Fare Thee Well: A Backward Look at Two Centuries of Historic American Hostelries, Fashionable Spas & Seaside Resorts*, New York, Crown Publishers, 1964.

Dubrow, Gail and Jennifer B. Goodman, editors, *Restoring Women's History through Historic Preservation*, Baltimore, The Johns Hopkins University Press, 2003.

Eisenman, Stephen F., *Nineteenth Century Art: A Critical History*, London, Thames & Hudson, 1994 and 2002.

Friedman, Donald, *Historical Building Construction: Design, Materials & Technology*, New York, W. W. Norton & Company, 1995, 2010, second edition.

Harris, Cyril M., editor, *Illustrated Dictionary of Historic Architecture*, New York, Dover Publications, Inc., 1977.

Harrison, Charles, Paul Wood, and Jason Gaiger, editors, *Art in Theory, 1815-1900: An Anthology of Changing Ideas*, Malden, Blackwell Publishing Ltd., 1998.

Holt, Elizabeth Gilmore, editor, *From the Classicists to the Impressionists: Art and Architecture in the Nineteenth Century*, Vol. II of *A Documentary History of Art*, Garden City, New York, Doubleday & Co., 1966.

Huxtable, Ada Louise, *On Architecture, Collected Reflections on a Century of Change*, New York, Walker & Company, 2008, see in particular two essays: "Beaux Arts—the Latest Avant-Garde," pp. 302-310; "Growing Up in a Beaux Arts World," pp. 455-458.

Johnson, Donald Leslie and Donald Langmead, *Makers of 20th Century Modern Architecture: A Bio-Critical Sourcebook*, Westport, Greenwood Press, 1997.

Kaplan, Justin, *When the Astors Owned New York: Blue Bloods and Grand Hotels in a Gilded Age*, New York, Plume, published by the Penguin Group, 2007.

Kimmelman, Michael, "Urban Renewal, No Bulldozer," *The New York Times*, June 1, 2014.

Kostof, Spiro, with revisions by Greg Castillo, *A History of Architecture, Settings and Rituals*, Second Edition, Oxford, Oxford University Press, 1995.

Lewis, Michael J., "The Battle between Polytechnic and Beaux-Arts in the American University," *Architecture School: Three Centuries of Educating Architects in North America*, pp. 67-89, Joan Ockman, editor, Cambridge, MIT Press; Washington, D.C., Association of Collegiate Schools of Architecture, 2012.

Martinson, Tom, *The Atlas of American Architecture: 2000 Years of Architecture, City Planning, Landscape Architecture and Civil Engineering*, New York, Rizzoli International Publications, 2009.

Mason, Randall, *The Once and Future New York, Historic Preservation and the Modern City*, Minneapolis, University of Minnesota Press, 2009.

Mumford, Lewis, editor, *Roots of Contemporary American Architecture: 37 Essays from the Mid-Nineteenth Century to the Present*, New York, Dover Publications, Inc., 1972.

Murtagh, William J., *Keeping Time: The History and Theory of Preservation in America*, Hoboken, John Wiley & Sons, Inc., 2006, third edition.

Nabokov, Peter and Robert Easton, *Native American Architecture*, Oxford, Oxford University Press, 1989.

O'Gorman, James F., *ABC of Architecture*, Philadelphia, University of Pennsylvania Press, 1998.

Pevsner, Nikolaus, *The Sources of Modern Architecture and Design*, London, Thames and Hudson, 1968.

Roth, Leland M., *A Concise History of American Architecture*, New York, Harper & Row, Icon Editions, 1980, second, corrected edition.

Rothschild, Joan, editor, *Design and Feminism: Re-Visioning Spaces, Places, and Everyday Things*, New Brunswick, Rutgers University Press, 1999.

Rybczynski, Witold, *A Clearing in the Distance, Frederick Law Olmsted and America in the 19th Century*, New York, Simon & Schuster, 1999.

Rybczynski, Witold, *City Life: Urban Expectations in a New World*. New York, HarperCollins, 1995.

Stern, Robert A. M., Thomas Mellins, and David Fishman, *New York 1880: Architecture and Urbanism in the Gilded Age*, New York, The Monacelli Press, 1999 and 2009.

Stern, Robert A. M., Gregory Gilmartin, and John Massengale, *New York 1900: Metropolitan Architecture and Urbanism 1890-1915*, New York, Rizzoli International Publications, 1983.

Stipe, Robert E., editor, *A Richer Heritage: Historic Preservation. in the Twenty-First Century*, Chapel Hill, The University of North Carolina Press, 2003.

Truman, Major Ben C., *et al.*, *History of the World's Fair: Being a complete and Authentic Description of the Columbian Exposition from its Inception*, Philadelphia, Mammoth Publish Co., 1893.

Twombly, Robert, editor, *Frederick Law Olmstead, Essential Texts*, New York, W. W. Norton & Company, 2010.

Tyler, Norman, Ted. J. Ligibel, and Ilene R. Tyler, *Historic Preservation: An Introduction to its History, Principles, and Practice*, New York, W. W. Norton & Company, 2000, 2009, second edition.

Upton, Dell, *Architecture in the United States*, Oxford, Oxford University Press, 1998.

Upton, Dell, "Before 1860," *Architecture School: Three Centuries of Educating Architects in North America*, pp. 37-65, Joan Ockman, editor, Cambridge, MIT Press; Washington, D.C., Association of Collegiate Schools of Architecture, 2012.

Ware, William R., *The American Vignola: A Guide to the Making of Classical Architecture*, New York, Dover Publications, 1994, original edition 1904.

Wilson, William H., *The City Beautiful Movement*, Baltimore, The Johns Hopkins University Press, 1989.

Woods, Mary N., *From Craft to Profession: The Practice of Architecture in Nineteenth-Century America*, Berkeley, University of California Press, 1999.

Wright, Frank Lloyd, *An Autobiography*, Scottsdale, The Frank Lloyd Wright Foundation with Duell, Sloan and Pearce, 1943; Pomegranate Communications, Inc. edition.

Internet

"Architect: Description," http://www.labor.state.ny.us/stats/olcny/architect.shtm.
AIA Buffalo/Western New York, http://aiabuffalowny.org/about_us/history/
"Cast Iron History," www.castironnyc.org/history.htm.
"Definition of Architect," http://www.architect.ca.gov/what_architect/definitions.shtml.
Gerou, Phillip H., FAIA, "AIA Code of Ethics," Rules Of Conduct: Distinction and Clarification, http://ncarb.org/~/media/Files/PDF/Mini-Monographs/EthicsConductMM.pdf.
"The Greenest Building: Quantifying the Environmental Value of Building Reuse," Preservation Green Lab of the National Trust for Historic Preservation's 2011, report, http://www.preservationnation.org/information-center/sustainable-communities/green-lab/lca/The_Greenest_Building_lowres.pdf.
"US Chronological List of Initial Enactment of Architectural Registration," National Council of Architectural Registration Boards, http://www.ncarb.org/en/About-NCARB/Regulation-of-Architecture.aspx.
Royal Architectural Institute of Canada, http://www.raic.org/index_e.htm.
Newfoundland and Labrador Association of Architects, http://www.newfoundlandarchitects.com/.
Architects' Association of Prince Edward Island, http://aapei.com/.
Architects' Association of New Brunswick, http://aanb.org/fr/.
Nova Scotia Association of Architects, http://www.nsaa.ns.ca/.
L'Ordre des architectes du Québec, http://www.oaq.com/.
Ontario Association of Architects, http://www.oaa.on.ca/.
Manitoba Association of Architects, http://www.mbarchitects.org/.
Alberta Association of Architects, https://www.aaa.ab.ca/aaa.
Architectural Institute of British Columbia, http://www.aibc.ca/.
Northwest Territories Association of Architects, http://www.nwtaa.ca/.

General References on the Gilded Age and Nineteenth to Twenty-First-Century-Related Subjects:

Brands, H. W., *American Colossus: The Triumph of Capitalism, 1865-1900*, New York, Doubleday, 2010.
Brown, Dee, *The Year of the Century: 1876*, New York, Charles Scribner's Sons, 1966.
Burns, Sarah, *Inventing the Modern Artist: Art & Culture in Gilded Age America*, New Haven, Yale University Press, 1996.
Calhoun, Charles W., editor, *The Gilded Age: Perspectives on the Origins of Modern America*, Boulder, Rowman and Littlefield Publishers, Inc., 2007.
Cashman, Sean Dennis, *America in the Gilded Age: From the Death of Lincoln to the Rise of Theodore Roosevelt*, New York, New York University Press, 1984.
Gilberti, Bruno, *Designing the Centennial: A History of the 1876 International Exhibition in Philadelphia*, Lexington, The University Press of Kentucky, 2002.
Greenstone, Michael and A. Looney, "Renewing Economically Distress American Communities," http://issues.org/27-2/greenstone.
Grusky, David B. and Tamar Kricheli-Katz, editors, *The New Gilded Age: The Critical Inequality Debates of Our Time*, Stanford, Stanford University Press, 2012.
James, Edmund J., *The Origin of the Land Grant Act of 1862 (The So-called Morrill Act) and Some Account of its Author, Jonathan B. Turner*, The University Studies, Vol. IV, No. 1, November, 1910, Urbana, University of Illinois, 1910.
Lienhard, John H., *Inventing Modern: Growing Up with X-Rays, Skyscrapers and Tailfins*, Oxford, Oxford University Press, 2003.
Maass, John, *The Glorious Enterprise: The Centennial Exhibition of 1876 and H. J. Schwarzmann, Architect-in-Chief*, Watkins Glen, American Life Foundation, 1973.
Nemec, Mark R., *Ivory Towers and Nationalist Minds: Universities, Leadership and the Development of the American State*, Ann Arbor, University of Michigan Press, 2006.
Trachtenberg, Alan, *The Incorporation of America: Culture & Society in the Gilded Age*, New York, Hill and Wang, 1982.

General References on Women's History

Baym, Nina, *American Women of Letters and the Nineteenth-Century Sciences: Styles of Affiliation*, New Brunswick, Rutgers University Press, 2002.
Baym, Nina, *American Women Writers and the Work of History, 1790-1860*, New Brunswick, Rutgers University Press, 1995.
Chadwick, Whitney, *Women, Art, and Society*, London, Thames and Hudson, 1997, second edition, revised and expanded.
Collins, Gail, *America's Women: 400 Years of Dolls, Drudges, Helpmates and Heroines*, New York, William Morrow, 2003.
Felder, Deborah G., *A Century of Women: The Most Influential Events in 20th Century Women's History*, Secaucus, Carol Publishing Group, 1999.

Gornick, Vivian, *The Solitude of Self: Thinking about Elizabeth Cady Stanton*, New York, Farrar, Straus and Giroux, 2005.
Kerber, Linda K. and Jane Sherron de Hart, editors, *Women's America: Refocusing the Past,* Oxford, Oxford University Press, 2004.
Matthews, Glena, *American Women's History, a Student Companion*, New York, Oxford University Press, 2000.
Matthews, Glena, *"Just A Housewife": The Rise & Fall of Domesticity in America*, Oxford, Oxford University Press, 1987.
McCarthy, Kathleen D., *Women's Culture, American Philanthropy and Art, 1830-1930*, Chicago, The University of Chicago Press, 1991.
Weatherfold, Doris, *American Women's History, an A to Z of People, Organizations, Issues and Events*, New York, Prentice Hall General Reference, 1994.

ACKNOWLEDGEMENTS

In Vancouver and Seattle, Washington, we would both like to acknowledge Jake Dykgraaf, who kindly gave us a tour of St. James Church, Vancouver, Washington, and Monte Hidden, for extending an invitation to us to visit the Academy. Yvette Payne, former on-site property manager of The Academy, took the better part of the day to show us Providence Academy inside out. Elson Strahan, President and Chief Executive Officer, and Alishia Topper, then Senior Director of Development, Fort Vancouver National Trust generously offered detailed explanations of the historic preservation process on which they have embarked, both at the Fort and eventually at Providence Academy, and gave us in-depth tours of the sites they oversee. Emily Dominick and Loretta Green, archivists, Providence Archives, Seattle, Washington let us examine the numerous collections in relation to Mother Joseph and Providence Academy and guided us through documents they have shared online ; Peter F. Schmid, Visual Resources Archivist, reproduced a couple of original documents for use in this book. Sister Susanne Hartung, Chief Mission Integration Officer, Providence Strategic and Management Services, found time in her incredibly busy schedule to talk with us about her role in the historic preservation campaign. Thank you all.

Carla Blank: "In Buffalo, New York, I would like to acknowledge the warm welcome and introduction to the Lafayette Hotel and Buffalo's architecture from architects Adriana Barbasch, Beverly Foit-Albert, and Jeffrey Albert of Foit-Albert Associates and Kelly Hayes McAlonie, past President AIANYS chapter; Clinton Brown, president of Clinton Brown Company Architecture, who with his architectural historian consultant Jennifer Walkowski, schooled me on the history of Buffalo and the Lafayette, thus helping me see the big picture, gave me a second tour of the Lafayette, and introduced me to architect Robert Coles who kindly shared his library; and Tim Jones, chief engineer of the Lafayette for eighteen years and maintenance supervisor, who let me view the Lafayette with my family, while it was in the process of renovation, explaining its past, present, and future plans. Also my thanks to Nancy Herlan Brady, descendent of William H. Fuchs, who just in the nick of time shared the rare and only known portrait of the three partners in Bethune, Bethune & Fuchs. To all these folks, great thanks, and most especially my gratitude to Kelly Hayes McAlonie, who generously shared materials and answered questions throughout the eight years I have been working on this subject.

"As an out-of-towner, I could not have done this work without the unfailing and speedy assistance of librarians Nancy Hadley, Manager, Archives and Records at The American Institute of Architects in Washington, D.C.; the Buffalo historical archives graciously accessed for me by Cynthia Van Ness, Director of Library and Archives at the Buffalo History Museum, assistant librarian Amy Miller and their library technician Shane Stephenson; and also Mike Castro of the City of Buffalo's Department of Economic Development, Permit & Inspection Services, who happened to answer his phone and immediately went searching through the old records to help prove Louise Bethune continued working into 1910. Additional thanks to Rare Book Curator Amy Pickard and all those librarians who helped locate materials on Bethune and Buffalo architecture archived in the Central branch of the Buffalo and Erie Public Library; and on pioneering women architects and the Gilded Age, at the New York Historical Society, the Chicago Art Institute, and McGill University libraries, and a special hats off to scholars and archivists of African-American artists, Corrine Jennings and Mary Rose Gentry, for taking up our question and researching the ancestry of Henrietta Cuttino Dozier."

We both extend our appreciative thanks to architect Jonathan Morris and his Carmina Woods Morris associate Pamela Timby-Straitiff who gave us an in-depth interview and tour of the Lafayette in 2013, and followed-up with supplying necessary images and answering research questions; Rocco Termini, President of Signature Development, who took the time to explain his work and vision for the Lafayette and Buffalo; and former Art Voices editor Geoff Kelly who shared his observations of Buffalo's current preservation projects and it's economy.

Tania Martin: "I am grateful to Annmarie Adams for having pointed Carla Blank in my direction and to Dell Upton for having encouraged me to take on this project. Jennifer Cousineau read drafts of the Foreword, The Introduction and Part I, helping me to restructure and clarify my narrative. To Jean Martin, my gratitude for lending me the Previa in summer 1998. To Lise and Sher Mohammad, thank you for accompanying me on that trip and for taking care of Pica while I was away on the 2013 research trip. I would also like to thank Dave G. Dewling and Lynda Hayward of the Newfoundland and Labrador Association of Architects, Judy Pestrak of the Manitoba Association of Architects."

Carla deeply thanks Tennessee Reed and Tania Martin, for their photographs, with further thanks to Tennessee for researching materials at the University of California, Berkeley libraries and her transcriptions of interviews. "Thanks also to William Littmann who graciously allowed me to audit his UC, Berkeley architecture history course. Thanks for the encouragement to go forward on this project, from literary agent Andy Ross, an early supporter, and Jeffrey St. Clair, editor of the online journal *Counter Punch* (September 13-14, 2008, and April 27, 2012) and Chris Farley, former editor at the *Wall Street Journal* (September 11, 2013), who both published my articles about Louise Bethune and the Lafayette Hotel."

We both appreciated receiving comments from each other, and from Ishmael Reed. And lastly, we want to express our gratitude and appreciation to Maja Romano for her careful copy-editing, Josée Lalancette for the smart book design, and especially to our editor and publisher, Robin Philpot of Baraka Books, without whose interest and support this project might not have become a book.

Carla Blank and Tania Martin,
October 15, 2014

MORE NONFICTION FROM BARAKA BOOKS

Barack Obama and the Jim Crow Media
The Return of the Nigger Breakers
Ishmael Reed

Going Too Far
Essays about America's Nervous Breakdown
Ishmael Reed

Journey to the Heart of the First Peoples Collections
Musées de la civilisation
Marie-Paule Robitaille, Director

America's Gift, What the World Owes
to theAmericas and Their First Inhabitants
Käthe Roth & Denis Vaugeois

The First Jews in North America
The Extraordinary Story
of the Hart Family, 1760-1860
Denis Vaugeois

Dying to Live
A Rwandan Family's Five-Year Flight
Across the Congo
Pierre-Claver Ndacyayisenga

Slouching Towards Sirte
NATO's War on Libya and Africa
Maximilian Forte

Rwanda and the New Scramble for Africa:
From Tragedy to Useful Imperial Fiction
Robin Philpot

Challenging the Mississippi Firebombers
Memories of Mississippi 1964-65
Jim Dann

The Question of Separatism
Quebec and the Struggle over Sovereignty
Jane Jacobs

The History of Montréal
The Story of a Great North American City
Paul-André Linteau

Justice Belied
The Unbalanced Scales
of International Criminal Justice
Sébastien Chartrand & John Philpot (editors)